ENTENTE IMPERIAL

To Auntie Laura,

I hope you enjoy this, despite the typos. Especially, pages 29-30 and 185-7, as well as some of the paintings, should meet your high standards! And yes, I realise its "Forbes" and not "Forbe's"....

Thanks for all your support since 1990!!

Lots of love,
Edward
xxx 22/2/22

ENTENTE IMPERIAL

British and French Power in the Age of Empire

EDWARD J. GILLIN

First published 2022

Amberley Publishing
The Hill, Stroud
Gloucestershire, GL5 4EP

www.amberley-books.com

Copyright © Edward J. Gillin, 2022

The right of Edward J. Gillin to be identified as the Author of this work has been asserted in accordance with the Copyright, Designs and Patents Act 1988.

ISBN 978 1 3981 0289 7 (hardback)
ISBN 978 1 3981 0290 3 (ebook)

All rights reserved. No part of this book may be reprinted or reproduced or utilised in any form or by any electronic, mechanical or other means, now known or hereafter invented, including photocopying and recording, or in any information storage or retrieval system, without the permission in writing from the Publishers.

British Library Cataloguing in Publication Data.
A catalogue record for this book is available from the British Library.

1 2 3 4 5 6 7 8 9 10

Typesetting by SJmagic DESIGN SERVICES, India.
Printed in the UK.

I am not whole,
Here you find a body, but not the soul.
Long ago I lost my heart,
And ever since, we've lived apart.
Though life and youth long have past;
It waits there still, at St Eustache.

CONTENTS

Acknowledgements   9

Introduction: Europe Ascendant   11

1 A World to Display: Britain and France at the Great Exhibition   28

2 Catastrophe and Collaboration: The Crimean War   53

3 Projections of Global Power: Cultivation and Commerce in China and Suez   79

4 Peace Secured: Free Trade and the Cobden-Chevalier Treaty   103

5 The Measure of Nations: Liberalism and the Metric System   118

6 Entente Diminished: The Fall of Palmerston and Napoléon   137

7 Imperial Rivals: The Anglo-French Divergence, 1871–98   156

8 Entente Renewed: The Drift to Global War   193

Epilogue: An Anglo-French World Order?   217

Bibliography   228

Endnotes   245

Index   274

ACKNOWLEDGEMENTS

Writing this book has been enormous fun thanks to brilliant conversations with some incredibly knowledgeable experts. The various parts of the work produced reflect these discussions and their range of specialist interests – and I hope provide a history of Anglo-French relations between 1815 and 1914 that unites the diplomatic, political, artistic, musical, military, scientific, technological, social, cultural, culinary, and architectural. Only by considering all of these can we have a true historical understanding of an age, or really analyse a complex theme like 'imperialism'. William Whyte, Geoffrey Tyack, Horatio Joyce, and David Lewis have all fuelled my passion for architecture, especially regarding John Ruskin and Amiens Cathedral. Graeme Gooday and Simon Schaffer indicated exciting avenues to explore within the history of science and technology. Robert Harding taught me all I know about the history of champagne, and David Trippett, Melissa Van Drie, Melle Kromhout, and Stephanie Probst have all helped me to consider musical questions within Anglo-French relations. Few possess so much knowledge of Anglo-French diplomatic history as Harry Mace: our conversations and sense of mischief have made this project a joy. I owe immense debts to Silke Muylaert, Robert Hall, Ben King, Rachel North, Keith Shepherd, Daniel Belteki,

Tim Marshall, Peter Roberts, Charles Fox, Rachel Morin, Michael and Caroline Carver, Carolyn Kennett, and Mike Jenks for their friendship and support. Fanny Gribenksi is to be credited with much of the inspiration for this work: from our discussions over musical pitch exchanges, an entire monograph has grown.

Much of the research for this project was done at Sherlock Close in Cambridge, where I was lucky enough to have the encouragement and entertainment of Amie Varney, Chlöe Gamlin, Tilda, and Bertram. The text was written on board the beautiful Ms *Marco Polo* while steaming around South America, through Panama, the West Indies, Africa, India, and back through Suez and the Mediterranean. Not only has this provided a crash course in the legacy of the French and British empires, from Mayotte and Cape Town to Bombay and Barbados, but I have benefitted from the good company of many passengers. To name a few, I must thank Geoff and Jane Evans, Rosie and Jim, Barry and Michael, Trisha, Kim Jeffs, Kaya Hutchinson, and Nick Roberts. Thanks go also to the lovely staff who kept the coffee flowing through the drafting, especially Nina Gatenadze, Essa, Stella Wais, and Septya. Finally, thanks go to Crosbie Smith for months of conversations and for enduring a week-long reading of the text. At Amberley Publishing, Connor Stait has been immensely enthusiastic and Nicola Embery has helped make the process of producing this book exceptionally easy.

Finally, I am grateful to my family and friends in Devon for everything they have done for me and all the patience they have shown over the past few years with my work and eccentric habits. Thanks go to my parents, Steve and Louise Spencer, my brother Alexander Teague, Montgomery Spencer ('the best of all of us'), Alfred Spencer the dog, Robert White, Laura Treloar, Peter Exell, June Sayers, Sid Sharma, Tommy Grimshaw everyone at Sharpham Vineyard, Warren, Victoria, Sebastian Max, and Reuben Putt-Gillin, Trisha Gliddon, and all of the Teague family, especially Steve and Pauline. The last word must go to the now legendary critic and wit 'Little Christopher Yabsley'.

INTRODUCTION: EUROPE ASCENDANT

Had you been a Chinese peasant on the banks of the River Pei-ho in late 1860, you would have seen a fearsome sight. Two foreign armies were returning in triumph from Peking. A hundred miles inland and with its colossal walls, the Chinese capital had long been considered impregnable. But just a few months earlier a British and French expeditionary force had invaded mainland China, advanced swiftly up the Pei-ho, and seized Peking with hardly a shot fired. Equipped with steamships, modern artillery, and rifles, the two European armies had annihilated all Chinese resistance. The celestial Xianfeng Emperor had fled the capital and his brother, Prince Gong, surrendered the city soon after. A once mighty civilization lay in ruins while Britain and France's global dominance was, by now, unquestionable. Four years earlier they had inflicted a similar humiliation on Russia and, in recent months, they had concluded the world's first free trade treaty. Together, this Anglo-French alliance had instigated a new world order. As a reminder to China of the dangers of challenging this European ascendency, the British and French had sacked the astonishingly beautiful Summer Palace. What had begun criminally as a mass looting descended into an outright act of vandalism with the Chinese Emperor's seat of power burned to the ground. Had you been on the banks of the river you might also have caught a final glimpse of the plunder taken from the palace, on its way back to the imperial capitals of London and Paris; among the stolen treasures, a pair of gold and jade sceptres destined for the sovereigns of the two most powerful nations on earth: Queen Victoria and Emperor Napoléon III.

This book is not about Britain's post-Brexit relationship with the European Union. It is a book about Britain's relationship with France in the 1850s. It argues that Britain was most dominant in global affairs when it collaborated with France, its leading European rival. Empire and industry did not engender an isolated Britain, rejecting external influences from the Continent. Rather, to exert its will throughout the world, Britain found France a crucial ally. Through military interventions, free trade, political integration, and shared scientific and commercial cultures, the entente cordiale produced an apogee of European power.

Britain's relations with Continental Europe have usually been strained, and in the twenty-first century these relations have been at the centre of discussions over Britain's place in the world. The empire is long gone, as is most of the industry, shipping, navy, and business. Hong Kong, the last genuine imperial asset, went in 1997, intensifying the uncertainty of the ex-superpower's dwindling global position. Since 1945, the preservation of its alliance with the United States helped Britain to maintain an inflated sense of international influence amid the rapid disintegration of empire, while relics from this imperial past continue to offer an aggrandized sense of Britain's standing. The Commonwealth, BBC World Service, Trident Nuclear Deterrent, and Wimbledon are all that is left to offer solace to those nostalgic over power. But essentially Britain does not know what it is. Should it accept a position as one among European nations, within an increasingly

Introduction: Europe Ascendant

integrated European Union? Or should it forge stronger links with the United States and other ex-colonies?

Today's commentators, keenly searching for answers, look to 'history'. If you want to know where Britain is going, why not look back to see where it has come from? It is a reasonable assumption. The problem is that, for the most part, politicians and journalists seem to take the wrong lessons from the past. Eagerly they look back on the days of empire as a time of great industry and prosperity, with all the global clout that this afforded. Roughly speaking we are talking about Britain from the early nineteenth century until the Second World War, or from about 1800 to 1945. Often the narrative is one of a brave Britain, standing alone, fighting the odds, capable of ordering the world as it liked without consultation.

The 1800s began with a series of wars against the First French Empire of Napoléon Bonaparte. While Bonaparte continually defeated the Prussian, Austrian, and Russian armies on land and snatched control of Continental Europe, Britain stood isolated as the one European power not at the French Emperor's mercy. It was the English Channel and the Royal Navy that kept Britain free. Bonaparte's final defeat at Waterloo in 1815 ushered in a golden century of British power, in which it dominated the oceans and built the largest empire ever seen, covering a quarter of the planet's land. Queen Victoria came to the throne in 1837: on her death in 1901 she was an empress, reigning over India, Canada, Australia, New Zealand, most of the West Indies, huge swathes of Africa from Cape Town to Cairo, and scores of cities, islands, and trading posts around the world. This dominance lasted until the outbreak of the First World War in 1914 and although the Britain that emerged victorious in 1918 was but a ghost of what it had been, its imperialism appeared unadulterated. Britain went into the Second World War in 1939 a superpower, but by 1945 it was certainly in the second tier of nations, in the shadow of a new American-Soviet world order. Yet even in the economic calamity of this second great war, historians, politicians, and journalists frequently portray Britain as standing alone, boldly resisting Nazi Germany. Its 'finest hour' came in the Battle of Britain where there were few allies to be found.

This narrative of 'splendid isolation' is a dangerous one, not least because it is a myth. Britain was at its most globally dominant when it worked with its Continental allies, not against them. When then, exactly, was this high point of influence? I would argue that it was in the 1850s. This was, after all, Britain's 'Age of Equipoise', as the historian W. L. Burn put it, in his classic study of the mid-Victorian generation. Burn's argument was that this was a period of unprecedented social and political calm, which allowed the nation to give an unusual amount of attention to foreign affairs.[1] Since its publication in 1964, *The Age of Equipoise* has provoked much debate about how this period should be conceptualised. This notion that the 1850s was a moment of profound stability is attractive, but Burn was himself writing amid Britain's post-war decline. Culturally and politically a Conservative, he saw the 1850s and 1860s as the climax of liberal Victorian 'civilization' that was in such contrast to the post-1945 welfare state that the Labour Party worked to build.[2]

Certainly 1850 to 1870 appeared calmer than the earlier decades of the nineteenth century, but there was still public disorder and political uncertainty at a local level. Arguably, however, the British state was adept at managing outbreaks of working-class unrest. Throughout the 1850s the infrastructure at hand for controlling public disorder grew quickly. The British army doubled in size between 1850 and 1860. The nation's railway and telegraphy networks expanded too. In 1852 there were 7,500 miles of railway track running across Britain, more than doubling by 1870. Steam-powered railways reduced travel times substantially, with the distance between London and Manchester reduced from a thirty-hour coach ride to just eight hours by train. This combined

Introduction: Europe Ascendant

military, telegraphy, and railway expansion meant that the British government, both at Westminster and locally, had more troops to deploy in moments of working-class unrest, and that these could be mobilised faster and despatched with greater speed than ever before. Telegraphy offered enhanced communication for local authorities to request support.[3] This infrastructure, though not guaranteeing stability, certainly contributed to it. Along with economic prosperity, growing wages and spending power, high employment, and relative political peace, this state apparatus contributed to a decade of domestic harmony.

Regardless of the extent to which this was Britain's Age of Equipoise, it is to this crucial decade that we must look if we want to know what Britain was when it was at the zenith of its power. Power itself is a hard thing to measure, but if we consider how Britain was performing relative to its competitors we get a sense of why the 1850s was such an auspicious moment. Industrially, Britain's lead was still unrivalled. Between the 1870s and the twentieth century it was clear that the flourishing, highly mechanized economies of Germany and the United States were surpassing British industry, while its own economic growth slowed sharply. Before the 1850s, Britain's industry was impressive, but its commercial and colonial possessions were still developing. The 1850s was, therefore, the one moment where Britain could claim to be the unrivalled global superpower. This was the decade of the Great Exhibition, that most euphoric celebration of national achievement: the ultimate moment of industrial, commercial, and technological hubris. In the same decade Britain fought a war against Russia on Russian soil, tightened its grip over its Indian empire, and humiliated China by capturing Peking. There appeared nowhere on Earth that Britain could not exert its authority.

Paul Kennedy, in his influential *The Rise and Fall of British Naval Mastery*, identified the period 1815 to 1859 as the age of Pax Britannica, but conceded that this really was not true until the middle of the century. 'If there was any period in history when Britannia could have been said to have ruled the waves, then it was in the sixty or so years following the final defeat of Napoléon. ... So unchallenged, so immense, did this influence appear, that people spoke then and later of a "Pax Britannica", finding the only noteworthy equivalent in history to be the centuries-long domination of the civilized world by imperial Rome', asserted Kennedy.[4] While this was not quite correct and comparisons with Rome's dominance proved short-lived, British naval power certainly gave the appearance of being unchallenged, as did the nation's industry. For less than £1 per person per annum spent on defence, the British state financed a vast navy without rival, costing no more than 2–3 per cent of the nation's income.[5] Although a far cry from 1815 when the Royal Navy consisted of some 214 ships of the line and 792 cruisers (though many were not in a seaworthy state), it was the Admiralty's policy to maintain 100 ships and 160 cruisers at all times. Though the navy rarely fulfilled this standard, this was a colossal peacetime force, intended to be superior to the navies of any other two nations who might unite against Britain. But in truth, no other nation had the resources or will to match the Royal Navy's supremacy.[6]

At the same time, Britain's overseas territories provided strategic bases around the globe from which to manage its informal empire. In the mid-nineteenth century, formal empire was not that popular with many Victorian audiences who favoured 'the imperialism of free trade', preferring informal influence over foreign territories. Rather than expensive military-secured colonial possessions, it was through trade, finance, and missionaries that liberal Victorians wanted to see global influence exerted, especially in West Africa, China, and the new republics of South America, where the British built up highly profitable trade hubs. Ports like Shanghai, Montevideo, Buenos Aires, and Valparaiso became invaluable commercial centres for

Introduction: Europe Ascendant

British business. As Kennedy pointed out, in the nineteenth century about 70 per cent of British emigration, 60 per cent of its exports, and 80 per cent its of capital flowed into regions beyond Britain's formal empire. However, Britain did seize vital strategic strongholds to keep the arteries of this informal empire open. The taking of Singapore in 1819 offered control over the western entrance into the China Sea, while the seizure of the Falklands in 1833 provided a valuable base overlooking Cape Horn. Aden was taken in 1839, guarding the entrance to the Red Sea, and Hong Kong's acquisition in 1841 was crucial for conducting trade with China. Further strategic bases were established around the world, including at Lagos, Fiji, Cape Town, Alexandria, Mombasa, Cyprus, Zanzibar, Sierra Leone, Ceylon, Malacca, the Seychelles, St Lucia and Tobago, Gambia, Ascension Isle, and Guiana.[7] No nation, before or since, possessed such a network of strategic strongholds from which to exert influence over global affairs.

As much as abroad, Britain's cultural, intellectual, and political dominance was evident at home. Back in London, Charles Barry and Augustus Pugin's new Palace of Westminster, home to Britain's revered Parliament, was opened. Following the completion of the opulent House of Lords in 1847, 1852 saw MPs take their seats for the first time in the Gothic glory of the House of Commons. Here was national confidence made manifest through highly romanticized Medieval architecture. Spectacular engineering projects abounded. Electricity offered rapid communication through telegraphy cables deep under the sea, conveying information around the globe in a way that some have described as a sort of 'Victorian Internet'.[8] Steam-powered railways and ships provided rapid travel. This was the decade of Isambard Kingdom Brunel's *Great Eastern* steamship; a colossal floating city built of iron, she was the largest moving man-made object to date. It was also a decade in which science appeared to offer man increasing mastery over nature itself.

Charles Darwin published his dramatic *On the Origin of Species* in 1859, revolutionizing perceptions of man's place in the universe. The first edition sold out within a few hours, sparking generations of arguments over God and evolution. Not many decades have witnessed quite so many historically defining moments. In the 1850s, Britain was unquestionably the place to be.

Despite all its wealth, Britain was also a place of extreme poverty, especially in the booming industrial centres of London, Liverpool, Manchester, Birmingham, and Glasgow. While the 1850s were politically very stable, the unrest and popular clamour for reform of the 1830s and 1840s was still fresh in the memory of the nation's ruling elites. For all that science and technology appeared to promise a Utopian future of material progress, new knowledge of geology, evolution, and astronomy provoked increasing religious controversy. In what was still an overwhelmingly Christian society, the natural sciences' assertions over the age of the Earth and fossilised animal life were causes for alarm. And as for the nation's industrial strength and grand imperialism, these were inseparable from doubts and anxieties. What if there was no God? What if India should be lost? What if the industrialized working classes should revolt? What if Britain's coal ran out?

One thing was certain: Britain was the foremost global power. There was no question of this. No politician embodied this national eminence quite so forcibly as Henry John Temple, Lord Palmerston. As Foreign Secretary for almost sixteen years between 1830 and 1851 (1830–34, 1835–41, and 1846–51), and then two terms as Prime Minister (1855–58 and 1859–65), he dominated mid-Victorian foreign policy. A rampant womaniser, he proudly recorded his sexual triumphs and failures in a series of pocket diaries. He was also found of hunting, eighteenth-century culture, and racing, but this lifestyle was expensive, compounding the considerable debts that he had inherited. More than half of his

Introduction: Europe Ascendant

land was in Ireland, and although he doubled his annual revenue from this to over £11,000 by 1840 through investing in a harbour, roads, drainage of bogs, and schools, the famine of 1845 to 1849 was bitterly felt and Palmerston attracted criticism for removing starving families from his land and sending them to North America.[9] Despite these mixed personal fortunes, few individuals have ever exerted so much international influence as Palmerston.

Palmerston's vision of Britain was of a powerful imperial empire with global punch. It was the inheritor of ancient Rome, a 'civilizing' force in a 'barbaric' world.[10] He was convinced that, throughout the world, Britain had a mission to 'extend, as far and as fast as possible, civilization', both through force and through treaties.[11] In 1850 during the Don Pacifico affair, these Roman comparisons were made most forcefully. When David Pacifico, a Jewish British subject from Gibraltar residing in Athens, was refused compensation from the Greek government for damage done to his house during an anti-Semitic mob while the police declined to intervene, Palmerston ordered a naval blockade of Greece until Pacifico received payment. This was a very public statement that Britain would protect the interests of its citizens wherever they were in the world, even by force if required. Palmerston's actions were popular, but enraged Queen Victoria and caused an intense debate over the extent of British foreign policy. Defending his course, Palmerston boldly declared to Parliament that 'as the Roman, in days of old, held himself free from indignity, when he could say *Civis Romanus sum*, so also a British subject, in whatever land he may be, shall feel confident that the watchful eye and strong arm of England will protect him against injustice and wrong'.[12]

This belief that Britain was the heir to Rome's global dominance even had architectural ramifications. When designing the new Foreign Office building at Whitehall, constructed between 1861 and 1868, architect George Gilbert Scott initially opted for a Gothic structure of elaborate Christian art, much in the fashion of his later railway station at St Pancras. Scott had in fact considered his first design quite French in inspiration, explaining that he had not aimed 'at making my style "Italian Gothic"; my ideas ran much more upon the French, to which for some years I had devoted my chief study'.[13] This would not do. Warning the architect not to try to 'Gothicize the whole country', Palmerston demanded Scott redraft the plans in a neoclassical style, reminiscent of the Roman Empire. He wanted a temple to imperialism, not some feudalistic church.[14]

Palmerston's reputation as an aggressive, but effective, Foreign Secretary was enhanced during the First Opium War between 1839 and 1842, which resulted in the British seizure of Hong Kong. Despite Tory opposition and claims that Palmerston had entered into an illegal war with China under the influence of opium traders, he recognised that securing this profitable market was crucial for British trade. In general, though, Palmerston opposed territorial acquisitions, preferring to exert influence rather than outright control. When Napoléon III suggested that Britain should seize Egypt and France take Morocco to secure their Mediterranean interests, he rejected this completely, preferring to work with local regimes and to build trade networks with them: 'Let us try to improve all these countries by the general influence of our commerce ... but let us all abstain from a crusade of conquest which would call down ... the condemnation of ... other civilized nations.'[15]

But Palmerston's confidence did not mean that Britain acted alone in world affairs or withdrew into isolation. Far from it, the 1850s was a unique moment of intense international collaboration between Britain and its only genuine European rival: France. Between 1848 and the early 1860s the two nations worked together to order the world as they saw fit. As allies they went to war with Russia in 1854 and China in 1860. As partners they negotiated the world's first free trade treaty between 1859 and 1860. They looked

Introduction: Europe Ascendant

with mutual interest to open up the Suez Canal and bring Europe closer to the subcontinent, Far East, and Australia. Even at the Great Exhibition, so much a festival of British industry, it was both France and Britain that offered economic lessons in manufacturing to the rest of the world (Chapter 1). And it was not just trade and war that brought them together. Though the workshop of the world, after 1851 Britain worked to adopt French approaches to the arts and by the end of the decade was looking to adopt France's metric system. Being the world's most eminent power did not mean enforcing its own views on its rivals, but actually respecting what its neighbours had to offer and embracing elements of foreign culture. Britain was greatest when it was looking to, and working alongside, France. As the flamboyant Chancellor of the Exchequer Benjamin Disraeli put it in 1858, Anglo-French cooperation was 'the key and corner-stone of modern civilization'.[16]

What then was France in the 1850s? In many ways, between 1848 and 1870, France was itself seeking a global role. Its Atlantic empire in the Americas was long gone, lost to the British in the eighteenth century. Not much remained in the West Indies either. Yet if Britain was the undoubted superpower of the nineteenth century, France was unquestionably the second imperial power. Like London, Paris boasted a splendid new foreign office, as much a projection of French imperial ambition as any architectural splendour Whitehall could boast. On the quay of the left bank of the Seine, architect Jacques Lacornée oversaw the construction of a beautiful new neoclassical building between 1845 and 1855, home to France's Ministry of Foreign Affairs. Although begun before Napoléon III came to power, this palace, popularly known as the Quai d'Orsay due to its location, was a fitting embodiment of the imperial ambitions of the new Emperor.

The lavish new Quai d'Orsay was just one part of a changing Paris, as Napoléon instigated an architectural transformation of the city into the capital of his new empire. Paris in the 1840s was a dark and disease-ridden place, with poor air and little sunlight. Its workshops and factories bred unrest and revolt, providing the ideal location for revolutions and barricades. Napoléon Bonaparte had long dreamt of refashioning this medieval realm into a modern utopia, lamenting his failure to complete this during his final lonely exile on St Helena. His nephew, Napoléon III, was determined to complete his uncle's vision. Impressed by London's wide streets and public parks, the new emperor appointed Georges-Eugéne Haussmann (1809–91) Prefect of the Seine in 1853. He gave him almost limitless powers and a huge budget, and ordered him to direct a massive renovation of Paris. During the next seventeen years, Haussmann demolished the city's overcrowded and narrow medieval streets, replacing them with expansive parks, squares, and boulevards. He extended Bonaparte's Rue de Rivoli from the Louvre to the Hôtel de Ville and modelled the Bois de Boulogne on London's Hyde Park. After the Rue de Rivoli's grand opening in 1855, the Rue Saint-Antoine provided a second east-west thoroughfare, divided by two north-south running boulevards, Strasbourg and Sébastopol. The tall street blocks that lined Haussmann's streets became symbolic of the French capital, with their uniformed layout of floors for shops, offices, superior living quarters, and flats neatly topped with forty-five-degree-angled mansard roofs and Dormer windows. Along with stunning new bridges bearing giant 'N's in their stonework, including the Pont Saint-Michel to connect the left bank to the Île-de-la-Cité, Haussmann's Gare du Nord provided a new industrial entrance to Paris. Built between 1861 and 1864, with vast iron pillars cast in Glasgow and a tasteful façade, this was emblematic of a new capital for a new age of steam-powered travel.[17]

A very central part of the social life of Napoléon's Paris was to be found on the rue de Faubourg St-Honoré, at the Hôtel de

Introduction: Europe Ascendant

Charost. Once home to Napoléon Bonaparte's stylish sister, Pauline Borghese, this was now the British Embassy, or the 'Residence' to those who knew it better. When the Duke of Wellington arrived as ambassador in Paris in 1814, he purchased the palace from Pauline for 861,000 francs and established it as Britain's permanent embassy. He had also had the choice of the Élysée, which would become the office for the French President in 1848, but this lacked the same taste and was unfurnished. Although considered too expensive throughout the 1820s and 1830s, the Hôtel de Charost was to remain the Parisian seat of British power and hospitality, becoming a favourite home-from-home for Queen Victoria and her son, Edward VII.[18]

Paris and London, then, were both imperial cities: great capitals of empire and centres of international diplomacy.[19] Despite few overseas colonies, France exerted economic and cultural influence on a global scale. Through what historians have called 'informal empire', French finance and the French language's centrality in scientific, commercial, and intellectual culture ensured it a leading role in Europe and the Mediterranean. It is significant that after 1815 these two global powers never went to war with each other.[20] Just as Britain opted for collaboration with its main European rival, so French politicians recognised that only by working with Britain could they extend their country's influence around the world.[21]

Throughout this book it becomes very clear that as Britain and France forged closer trade links and collaborated in military expeditions, relations were constantly strained. British and French politicians, generals, engineers, and merchants could not help but view their allies with suspicion and jealousy. Petty arguments were rife. Often British audiences suspected that at any moment the French might turn from partner to invader. It was, after all, traditionally the enemy and the spectre of centuries of war could not easily be dispelled. Invasion panics were a common occurrence throughout the decade. At the same time, British commentators looked down on France as a decadent, materialistic, and politically radical state, under the rule of Emperor Napoléon III, himself a supposedly despotic, militaristic dictator. The Victorians prided themselves on their liberal politics and system of government in which a constitutional monarch was answerable to an elected parliament. These contrasts became particularly noticeable during the post-1848 political upheavals in France and subsequent Great Exhibition in 1851.

It was, after all, during the invasion panic of 1859 that Charles Dickens wrote his hugely popular historical fiction *A Tale of Two Cities*, itself a commentary on the close relations between Britain and France during a period of political unease. Dickens' work took much inspiration from Scottish philosopher Thomas Carlyle's *The French Revolution: a History*, published in 1837 and revised in 1857. This authoritative work adopted an unusual style in which Carlyle and his readers appeared as observers of historical events as they occurred, providing a simulation of the horrors of the Reign of Terror during 1793 and 1794, and the chaos of revolutionary France. Dickens' *A Tale of Two Cities* was equally explicit over the injustice and bloodshed of the French Revolution of 1789, but this was an account of France that would have been very pertinent to Victorian readers in 1859. Dickens was growing increasingly despondent over the rise of nationalistic sentiment in both Britain and France during the late 1850s, especially surrounding the Orsini controversy of 1858 (Chapter 4).[22] In *A Tale of Two Cities*, centred around the Anglo-French Tellson's Bank, Dickens provided a warning of the dangers of prolonged social inequality that might lead to public unrest, as well as revolution, which usually ended in chaotic violence and mob rule. The aristocratic 'Monseigneur', who required four servants to be capable of consuming his morning hot chocolate, was out of touch with his tenants and the affairs of state, being symbolic of an entire class heading irrevocably towards annihilation in the upheaval of 1789.[23] Monseigneur himself summed up French autocracy and totalitarian government, asserting that 'Repression is the only lasting philosophy. The dark deference of fear and slavery.' In contrast, though its legal system was not that much superior to France's revolutionary justice, Dickens portrayed England as a haven for political refugees and those eager to make their own way in the world, far from the trappings of inherited wealth and titles.[24]

And yet Dickens also depicted Paris and London in the 1780s and 1790s as inseparably connected, both culturally and economically. Both were cities where miscarriages of justice and poverty were rife. Both were places never too far from social unrest and mob violence. When Monseigneur's class flee France, they go to London, where their 'great gathering-place' was Tellson's Bank, the weighty financial unifier between the two countries and symbol of stability.[25] Above all else though, Dickens used France to convey the horrors of revolution to English readers. With a very graphic account of the violence of 1789 and acts of vengeance by Paris' starving masses, it was the guillotine that held sway in Dickens' portrayal of 1790s France. This gruesome instrument of execution was 'the best cure for headache, it infallibly prevented hair from turning grey, it imparted a peculiar delicacy to the complexion, it was the national razor which shaved close … It was the sign of the regeneration of the human race. It superseded the cross … It hushed the eloquent, struck down the powerful, abolished the beautiful and good.'[26] For Dickens, the guillotine was the ultimate symbol of revolutionary mob justice and served as a grim reminder on the dangers of extreme poverty. But it was significant that *A Tale of Two Cities* appeared at the very moment that Britain's relations with France were most strained. This was a book that confirmed fears that Britain and France were, while connected, also inherently different.

Despite these differences, the two nations found common cause. In the snows of the Crimea and the mysteries of mainland China, French and British soldiers shared bread, wine, and the hardships of battle (Chapters 2 and 3). In Paris and London politicians looked to secure peace and promote commercial enterprise. Crucially, alliance involved a certain amount of political integration. As the Victorians found out, it was hard to act in unison with the French without some political flexibility. The decade ended with Britain and France concluding a free trade treaty (Chapter 4). No 'liberal' measure was so celebrated in Victorian Britain as free trade. To extract state intervention from the economy, remove tariffs, and allow the markets to reign unrestricted was broadly considered the epitome of a modern, liberal nation. No country committed to free trade could truly be autocratic or bent on war, or so Victorian political economists believed. So getting France, long a bastion of protectionism, to agree to free trade was an unprecedented coup.

However, free trade raised profound questions over measurement standards (Chapter 5). To trade without restriction, sharing the same system of weights and measures was crucial. The problem was that while France's interventionist state was capable of enforcing the metric system on its population, in liberal Britain where minimal state action in the nation's social and economic life was so celebrated – *laissez-faire* government as Victorians called it – it was hard to instigate the regulation required to assist international trade. Free trade and commercial unity therefore involved controversial questions over political integration. It was difficult to operate a truly open market without addressing concerns over the role of Parliament and the freedoms of individuals within society. What we would today call 'red tape' was as pertinent an issue for buccaneering Victorian capitalists as

Introduction: Europe Ascendant

it is for today's disciples of the free market. Importantly though, despite its global dominance, vast empire, and rampant industry, Britain did not reject European influence outright. Rather, it sought ways to embrace it.

Revealingly, it was what followed this Anglo-French moment of integration that demonstrated the crucial importance of collaboration in exerting global order. In the decade that followed Britain and France's trade integration, the two nations drifted apart. Throughout the 1860s, Napoléon III became an increasingly unreliable partner, while British politicians lost direction and shied away from Continental commitments. The Franco-British world system of the 1850s began to break up (Chapter 6). In Europe, a new power superseded France, the German Empire, that would bring about the fall of the ageing French Emperor in 1871. In this new political landscape, deprived of its French allies, Britain found it very difficult to exert the authority within Europe that it had enjoyed during the 1850s. The late nineteenth century was marked not by Anglo-French cooperation, but imperial rivalry, culminating in a virtual British isolation from the Continent by 1900 (Chapter 7). In the early twentieth century, however, it was apparent that the two nations needed each other, not in order to revive the global hegemony of the 1850s, but simply to survive in the face of growing German and American competition (Chapter 8). In 1904, the entente that had disintegrated in the 1860s was recast. It would be a partnership that would see Britain and France revive the alliances of Palmerston and Napoléon as the two fading powers entered a global war dependent on each other to weather the challenge of German militarism between 1914 and 1918. As much as the 1850s had demonstrated the virtues of European cooperation, the subsequent decades provided a harsh lesson on how difficult it was, both for France and Britain, to keep their grip on world power without a powerful ally.

I

A WORLD TO DISPLAY: BRITAIN AND FRANCE AT THE GREAT EXHIBITION

On the bloodied Belgian fields of Waterloo on 18 June 1815, peace was finally restored to Europe after the Revolutionary and Napoleonic Wars that had engulfed the Continent for over a quarter of a century. Britain had, since the French Revolution of 1789, become increasingly isolated from European science and learning. Now, with Napoléon Bonaparte's second and, this time, permanent exile to the tiny South Atlantic island of St Helena, Britain was finally opened up to European audiences and ideas. But after almost twenty-five years of conflict between Britain and France, the great question that troubled political and economic thinkers on the other side of the English Channel was simple: why had Britain won? Given the obvious military genius of Napoléon and the almost inexhaustible supply of conscripts, France's defeat was mystifying. The answer, surely, was to be found in Britain's industrialization and expansive use of steam power.

During the late 1810s and 1820s, visitors from the Continent travelled to England to witness her steam-powered industry. Businessman Jean-Baptiste Say (1767-1832), for example, found the island covered in thousands of steam engines, compared to just a handful that he witnessed on his visit before the Napoleonic Wars.[1] After a similar investigation, the mathematician and economist Baron Pierre Charles François Dupin (1784–1873) reached a similar conclusion: Napoléon had lost because of Britain's industrial use of coal.[2] Although he did not know it, Dupin's investigation into British industry would shortly inspire the first fictional detective: inspector C. Augustus Dupin. The central character in Edgar Allan Poe's (1809–49) *The Murders in the Rue Morgue* and two subsequent novels, Dupin provided a deductive model that would later inspire both Arthur Conan Doyle's Sherlock Holmes and Agatha Christie's Hercule Poirot. But Poe's original embodiment of machine-like reasoning took the name from an economist determined to resolve a riddle every bit as troublesome as any murder or crime. In 1820s France, British steam power was the great question of the day.

Above all, it was to the Atlantic mining district of Cornwall that French economists looked with wonder in the years after Waterloo. Writing in the prestigious *Annales de Chimie et de Physique*, mathematician Jean-Baptiste Biot (1774–1862) identified the supremacy of Britain's steam-powered industry and, specifically, the immense economy of engineer Arthur Woolf's Cornish high-pressure steam engines. Rather than the low-pressure engines of eighteenth-century engineers Thomas Newcomen and James Watt, Woolf's new machines operated at a higher pressure in which steam was channelled into a confined space from which more work could be extracted for the same consumption of fuel. Though rich in tin and copper ore, Cornwall lacked a cheap supply of coal, which was crucial to keeping the pumping engines working on which the mines relied to prevent flooding. Eager to find ways of economising on fuel consumption, Cornwall's mine owners looked hopefully to the high-pressure engines of Woolf and his rivals, including the much-celebrated Richard Trevithick.

Cornwall offered a valuable model for France, with both regions lacking coal, and both economies tormented by the question of fuel consumption. To the French, still employing old low-pressure engines, Woolf's compounds appeared attractive: post-Napoleonic France was a fruitful market for Cornish steam-engine technology.[3] Sadi Carnot's (1796–1832) *Reflections on the motive power of fire* (1824) was central to this French investigation into British, and specifically Cornish, steam power. A military engineer, mathematician, and son of Bonaparte's final Minister of the Interior, Carnot sought to explain the efficiency of steam engines in terms of their potential to conserve energy. For him, the key question for engineers who were eager to emulate British standards of steam engine economy was how to extract the most work from a given amount of heat; work being the result of a conversion of energy, or 'caloric', from a warm to a cool temperature. The ideal engine, Carnot surmised, was one in which no heat was wasted, but all caloric was transformed into useful work.[4] He portrayed Woolf as something of a hero in this drive towards engines of increasing economy.[5]

In the wake of Carnot's work, France came increasingly to celebrate Woolf's high-pressure steam engines. Woolf's associate, Humphrey Edwards, began importing such machines to France in 1815, before commencing the construction of similar engines at the Chaillot Works in Paris from 1817. The French were rapidly replacing their pre-1789 steam engine technology.[6] There was some truth in Carnot's blunt assertion that Britain's steam engines had been more important in the recent wars than her navy.[7]

It was not just France that had much to learn through this post-1815 exchange of scientific and industrial knowledge. For all that Britain had delivered a tour de force in steam-powered industry, English audiences eyed enviously the eminence of the French natural sciences. France was at the centre of European mathematics by the early nineteenth century, but its new post-Newtonian analytical methods were controversial in Britain due to their revolutionary connotations. In his *Exposition du système du monde* (1796), Pierre-Simon Laplace (1749–1827), the doyen of French mathematics, provided a sublime vision of a mechanical universe which operated according to a series of governing mathematical principles. The mathematics was impressive, but carried with it troubling implications for British audiences: Laplace portrayed the universe as a godless place, in which all could be accounted for by pre-existing laws. When Napoléon apocryphally asked where God fit in this account, Laplace allegedly declared that he had no need of such a hypothesis. French mathematics was political, radical and religiously dangerous.

However, with the end of the Napoleonic Wars in 1815, such mathematics slowly became more acceptable, as British reformers looked to implement French-style analysis. The University of Cambridge was at the centre of this renaissance of mathematical education. Along with George Peacock and Charles Babbage, astronomer and mathematician John Herschel led a revival of Cambridge's mathematics by introducing Continental-style techniques. Cambridge's radical reformers took what had been a French academic preserve and transformed the university into a bastion of mathematical learning.[8]

For all these exciting exchanges in science and industry, the character of French and British politics remained radically different throughout the 1820s and 1830s. As France endured royal comebacks and revolts, Britain experienced a growing number of liberal reforms. Along with a series of free trade measures, church and local government reforms, and the abolition of slavery throughout the British Empire in 1833, the greatest scalp of all, the reform of Parliament, came in 1832 with the Great Reform Act. This controversially extended the franchise from about 500,000 to 813,000 voters, giving greater political representation to Britain's booming industrial towns and largely remedying the corruption of rotten boroughs.

*

By the late 1840s, revolution was in the air on both sides of the Channel. Throughout 1848 a dangerous wind blew across Europe. In Hungary, the German States, Switzerland, Sweden, and Austria, the old monarchical regimes strained under the clamour of popular unrest and looked certain to fall: in France it actually did. Paris was accustomed to political upheavals. Since the Revolution of 1789 the Bourbon monarchy had been restored in 1814 and, after an interlude, again in 1815. But the revolution of 1830, in which King Louis Philippe of Orleans usurped the Bourbon throne, reminded those in power of the fragility of their control. In 1848 another revolution overthrew the French monarchy, this time for good, with Louis Philippe forced into exile in England. He would be the last king of France and died in Surrey in 1850.

On the other side of the Channel there was more unrest. In London the largest ever gathering of Chartists seemed likely to escalate into an outright British revolution. These working-class protestors from the booming industrial cities of the north demanded a truly radical reform of government, including annual parliamentary elections and suffrage for all men aged over twenty-one (not women). Queen Victoria and her family sought refuge at Osborne House on the Isle of Wight. In that spring of 1848 it really seemed that the French contagion of revolution would spread to Britain. And with it, that Victoria might go the way of Louis XVI and Marie Antoinette, guillotined at the hands of the mob in 1793.

A World to Display: Britain and France at the Great Exhibition

Despite the panic, the nation escaped the bloody chaos of revolution and the Chartist threat subsided with little more than a whimper. The royal family remained unharmed. France's 1848 revolution was actually rather conveniently timed for Britain. In 1843 the two countries had agreed to cooperate, forming what was proclaimed as an *entente cordiale*. As Foreign Secretary under the Conservative premiership of Robert Peel, Lord Aberdeen pursued a diplomatic policy aimed at improving relations with Britain's oldest enemy. Between 1841 and 1846 he built a friendly understanding with France's Premier, François Guizot. Aberdeen's predecessor at the Foreign Office, the provocative Lord Palmerston, had seen a deterioration in relations between Britain's Liberal government and Louis Philippe. Aberdeen ensured the Conservatives would redress this.[9] But when the Liberals seized power and Lord John Russell replaced Peel as Prime Minister, relations again disintegrated. Palmerston, returning as Foreign Secretary, clashed with Guizot over the marriages of Queen Isabella of Spain and her sister, Luisa Fernanda. Palmerston wanted Isabella to marry Leopold of Saxe-Coburg, a cousin of Victoria's husband, Albert. Guizot had different ideas, preferring a Spanish match with a French prince to secure Louis Philippe influence in the region. To Palmerston's annoyance, Guizot got his way, with the Bourbon Duke of Cádiz marrying Isabella and the Duke of Montpensier, son of the French king, marrying Luisa Fernanda.[10] Palmerston and Guizot never resolved their differences over the Spanish marriages. Luckily for the British Foreign Secretary, the revolution of 1848 meant he never had to.

Palmerston's initial response to the overthrow of Louis Philippe was cautious. Unsurprisingly, the fall of the king sent shudders through most British politicians. Who did not fear that 1848 might be another 1789 and that revolution would be followed by the tyranny of a second Reign of Terror? The revolutionary governments of the 1790s, ruling through the power of the mob and the dread of the guillotine, presented a chilling spectre. But by the end of 1848, Russell's Liberal government found unlikely reassurance in the rise of Louis Napoléon, nephew to the long-dead 'bogeyman' of Europe, Emperor Napoléon Bonaparte.

The son of Bonaparte's younger brother, Louis, and the daughter of Napoléon's wife Joséphine, Hortense de Beauharnais, Louis Napoléon was born in 1808. As Joséphine was too old to provide the emperor with an heir, the marriage was intended to furnish Bonaparte with a successor, but with his fall from power in 1815, Louis and the Bonapartes fled France into exile. With his second wife, Marie Louise, Bonaparte did have a legitimate heir, a son, whom Bonapartists in France proclaimed as Napoléon II between 1821 and his death in 1831, when Louis again became the heir to the Bonaparte claim to the French throne. Convinced that there was popular support for a Bonapartist coup, Louis planned a return to Paris in the 1830s, arriving in Strasbourg in 1836 to lead an uprising against the Orleans regime, but this ended in disaster as Royalist troops put down the would-be revolution, and forced Louis to flee back to Switzerland. He travelled to London, Brazil, and New York, before again returning to Switzerland for the death of his mother in 1837. In 1838 he went to live in London, where he enjoyed a genteel lifestyle in a fine town house, socialising with the city's elite politicians and scientists. After two years of this easy life, he made a second bid to seize power in France, sailing to Boulogne in 1840 with sixty armed men aboard the *Edinburgh-Castle*. As in Strasbourg, this ended badly, with the revolutionaries failing to get beyond the beach before they were arrested, with Louis imprisoned for life. After years in prison, busily spent writing, he escaped in 1846 disguised as a labourer and returned to London. When revolution broke out in France in 1848, Louis Napoléon was convinced that his time had come. In Legislative Assembly elections of June, he ran successfully as a candidate, making the most of his Bonapartist credentials, which carried great political weight in revolutionary France. After remaining in London during the summer, he returned to Paris in September and in the election of that month prepared to stand as the first ever elected President of France. In December 1848, Louis Napoléon did indeed become President of the Legislative Assembly, heading a government of moderates who respected private property and the rule of law. This was a France that Britain could do business with.[11]

On 2 December 1851 this tranquillity was shattered. On the anniversary of Bonaparte's greatest victory, the Battle of Austerlitz, Louis Napoléon seized absolute power in a brilliant *coup d'état*, promoting himself from president to emperor. Alarm sounded across the Channel. British audiences could not help recalling that another Napoléon had also crowned himself emperor, back on 2 December 1804, preceding a decade of war. The shared date of Austerlitz and Bonaparte's crowning was as troubling for the British as it was auspicious for the French.[12] Surprisingly though, Palmerston endorsed the coup, believing it a harbinger of stability. His foreign policy, though often appearing jingoistic, actually involved cultivating good relations with France. An alliance was safe, despite public displays of hostility to the old rivals being politically popular. As Palmerston put it, Britain had 'no eternal allies' and 'no perpetual enemies', only 'eternal and perpetual interests'.[13] Above all, this Foreign Secretary was a pragmatist and a French emperor promised a vastly more reliable ally than a revolutionary government.

Unfortunately for Palmerston, his endorsement of Napoléon's coup was premature. Out of sync with public alarm, he was promptly sacked. By this point Palmerston had served as Foreign Secretary in the governments of Earl Grey, Lord Melbourne, and Russell for almost sixteen years, since 1830. His departure changed little of Britain's foreign policy. In February 1852 the Earl of Malmesbury took over the Foreign Office as part of the Earl of Derby's new government. It was a brief but crucial tenure. Malmsbury was a personal friend of Napoléon, an acquaintance of some twenty-three years. Based on little more than that the new emperor shared the name of his uncle, the military genius, Britain spent 1852 in the grip of an invasion panic. But Malmsbury did not share this paranoia towards France. Like Palmerston, he recognised that Napoléon provided a reliable partner on the Continent. Indeed, in 1850 Napoléon told Malmsbury that should their two nations act in unison, 'France and England could remodel everything.'[14]

At the end of 1852 Napoléon held a plebiscite over the establishment of a new empire. Again this seemed reminiscent of his uncle's rise to power. His styling of himself as 'Napoléon III', rather than 'Napoléon II', was also a contentious point. To do so suggested Napoléon Bonaparte's son, who died in 1832, had been emperor. This simply ignored the rule of the Bourbon and Orlean regimes between 1815 and 1848.[15] Malmsbury, however, showed his support of Napoléon III in Parliament, delivering a speech praising the French emperor. Like Palmerston a year earlier, he got carried away, appearing far too pro-French. As his Prime Minister, Derby, listened with both hands covering his face in horror, Malmsbury's enthusiasm for Napoléon III was overdone. His speech opened the Conservative government up to sharp criticism and before long the Liberals were back in power and Palmerston back in the Foreign Office.[16] Malmsbury's speech weakened Derby's administration, but it was Benjamin Disraeli's budget defeat that brought the Conservative government down. Rich with words, but poor with numbers, Disraeli made a lamentable Chancellor of the Exchequer and his great Liberal rival, William

Ewart Gladstone, savaged his debut budget. It failed to pass in the House of Commons by 305 votes to 285. No government could last long once it had lost control of the nation's finances.[17]

Again a change of government, but Palmerston's and Malmsbury's foreign policies were consistent. To keep France on side and maintain relations with Napoléon, that was the key to European stability. Yet in the early 1850s France was not an obvious partner for Britain. Amid continual invasion panics, British audiences beyond the Foreign Office saw in France a potential invader, not an ally. Politically and culturally, it seemed the very opposite of all that Britain was. Napoléon's autocracy provided a productive comparison for defining Britain's own national identity. While France was militaristic, Catholic, and dictatorial, Britain claimed to be a bastion of constitutional monarchy, parliamentary accountability, liberal politics, free trade, and religious toleration. For evidence, contented Britons viewed the nation's political stability as being in sharp contrast to France's addiction to revolution. Historian Jonathan Parry has argued that the Liberal Party's dominance of mid-Victorian politics was in part due to these readings, in which to be liberal was to be English and to be autocratic was to be French.[18] Even Napoléon's use of referenda to confirm his own rule seemed more an appeal to the mob than an honest move towards liberalism. Along with his wielding of patronage, the luxury and material decadence of Paris, and Napoléon's obsession with his own dynasty, France seemed morally inferior.[19]

For all that France was to be condemned, Britain was to be celebrated. And in the same year that Napoléon took the ultimate step of declaring himself emperor, Britain embarked on perhaps the ultimate celebration of national industry and progress. In the post-1848 political calm, the country had been preparing for a demonstration to the world that Britain was the first among nations. What was created in London's Hyde Park was to become famous as the Great Exhibition.

Although a celebration of the natural and man-made produce of the world, the 1851 Great Exhibition was above all a festival of British industrial and economic eminence. The brainchild of Queen Victoria's husband Prince Albert, himself a German from the Saxon duchy of Saxe-Coburg-Saalfeld, this was proclaimed as a great spectacle to encourage the world's arts, enhance international trade, and stimulate scientific progress. It was also supposed to bring the manufactures of each nation together and, through comparison and competition, to deliver a very clear message: that British industry, science, and engineering provided the model of a progressive nation. The lesson to the world was a simple one: by harnessing steam power and industrialising as quickly as possible, other nation's would move closer to Britain's prosperity. This was the future and it was to be built on iron and coal.

Housed in Joseph Paxton's colossal Crystal Palace, the enormity of the exhibition provided one of the undoubted wonders of the century. Built with glass and iron on an unprecedented scale, the palace stretched 1,851ft in length by 456ft in width, being four times the length and double the width of Christopher Wren's St Paul's Cathedral.[20] Queen Victoria was certainly impressed. On attending the opening ceremony on 1 May 1851 she noted in her diary that it was one of 'the greatest & most glorious days of our lives'. Hyde Park had never looked so fine and, after a light sprinkling of rain, 'the sun shone & gleamed upon the gigantic edifice, upon which the flags of every nation were flying'. Hardly lacking in vanity, it was not so much the celebration of British industry that satisfied the thirty-one-year-old queen, as the credit she felt her husband Albert could take for the exhibition's success.[21]

As you entered, the exhibition was divided into two halves. On your left were the products of Britain and its empire. To your right, the rest of the world was on display, including France, Turkey, Spain, Italy, Egypt, China, Brazil, and the United States. Within this 'vast greenhouse' 50,000 visitors a day goggled at the exhibits of scientific wonder and technical skill. This number rose to over 70,000 when the entry price was cut to a shilling. On these 'shilling days' the glass and iron palace would be full of country folk, who would 'arrive in their rustic dresses, with their wives, their children, and provisions'.[22] Thanks to specially reduced railway fares, whole parishes from all over the country visited, often under the guidance of their local clergyman. On the same days you could see soldiers, sailors, and hundreds of 'charity children' dressed all in blue with yellow stockings. Saturday mornings were reserved for invalids and the infirm, who would be drawn about in small carriages; this was a spectacle for the whole nation, regardless of class, gender, age, or disability. No wine, beer, or spirit was permitted inside but, as one French tourist observed, 'of course there is tea'. That same Frenchman also lamented the food on offer: several buffets sold 'all kinds of fearful pastry, and horrible creams that would be ices'.[23]

But visitors did not come for the cuisine. They came for the spectacular array of manufactures, arts, natural products, scientific wonders, and technical innovations. Notable among Britain's manufactures was the collection of Bibles in the known languages of the world. But nothing provoked so much excitement as the jewellery, which caused queues and blocked circulation through the exhibition as the police struggled to keep wide-eyed ladies moving past these valuable treasures. Particularly popular was the recently re-cut Koh-i-noor diamond, displayed next to its crystal-cut replica to appear like two drops of water. These attracted a constant crowd. Yet the 'real diamond' on display was in fact 'the huge block of coal, which decorates one of the entrances to the Exhibition'. For the French correspondent of the influential *Journal des Débats, Politiques et Littéraires*,

John-Marguerite-Émile Lemoinne, this lump of coal was 'the real diamond of England' while the Koh-i-noor was itself 'but a species of coal'.[24] Lemoinne agreed that the exhibition confirmed Britain's prowess in machinery and science. In England 'Fire, air, water, steam, electricity, are all exerting their agency' thanks to the nation's 'supremacy of science'.[25] Indeed, Britain's evident mechanical ingenuity led many foreign tourists, surprised at finding the sun shining over London, to speculate that the English had 'invented some process to warm their climate'.[26] Even the demeanour of Londoners appeared to foreigners to have changed. 'Offering hospitality to the whole world', tourists found the English to have abandoned their traditional reserve and become sociable, entering freely into conversations with strangers across the capital. As much as the world was put on display before all of Britain, all of Britain was on display to the world, and its performance was impressive.

William Whewell had no doubts over the exhibition's true meaning. Master of the enormously wealthy Trinity College Cambridge, Whewell had coined the words 'scientist' and 'physicist' as well as a catalogue of terms for describing electrical science, including 'cathode', 'electrolyte' and 'electrolysis'. He was the most eminent historian and philosopher of science of his day. What truly made the Great Exhibition a triumph, according to Whewell, was that in bringing the manufactures of the world together, side by side, Britain had annihilated the space which separated each nation and, in doing so, also 'annihilated the time which separates one stage of a nation's progress from another'.[27] By exhibiting the world's produce in a single building it was possible to measure exactly where Britain stood relative to other nations. Whewell warned that there was much produced abroad, including 'the work of savage hands', that might make Englishmen despair of their own products. He conceded the superior beauty of ornamental

A World to Display: Britain and France at the Great Exhibition

and tissue works from Persia and India, as well as silks, shawls, embroidery, jewellery, and carvings from the Orient.[28]

Despite this, Whewell was satisfied that Britain's 'superiority' had been proven. But what was this superiority? The nation had undoubtedly accumulated considerable riches in skill and capital, and its 'mechanical ingenuity and mechanical power' were clearly immense. Yet its goods were in many respects inferior to those of less industrialised countries. The answer then, according to Whewell, was that Britain's superiority was mass production. Through ingenious inventions and intricately calibrated

Intellectual powerhouse, polymath and Master of Trinity College Cambridge William Whewell celebrated the Great Exhibition's display of British mass production and mechanised labour. (Author's collection)

machines, Britain satisfied the demands of vast populations. The mechanised production of textiles clothed people of all classes. This was the true meaning of Britain's industry: that 'the machine with its million fingers works for millions of purchasers, while in remote countries, where magnificence and savagery stand side by side, tens of thousands work for one. There Art labours for the rich alone; here she works for the poor no less.'[29] In other words, British-style industrial progress was synonymous with social progress because to harness steam power in manufacturing was to make products affordable for all. Whewell's message was clear: mechanised labour and factory production had a crucial moral value.

Yet for all the emphasis on progress and science, in 1851 Britain was still an immensely religious nation and the Great Exhibition, though a celebration of industry and commerce, was subject to Biblically informed interpretations. About 7¼ million attended church each Sunday out of a population of some 18 million, while the Church of England was still politically powerful, through its Supreme Head, the Queen, twenty-six bishops in the House of Lords, and its extensive land and wealth.[30] So for all that we may look back and see the Great Exhibition as startlingly familiar, modern even, many Victorians saw it in religious terms. On the Sunday after its opening, hundreds of sermons across Britain addressed the subject and, for those attending the exhibition, religious guides were on sale offering advice on where to worship.[31] But clergymen did not always see the Great Exhibition as something to celebrate. Among Anglicans there were fears over the influx of foreigners, especially Roman Catholics, to the capital, which some churchmen likened to Belshazzar's Feast. Depicted in the Book of Daniel, the fall of the decadent and ostentatious Babylon was predicted at the feast by the original writing on the wall. With London's material wealth likened to godless Babylon,

A World to Display: Britain and France at the Great Exhibition

The 'Machinery Court' of the Great Exhibition in 1851, exhibiting the technology of mass production that Whewell thought so important to British economic success. (Author's collection)

clergymen cast the Great Exhibition as a harbinger of doom. Both the feast and the Exhibition were acts of hubris which could not escape divine punishment.

Likewise, the chaos of a capital filled with foreigners speaking diverse languages drew comparisons with the Tower of Babel as described in Genesis.[32] Other prophetic interpretations of the Crystal Palace found the Book of Revelation's account of the heavenly city revealed on Judgement Day as made of 'pure gold, like unto clear glass' highly apt. Unamused, *The Times* dryly observed that, with 'rather violent Scriptural analogies, a certain class of pietists have run wild on the catastrophes which they conceive to be a natural and proper retribution for any great scheme of secular unity'.[33] While the Great Exhibition evidently fuelled much pride in Britain's industry, it also triggered anxieties that such material decadence and national hubris would surely provoke God's retribution. While promoters portrayed the exhibition as a symbol of progress, a significant number of Victorians looked to the Bible for the exhibition's meaning.

It was not only religious concerns that surrounded the Crystal Palace. Not everyone shared in the eulogising of the economic shrewdness of the exhibition. One disgruntled manufacturer condemned Albert for plunging the nation 'headlong into a vortex of extravagant display' which was certain to 'bring ruin and desolation to the homes of thousands'.[34] The Exhibition appeared to threaten the British workman, not only for revealing all his skills to foreign rivals, but by advertising the superior wares of other nations. The manufacturer feared the Great Exhibition was nothing but a scheme for encouraging foreign labour into Britain at the expense of workers at home. In particular, a recent French exposition in George Street on Hanover Square, which had secured large orders for French manufacturers, was further proof of how Britain had 'for years been struggling against the growing

A World to Display: Britain and France at the Great Exhibition

and deep rooted taste of the British public for French silks, shoes, gloves, &c., and other foreign produce'.[35]

Most worryingly for British audiences, it did indeed seem that France had outperformed the host nation. If there was anything worse than encouraging foreign competition or invoking divine retribution, it was the thought that Britain's arch rival had provided the world with a superior model of industrial development. And this was certainly what many felt. French manufacturers dominated the production of luxury goods, especially furnishings and clothing, but above all what were known as *articles de Paris*: small and delicate goods of a valuable nature, including decorative boxes, fans, buttons, artificial flowers, and fine combs. Economists and journalists alike declaimed that France's bourgeois consumers provided a preferable industrial future, in which style and quality trumped mass production. Joseph Garnier and Hippolyte Dussard, both French political economists, proudly boasted that the lesson of the Great Exhibition was that 'the United States can feed the world, England can clothe it, and France can beautify it'.[36] Lemoinne certainly had no doubts over France's performance. In works of 'taste', especially luxury silks, porcelain, carpets, jewellery, and lace, his country excelled. France's industry was art and Frenchmen could 'look at the Crystal Palace with pride. In this festival of nations, in this pacific and glorious competition of human industry, France stands pre-eminent in the products of art, taste, and imagination.'[37] Michel Chevalier, another political economist, put it equally succinctly: 'The Frenchman engages in industry as an artist, the Englishman as a merchant.'[38] France's confidence in its luxury products was well grounded, with its exports booming in the years following the Exhibition. A survey of Parisian industry between 1847 and 1848 found that almost all luxury goods were sold within France, but a similar survey in 1860 discovered that Parisian exports had expanded rapidly. Although

75 per cent of products sustained domestic consumption, 14 per cent of furnishings, 17 per cent of clothing, and 26 per cent of *articles de Paris* went abroad.[39]

But why was it that luxury French manufactures were so much better than everyone else's? If you asked most Victorians, they would have told you that France's superiority was due to the taste of its consumers and the quality of its workmanship, and that both had developed thanks to the consumption of bourgeois French women. In France it was usual for wives to assume responsibility for the decoration of the home but, unlike in Britain, they also took control of household spending. Contemporaries believed that this feminine purchasing power, especially among fashionable Parisian women, was why France's wares had fared so well in London. French women had taste, they had style, and they had the cash to back it.[40] Britain's mass production certainly offered an economic model for other nations, but for France this was not a model to follow.

Count Léon de Laborde, art critic and economist, argued that it was obvious from the Exhibition that low prices and mass mechanised production degraded art. He confidently asserted that France, not Britain, had taken a lead in industry by emphasising the importance of artistic skill and quality in manufacturing.[41] Laborde determined that, instead of mechanising, France should protect its artistic superiority. And the key to this would be to mobilise the nation's women. Laborde believed that mothers were the foundation of French economic success because they decorated the home and because they instructed their children in taste. As he explained, women 'paint, sculpt, engrave, make lithographs, design embroidery and fans, and produce a thousand delicate art objects called *articles de Paris* without leaving the mother's protective roof, without losing sight of the baby's cradle, without placing a foot in these places of corruption called factories, veritable prisons of communal labour'.⁴² Rather than British steam-powered machinery, it was French women of taste who would provide the basis of French prosperity. While the women of London were not exactly considered as stylish as their Parisian sisters, Britain also responded to the Great Exhibition by instigating a series of art reforms intended as a counterbalance to the influence of machinery and to follow France's example.

British industry attracted criticism of a much darker nature. While admiration for French taste and quality cast a shadow over Britain's manufacturing prowess, the increasing use of machines and techniques of mass production carried with it alarming social and moral implications. No one summed this up with more beautiful prose than the celebrated art critic and social reformer John Ruskin. Although most famous for his early patronage of the Pre-Raphaelite Brotherhood of artists, and remembered today for his failure to consummate his marriage to Effie Gray (who later married Ruskin's prodigy, John Everett Millais) and subsequent desire to marry his fourteen-year-old student Rose La Touche, few commentators commanded so much authority within Victorian society. When Ruskin looked at Britain's industrial machinery and factory production, he was horrified. Just two years after the Great Exhibition, Ruskin encouraged his readers to 'look round this English room of yours ... the work of it was so good and strong, and the ornaments of it so finished. Examine again all those accurate mouldings, and perfect polishings, and unerring adjustments of the seasoned wood and tempered steel.' Was this precision and finesse not cause for national pride? Not for Ruksin. 'Alas!' he exclaimed, 'if read rightly, these perfectnesses are signs of a slavery in our England.'⁴³ This 'slavery' was that of factory precision: machines relied on standardisation, both in terms of parts, calibration, and produce, but such regulation involved the dehumanising of labourers.

The coal-powered machines of Britain's industry depended on intricate regulation and the deskilling of workers. Real beauty in art was not due to accuracy and perfection, but to human thought and craft. Ruskin argued that a worker could either think as a man or operate as a machine:

> You can teach a man to draw a straight line, and to cut one; to strike a curved line, and to carve it; and to copy and carve any number of given lines or forms, with admirable speed and perfect precision; and you find his work perfect of its kind: but if you ask him to think about any of these forms ... you have made a man of him ... He was only a machine before, an animated tool.[44]

For Britain's labourers and the future of its industry, the nation faced a choice. Ruskin warned that 'Men were not intended to work with the accuracy of tools, to be precise and perfect in all their actions. If you will have that precision out of them, and make their fingers measure degrees like cog-wheels, and their arms strike curves like compasses, you must unhumanise them.'[45] The very exactness of workshop production that the Great Exhibition was intended to celebrate, in Ruskin's view, degraded man, reducing him to a machine part.

As ever, Ruskin looked to architecture for the basis of this interpretation, but for many Victorians what he was saying carried extremely troubling religious implications. In his hugely popular *The Stones of Venice*, published between 1851 and 1853, Ruskin argued that architecture was linked to nature in terms of climate, vegetation, and animals. There was, for instance, a 'mountain brotherhood between the cathedral and the Alp', while the cosy-looking homes of little English villages reflected the need for warmth and comfort on these damp Atlantic islands.[46] But, more importantly, architecture was also an index of religious principle and, in this respect, the Gothic of Northern Europe was morally exalted above all other styles. Medieval Christian Gothic was, Ruskin argued, savage in nature, but this was in fact a crucial part of its noble character. By 'savageness', Ruskin explained that the Gothic lacked the precision and uniformity of Classical Greek or Assyrian architecture. In Classical buildings, workmen were required to produce accurate carvings and replicate precise forms which, in the same way as Victorian Britain's mechanised industry, reduced skilled craftsmen to slaves. In contrast, though impressive works of engineering, Gothic architecture was 'savage' because it was imperfect; because there was little uniformity or precision in its carvings, the forms of which were entrusted to the labourer rather than standardised. Emphatically, Ruskin claimed that 'in the medieval, or especially Christian, system of ornament, this slavery is done away with altogether; Christianity having recognised ... the individual value of every soul.'[47] The medieval Christian workman was asked to do the best he could, as truly as he knew how or his skill permitted. The results were imperfect, being 'the labour of inferior minds' to the perfect architecture of ancient Greece, but such imperfections were morally superior to slavery-secured perfection.

This was, very obviously, a hugely romanticised portrayal of feudal medieval Europe. But it really did not matter: Ruskin delivered his rejection of mechanised industry and factory labour in a highly persuasive manner. His silky prose and rich rhetoric ensured that even readers who did not share in Ruskin's romantic socialism could still sympathise with his calls for a return to simpler forms of manufacturing based on the skill and ideas of craftsmen, rather than the calibration of a machine. Indeed, during the second half of the nineteenth century Ruskin's arguments underpinned the core values of William Morris's Arts and Crafts Movement and its rejection of industrial slavery through hand-made produce.

Fifty-four years after the Great Exhibition, at the 1906 General Election, the first in which the Labour Party secured a significant share of seats in the House of Commons (twenty-nine), this first generation of Labour MPs identified Ruskin's writings as having the most significant influence on their beliefs, placing him just ahead of the Bible, and well above Karl Marx.[48]

*

The Great Exhibition ended on 25 September 1851, with Queen Victoria drawing the proceedings to a close. At this very moment Britain and France, for all the observed differences in their economies, moved closer together than ever before. On the same day, a dramatic announcement was made at the Crystal Palace: France and Britain had been connected by a telegraphic cable, the ultimate symbol of Victorian progress. Delivering the proclamation was Thomas Crampton, who had himself half-funded the project and, with his experience as engineer to the London, Chatham, and Dover Railway Company, overseen the operation. This technological wonder, a working submarine cable, was perhaps the most important of the Exhibition. It meant that a message could be transmitted under the English Channel by Morse code, as was the practice in Continental Europe from 1851, or by the Cooke and Wheatstone system, as was customary in Britain. While Morse code consisted of a series of dots and dashes, transmitted by the making and breaking of an electrical current, the Cooke and Wheatstone method was to employ a device which displayed a series of needles that pointed at different letters to spell out words. Electric telegraphy was not new; it had been in increasing use on land throughout the 1840s. But submarine links were tricky.

In fact a line had already been established from Shakespeare's Cliff at Dover to the headland of Cape Gris-Nez, halfway between

A World to Display: Britain and France at the Great Exhibition

Calais and Boulogne in August 1850. This cable had worked briefly before an enterprising French fisherman had scooped up the line. The connection was lost. The 1851 venture, however, deployed a stronger cable of four copper wires (rather than one, as in 1850) sheathed in gutta percha, then wrapped in spun yarn in tar and clothed finally in rope made from ten galvanised iron wires. Under the direction of the Submarine Telegraph Company, Britain and Europe had been united as never before. Though it was often unreliable, electric telegraphy promised almost instantaneous communication. The satirical periodical *Punch* celebrated the historic moment by depicting John Bull and the Emperor Napoléon as 'Siamese twins' linked by 'electric wire'. *Punch* had always had an odd sense of humour.

In November 1851 the cross-Channel connection opened to public use. An entrepreneur by the name of Paul Julius Reuter saw

THE NEW SIAMESE TWINS.

Punch's depiction of Britain and France's uniting by electric telegraph in 1851 with the opening of the Channel cable. (Author's collection)

an opportunity, using the line to relay information on commodity prices between London and Paris, conveying news and stock market updates. Seven years later the first transatlantic telegraph cable briefly connected Britain and America before contact was lost. A new line was laid in 1865 but this soon broke and had to be repaired in 1866. By the end of the century, Britain's cables encircled the globe, uniting its colossal empire.[49] It is true that telegraphy often failed to live up to expectations. The problem of electrical resistance, in which the sending of messages slowed and eventually ceased, accompanied the propensity of submarine cables to break. Locating the point of disruption was challenging to say the least. Equally annoying was that gutta percha, the gum-like insulation that was so crucial to protecting the copper wire from salt water, made a tasty meal for deep-sea worms. But in 1851 these difficulties were all to come. For Britain and France, telegraphy had undeniably brought London and Paris closer together. A message sent from Westminster at breakfast could be in the Tuileries Palace before lunch. News of public unrest on the Place de la Concorde could be in Whitehall within the hour. So long rivals, Britain and France began the Great Exhibition separated by days of travel and nearly 21 miles of sea. They ended it in direct communication.

2

CATASTROPHE AND COLLABORATION: THE CRIMEAN WAR

Off the Devon coast of Torbay and Plymouth was the nearest Napoléon Bonaparte ever got to England. That was in 1815 and the deposed French emperor, so long the terror of all Europe, was on his way to a second exile, this time on the Atlantic island of St Helena. He would not return, alive at least. His nephew, Emperor Napoléon III, did considerably better. In the spring of 1855 he landed at Dover, bound for London. At Windsor Castle, Napoléon and his empress, Eugénie, met Victoria and Albert on 16 April. The queen recorded her first impressions in her journal: 'The 'Emperor is extremely short, but with a head & bust, which ought to belong to a much taller man.'[1] Given that, at barely 5ft, she herself was pint sized, Napoléon's lack of height must have been striking.

Over the next few days the two couples, one royal, one imperial, made quite the set. Dining, dancing, and wondering at London's marvels, Napoléon treated Victoria to a masterclass in charm. She fell completely. On 17 April they attended a parade by day, and by night Victoria and Napoléon danced a quadrille, ironically in a room named after the last time British and French armies had danced on the battlefield. 'Really to think of a G^d Daughter of George IIIrd, dancing with the nephew of our great enemy, the Emp^r Napoléon now my most firm Ally, <u>in</u> the <u>Waterloo Gallery</u> – is incredible!' mused the queen.² She certainly knew how to be diplomatic. Another night they attended *Fidelio* at Covent Garden. Receiving an enthusiastic reception from the audience, Victoria and Eugénie provided a spectacular contrast. Elegant and refined, the empress wore a white tulle crinoline, edged with white marabou feathers. Stylish to say the least. Accompanying Victoria's blue and gold dress was a diadem of diamonds and a necklace of huge Indian rubies. Inelegant, the uncharitable might conclude.³

The party did not end there. Napoléon invited his new royal friends for a return leg in Paris and, on 18 August, Victoria and Albert set sail for Boulogne aboard the royal yacht.⁴ As they came into harbour the emperor himself awaited them, along with a modest reception of 40,000 French soldiers. Napoléon welcomed the couple to France and they quickly made for Paris. Victoria later noted that all along the way crowds cheered 'Vive la Reine d'Angleterre'.⁵ How long ago Waterloo must have seemed. Paris dazzled in the sun, its streets lined with troops, flowers, flags, and wide-eyed Parisians. At dinner the emperor confessed to Victoria 'that such enthusiasm as we had witnessed today, had <u>not</u> been known in <u>Paris</u>, - not even in the time of the 1^rst Emp^r Napoléon's triumphs!'⁶ He might have been slightly envious, but he certainly knew how to seduce. Rooms were ready for Victoria and Albert at the Palace of Saint-Cloud, the same suite that had belonged to the ill-fated Queen Marie Antoinette. Napoléon had ordered these redecorated at vast expense in white and gold, with ceilings painted to appear like sky, resembling Victoria's own apartments at Buckingham Palace.⁷ She loved it. Naturally, good food followed, with breakfast and luncheon served on china dating from the first emperor but repainted with royal fleurs de lis.⁸ The ghosts of France's political past manifested themselves all around. With his German love of utility and austere eye, Albert found much of this ostentation distasteful. Albert had never been impressed with Napoléon, once describing him as 'a walking lie'.[9] But then, he was not the head of state, and this was very much a show for Victoria, the real power in the relationship.

Above all, it was Paris that stole her heart. Under an immense rebuilding project, the city had never looked so good. Ever on the arm of Napoléon, Victoria visited the newly completed Arc de Triomphe and the Exposition Universelle, including the Palais de L'Industrie. They toured the Hotel de Ville, the site of Louis XVI's execution, and the wondrous Gothic splendour of Sainte-Chapelle, which Victoria thought to be 'of the purest early Gothic architecture'. Notre-Dame followed, though she thought it a bit dull inside, despite a glorious exterior.[10] Victoria had, perhaps, never known such prolonged excitement. In her journal she wrote, ecstatically, 'Everything, so gay, so bright, & though very hot, the air so clear & light. The absence of smoke keeps everything so white & bright, & this, in Paris, with much gilding about the shops, green shutters, &c – produces a brilliancy of effect which is quite incredible.'[11] For once, British coal-powered industry was to be regretted, with the smoke-stained cities of Britain a far cry from the beauty of Paris. It was a long and bustling visit, but daily telegrams kept the royals informed of their children's health and movements.

Paris had excelled, Victoria and Albert had sparkled, and Napoléon and his empress had charmed. As state visits go, this was an absolute triumph. Even the weather approved. 'Most truly do the Heavens favour & smile upon our visit & upon this happy alliance,' a thoroughly satisfied Victoria declared.[12] Yet the context had been a grim one and the meetings in both London and Paris of tremendous importance. Throughout, a dark shadow hung over all the glamour and finery. A spectre-like subject had been on the edge of all conversation: the war in the Crimea. The 'happy alliance' between Britain and France had been a strained one. Together they were at war with Tsarist Russia: a long, drawn-out affair stretching from the spring of 1854 well into 1856. The two meetings between monarch and emperor were intended to shore-up relations between the two great powers. The publicity and popular appeal they aroused on either side of the Channel could not have come at a more critical moment. Victoria and Albert had dispensed a sorely wanted sprinkle of celebrity on an alliance that was in danger of falling apart.

*

Britain and France had very different reasons for war in 1854. For Britain, it was the threat of Russian naval access to the Mediterranean, from the Black Sea via the Dardanelles. Russian influence over such a vital line of communication between Britain and India was bound to unsettle British politicians. France, on the other hand, had political and religious interests. For both nations the problem was the rapid decay of Turkey, the 'Sick Man of Europe'. The growing political instability of this once great Islamic power, the Ottoman Empire, became obvious during the 1820s with a rebellion in Greece. After a bitter guerrilla war, Greece secured independence from Turkey in 1829. Then, in 1831, Egypt followed, promptly launching an invasion into Syria. In desperation to prevent the empire's impending collapse, Sultan Mahmud II sought help from Tsar Nicholas I, who despatched the Russian fleet to the Mediterranean. Shaken by Russia's eagerness to exert influence in Syria, Britain and France demanded the sultan refuse Russian aid and accept that Egypt should be allowed to keep the region. This he did. A failed

Ottoman attempt to recapture Syria in 1839 confirmed Turkey's decline. Determined to prevent any further Russian influence in the eastern Mediterranean, France entered into a secret treaty with the Ottoman Empire, promising to assist it in case of invasion. Austria, Prussia, and Britain signed a convention in 1840 offering similar terms, as did Russia. But Nicholas' plan was to expel the Turks from Europe once and for all. And in 1850 he found the perfect excuse to do just that.

Since 1815 France's standing in Europe had been contained. After the Congress of Vienna that followed the Napoleonic Wars, France was largely denied international influence. Determined to change this, the newly elected Louis-Napoléon saw an opportunity to rebalance European politics. As ever, the dispute was over the Holy sites of Jerusalem. Under the terms of an almost forgotten treaty between France and the Ottoman Sultan in 1740, Roman Catholic monks were entitled to have the key to the main door of the Church of Bethlehem and keys to each door to the Sacred Manger. It was also agreed that a silver star bearing the arms of France was to be placed in the Sanctuary of the Nativity. This Turkish-French treaty was an assertion of Roman Catholicism in Palestine that would be backed by French naval power if required. Until 1850, no one really cared enough to enforce the treaty's terms, but Napoléon saw his chance. The keys to the holy sites were in the hands of Greek Orthodox priests and Russia had a 'right of intervention' into the Ottoman provinces of Wallachia and Moldavia, specified in the 1812 Treaty of Bucharest, should it feel the Greek Orthodox Church was under threat from the Islamic state. By enforcing the terms of the Ottoman-French treaty of 1740, Napoléon would not only provoke Russia into a war that might enhance French international influence, but his defence of the rights of the Catholic Church could well secure him invaluable religious support in France, stabilising his political position.

Entente Imperial

When Napoléon demanded Sultan Abdülmecid, ruler of the Ottoman Empire since 1839, conform with the terms of the 1740 treaty, he refused. But when the French emperor insisted, threatening to send the French fleet to close the Dardanelles, the sultan had little choice but to remove the keys from the Greek Orthodox Church and hand them over to Roman Catholic monks. In December 1852 the silver star went up in the Sanctuary of the Nativity. Riots followed, some Orthodox priests were killed, and by March 1853 the Tsar demanded the Orthodox Church's privileges be restored. The sultan refused, emboldened by the promise of French naval support. In May, Russia broke off diplomatic relations with Turkey, soon followed by an ultimatum. This was rejected and, by July, Russian troops had marched into Moldavia and Wallachia. This advance on the Danube was accompanied with an invasion through the Caucasus towards Persia and a Russian fleet deployed for Constantinople. By October, Turkey and Russia were at war.

Humiliatingly for Nicholas, it took only a month for the apparently feeble Turkish forces to bring Russia's armies to a standstill. Desperate for a victory, the Russian Black Sea fleet launched an attack on a Turkish naval squadron sheltering from bad weather at Sinope. Given that the Turkish ships consisted only of a few frigates, a steamer, two schooners, and a handful of transport vessels, the Russian fleet's six fully armed battleships, two frigates, and four steamers had an overwhelming amount of firepower. Predictably, a slaughter ensued. The destruction of the Turk squadron was so complete that Sinope could be seen as little else but an atrocity. France and Britain, hovering on the edge of war, felt bound to act. Together they demanded the Russian Black Sea fleet return to its port, Sebastopol, but the Tsar chose instead to break off diplomatic relations. An Anglo-French ultimatum followed in February 1854, but on receiving no response Britain and France declared war on Russia on 28 March.[13]

Using its vast naval superiority, Britain sent a fleet to the Baltic to blockade the Gulf of Finland. But Napoléon and the British cabinet, a coalition of Whigs, Free Traders, and Peelite Tories under the premiership of Lord Aberdeen, soon agreed that the centre of operations would be in the Black Sea, on the Crimean Peninsula. Here they would land an expeditionary force combining both armies that would swiftly seize the port of Sebastopol and neutralise Russian naval power in the Black Sea. By June 1854, Anglo-French blockades in the Black and Baltic seas ensured the Russian fleets could not leave port, but this was not enough. In France, Napoléon wanted a great victory on land. The political value of this was obvious, reminiscent of the great military victories of his uncle, Napoléon Bonaparte. In Britain *The Times* also called for an attack on Sebastopol. It had taken Aberdeen time to get used to the idea that his government should ally with France against Russia, but the massacre of Sinope shook his conviction that the Tsar did not want conflict. Hesitatingly, the Prime Minister was drawn towards war. On the outbreak of hostilities, Aberdeen considered resigning but the queen, in tears, begged him not to abandon her to Palmerston and his supporters, who had promoted British intervention against Russia.[14] At the end of June, the Duke of Newcastle, Minister of War, ordered an assault on the Black Sea port.

This was easier said than done. Britain's peacetime army was woefully small and its contribution to the expedition numbered about 27,000 troops under the command of the sixty-six-year-old Lord Raglan. The French army would therefore have to do the bulk of the fighting. More worrying was that the British general staff lacked experience, with half of the divisional commanders having seen no action. Of those that had, the French had been the enemy, not the ally. Raglan himself had served as an aide-de-camp on Wellington's staff from 1808 until 1814 in Portugal, Spain, and

France, and again at Waterloo. Here he had lost his right arm and that was to be his final taste of battle until the Crimea, thirty-nine years later.

In contrast, the French command was supposedly superior, having seen combat in France's recent war in Algeria; at least this was the theory. Marshal Jacques Leroy de Saint-Arnaud was in overall charge of the French forces. Unlike Raglan who, as one of Wellington's staff officers, had no direct experience of commanding units in battle, Saint-Arnaud had cut his teeth throughout the 1840s in the protracted French Algerian campaign. Yet his appointment to command the Crimean expedition had more to do with his political connections. Or so his critics would have us believe. Saint-Arnaud's support of Napoléon had been crucial to the emperor's rise to power. A fellow conspirator, he had secured Napoléon the army's loyalty and ensured reliable troops were in the right place at the right time during the 1851 coup. But Saint-Arnaud was, by 1853, a sick man; by 1854 he was a dead man walking. What began as a persistent stomach infection was, in fact, aggressive stomach cancer. Time was running out for the marshal and he knew it, adding much to his sense of urgency. To his credit, Saint-Arnaud's English was excellent and this was a contributary consideration in his selection.[15]

From the start it was clear things between the French and British would be difficult. The task facing Raglan and Saint-Arnaud was immense. Not only had they to land an expedition on Russian soil, but they had to do this in collaboration with an ally with whom, for centuries, they had traditionally fought. Captain Nigel Kingscote, aide-de-camp and nephew to Raglan, provided an example of how the British commanders viewed their new partners: 'I hate the French and all Saint-Arnaud's staff, with one or two exceptions, are just like monkeys, girthed up as tight as they can be and sticking out above and below like balloons.'[16] And this coming in May 1854, before the staffs had even tried working together.

After passing Constantinople and the Dardanelles, the two armies gathered at Varna. After organising throughout August, Saint-Arnaud took the final decision to sail for the Crimea. Napoléon wanted a swift victory, having little enthusiasm for Sebastopol in particular; this was a British plan due to the port's obvious naval significance. But eager to put an army in the field and with things deadlocked on the Danube, the ailing Saint-Arnaud sought and secured approval from Paris and London. Stressing his doubts over his allies, Saint-Arnaud felt that 'the English have come with the part taken of not to take part. I will make them go to the Crimea in spite of themselves.'[17] Prince Napoléon, cousin to Napoléon III, shared these anxieties over Britain's commitment, emphasising to the British general staff that failure in the Crimea would bring down his cousin's dynasty. For Britain, failure would mean little more than a new cabinet.[18]

Departing Varna, Saint-Arnaud complained of the sloth the British exhibited. French troops embarked on 28 August, but had to wait until 7 September for their partners to be ready. The Royal Navy's claims that the French did not understand the importance of wind for sailing ships carried little weight with the French marshal, ever conscious that his time was running out.[19]

The allied expedition landed on a sandy beach along the ominously named Calamita Bay. Thirty miles north of Sebastopol, the disagreements between the two general staffs intensified. The French felt that their allies were a constant drag on operations. Having landed in the Crimea on 14 September, Saint-Arnaud wanted to move swiftly on to Sebastopol, leaving Calamita Bay by the 17th, but the British were not ready to leave until the 19th. By Varna, Saint-Arnaud knew he would not survive the war and his only hope was to seize Sebastopol before his own death. On landing at Calamita Bay, he wrote to his brother that it 'has now been made quite apparent to the English that I was right ... I have a military flair which I can count on and the English have not made war since 1815.'[20] His confidence was reasonable, if premature; the Russians were trapped to the expedition's south and would be forced to defend Sebastopol. But speed was of the essence. While the British struggled to unload their cavalry in the heavy surf, Saint-Arnaud sat on the beach in the sun reading a newspaper.[21]

Having finally departed, the Anglo-French force found the Russians holding a very strong position on the River Alma. Facing some 39,000 troops and ninety-six guns, Saint-Arnaud formulated a cunning plan in which the French would provide a flanking manoeuvre, with the British making a decisive assault on the Russian 'Great Redoubt'.[22] In the semi-official report of the war, written with Napoléon's sanction, César Lecat de Bazancourt, the emperor's official historian, provided a French account of Britain's performance throughout the expedition. Though an allied victory, Bazancourt reported that at the Alma Raglan had delayed issuing orders to his divisional commanders so that the French-planned 7 a.m. assault did not begin for another three and half hours. This bizarre error gave the Russians time to reorganise their defences, strengthening the flank on which Saint-Arnaud intended to concentrate his attack. The day after the battle, the French marshal planned to push on to Sebastopol. But still the British delayed, apparently incapable of organising in time. Another day and further initiative was lost.[23] 'My soldiers run; theirs march,' Saint-Arnaud noted scornfully.[24] Bazancourt was equally blunt: 'The English, intrepid and indefatigable in action, appear not to understand the vast importance of a day, or an hour of delay, in a warlike operation.'[25] Bazancourt admired the order and bravery the British displayed at the Battle of the

Alma, despite tough terrain and heavy artillery fire. The battle had been a great demonstration of what a formidable alliance the two powers forged: the 'distinctive genius of the French and English nations, and the individual character of each people, were strikingly manifested on this occasion'.[26] But overall, the French were dissatisfied with their partners. Though brave, the British army showed little initiative; at the Alma it 'was completely wanting in pliability', complained Bazancourt.[27]

For Raglan's part, it had been the French who had dithered at the Alma. The evening following the battle, having a whole division fresh in reserve, he had wanted to push on, but found Saint-Arnaud unwilling on account of his soldiers having shed their knapsacks at the start of the assault. The French would not advance without these, so spent the end of the day retracing the battlefield to collect them. Angrily, Raglan reported to the Duke of Newcastle:

> The French Army accomplished what they undertook perfectly well but Lord Burghersh will tell you *confidentially* what is the general conviction in the English Army that if Marshal Saint-Arnaud had kept moving on after he had turned the Enemy's left, the results of the victory would have been immediate, large bodies of prisoners would have fallen into our hands and the dispersion of the Russian Troops would have been extensive.[28]

The French certainly knew how to add insult to injury. During the assault on the Great Redoubt, a formidable defensive work, the British had captured two guns, highly prized trophies indeed. However, seizing them from the Russians was one thing, holding on to them the following morning quite another, as a captain on Raglan's staff explained: 'Ld R[aglan] sent this morn to have the guns *we* had taken brought down & parked close to his Tent, can you conceive the *French* having had the bad taste to send two limbers with 6 Horses to take them away? Ld R could not help laughing at the impudence ... They give us the brunt of the Action, & when we take the Battery ... have the face to attempt to take the Guns *we* captured away from us the next day.'²⁹ Raglan might chuckle, but the strained relationship between the allies was quickly becoming a major obstacle.

There was also suspicion that Saint-Arnaud's poor health had much to do with his refusal to press the allied advantage immediately. Not long after, Saint-Arnaud stood down, with General François Canrobert replacing him in command. Despite their differences, Raglan and Saint-Arnaud had managed to keep friendly relations. Resigning on 25 September, Saint-Arnaud was dead by the 29th. His body was returned to France for a grand burial, full of pomp and ceremony, and Napoléon rewarded his widow with a large annuity. *The Times* correspondent William Russell considered that, though his 'private character ... was far from a model for imitation', had Saint-Arnaud lived to direct the ensuing siege of Sebastopol, he was sure that 'the operations would doubtless have been more bold, if not more successful, than they have proved to be under Lord Raglan and General Canrobert'.³⁰

Even with the delay at the Alma, the allies had to leave some 750 injured casualties on the battlefield. In *The Times*, Russell described the savage scene, with the dead 'festering in heaps around the sick and dying'. Only 340 made it to a ship for evacuation.³¹ Alma had been tough, but the real foe was cholera. Since landing, the allies had been dogged by disease and this continued to plague the troops on the march to Sebastopol. By 4 October the French were ready to lay siege to the port, but due to further delays the first shots were not fired for twelve more days. Lieutenant-General Sir Charles Windham blamed Raglan. 'We decidedly have no Wellington here,' he wrote home.³²

Sir George Brown, commander of the Light Division and veteran of the Napoleonic Wars, resented accusations of dawdling and thought it was the French who had put up a poor show. Believing the British infantryman to be the finest in the world, he reported the French staff had been so impressed at the discipline of his own men that they had implemented British army exercises and drill. The French were also, apparently, envious of the respect British soldiers paid their officers. Brown claimed that those who thought the British had 'everything to learn from the French' were mistaken.[33]

Despite such pride, there was a strong sense that the British had had to be guided through the campaign. One anonymous French general officer serving in the Crimea, almost certainly Prince Napoléon, called for the campaign to be abandoned as, by 1855, there was no prospect of success. It was his opinion that the French emperor had only to take the initiative in this matter for the British to follow. Indeed, he thought that with Napoléon III's influence, Britain would follow France 'to the edge of the world'.[34]

To be fair, many British officers had equal doubts over the competence of their seniors. Captain Louis Nolan, for example, was infuriated at Raglan's reluctance to deploy the cavalry to pursue the retreating Russian army from the Alma. As the allied armies moved south and laid siege to Sebastopol, this discontent mounted, with reasonable cause. Having regrouped after the Alma, the Russian army made a bid to relieve the besieged port. The allies had employed the small fishing town of Balaklava to supply the entrenched troops around the city, but this created a very exposed line of communications. On 25 October General Pavel Liprandi, the Russian army's commander, took his chance, pushing forward along the road connecting Balaklava and Sebastopol. With the French engaged in the siege, Raglan was woefully vulnerable, having only the cavalry division, 1,200 marines, a few Turkish units, and the 93rd Highlanders to hold back 25,000 Russians. After brave Turkish resistance, the Russian onslaught captured the allied defences. Seeing the danger, Raglan ordered two divisions up from the siege, while the 93rd held off the attack. Russell of *The Times* immortalised this action, famously referring to it as the 'thin red line'. A hugely successful heavy cavalry charge followed. About 300 British cavalrymen threw back some 3,000 Russian chargers, relieving the 93rd.[35]

All seemed calm, but the British general staff knew how to snatch defeat from the jaws of victory. Looking to press the advantage, Raglan hoped to attack with infantry and the Light Brigade, but the divisions from the siege had still not arrived. When the Russians began moving British guns from the defences they had captured in the morning, Raglan ordered the cavalry to charge, but through a confused message which Captain Nolan delivered to Lord Lucan, commanding the cavalry division, the Light Brigade charged the wrong guns. Instead of recapturing British guns, Lord Cardigan led his brigade of Light Dragoons, Lancers, and Hussars straight into a battery of Russian guns, flanked on either side by more guns and infantry.

In what became notorious as the 'Charge of the Light Brigade', of some 673 cavalrymen, 260 were casualties, with 475 horses lost. This was a monumental calamity and appeared irrefutable proof of the incompetence of Britain's officers, including Raglan.[36] Above all though, it was the Earl of Cardigan and his brother-in-law Lord Lucan who epitomised the lack of professionalism prevalent within the British general staff. Both had purchased their commands and had no military experience. Since the militaristic rule of Oliver Cromwell in the 1650s, British politicians had feared allowing the army too much influence. To ensure it did not become a politically dangerous organ, the purchase system in which wealthy men paid for their rank ensured the ruling aristocracy were connected with the army in a way that would not risk political stability. But this did not make for competent officers, as the Crimea painfully demonstrated. Worse still, Lucan and Cardigan hated each other, being rivals since Lucan married Cardigan's youngest sister, Anne, in 1829. Raglan had shown profound stupidity in appointing Cardigan commander of the Light Brigade which, as one half of the cavalry division, was under Lucan's direction. A worse pairing could hardly have been found.[37] Cardigan left the Crimea in December on medical grounds and in January 1855 the Minister of War recalled Lucan. Neither were missed.[38]

Though Lucan and Cardigan provided the most notorious examples of incompetence and the Charge of the Light Brigade by far the most dramatic disaster, this was no isolated example. If the French distrusted their allies, they probably had good reason. After seeing the inexplicable charge, Liprandi took a lot of convincing that the cavalrymen had not all been drunk. The French were equally shocked at the stupidity of their partners. Famously, the French General Pierre François Bosquet proclaimed it 'magnificent, but not war'.[39]

Following another failed attempt to lift the siege at what became known as the Battle of Inkerman, both sides settled down into the grim deadlock of trench warfare. Anglo-French disputes persisted. When Canrobert ordered Raglan place what remained of the cavalry on the flank of the besieging troops, Lucan refused. He worried that this was too far from Balaklava to supply the horses with fodder. By November the roads were in a woeful state, so Lucan's concern was well placed. But Canrobert pressed the point, fearing that not to put the cavalry into the line would reveal to the Russians how weak it was. Raglan agreed and Lucan's prophecy was fulfilled: the horses starved. The few surviving animals were

A French rifle pit before Sebastopol, revealing the grim deadlock of trench warfare. (Author's collection)

taken back to Balaklava and stabled in a series of deep cave-like holes which promptly filled with rats. This was a sad end for those creatures lucky enough to have survived the charges of Balaklava. By January 1855, Anglo-French disagreements ensured that there was hardly a horse left.[40]

Going into the winter of 1854/55 the British had about 25,000 troops in the peninsula, compared to 40,000 French, which rapidly increased to over 75,000. By January, France had four times the number of British soldiers in the Crimea. During this winter, it often seemed that the French had the only effective army in the field. British organisation was shambolic. Lieutenant-General Windham conceded that the 'organisation of the French is beautiful, ours is a perfect disgrace'. While British rations were issued individually, to be prepared in any way a soldier could manage, the French implemented mass hot food production. Each regiment had its own baker. British soldiers relied on French charity for their daily bread. On one day alone, the French provided some 35,000 loaves for their starving allies.[41]

When Canrobert returned to Paris in August 1855 he was perhaps diplomatic in his review of the war's conduct. Seated next to Queen Victoria on her stay at Saint-Cloud, he delivered a glowing account of the recently deceased Raglan and the English in general. In her diary, Victoria recorded how she dined with the general, fresh 'from the trenches'. Canrobert assured the queen of the bravery of her troops and the competence of her generals. A man untroubled by the demands of veracity you might think, but not Victoria. 'Such an honest good man, so sincere & friendly, & so fond of the English', she wrote. Before leaving Paris she rewarded the general with the Order of the Bath, presumably for his honesty.[42]

Among the rank and file there were mixed experiences of the Anglo-French alliance. Surgeon Douglas Reid had recently completed his medical degree at the University of Edinburgh, just weeks before leaving for the Crimea. In January 1855 he had great hopes that the French army's size, now at almost 100,000 troops, would ensure Sebastopol would fall swiftly, but after several months in the trenches he was sorely disillusioned. When a shell exploded at a battery near his camp, injuring a French soldier, Reid reported how this 'made a lot of others take to their heels. Certainly the French are splendid soldiers, *to run*.'[43] However, Reid was in a minority. While the generals and staff officers bickered, in the camps and trenches before Sebastopol, British and French soldiers shared in the horrors of the campaign. Here there was respect and often outright friendship.

Harry Powell was a lucky man. The son of a soldier, born and raised in India, he had joined the 13th Light Dragoons and charged with the Light Brigade at Balaklava. In the weeks after this haunting encounter, Powell found a rare moment of pleasure through his comradeship with French soldiers. Encamped around Sebastopol, Powell enjoyed drinking hot coffee and wine with his Gallic partners, who would always welcome the young cavalryman to their camp, addressing him as '*Bone* English'. Twenty years later, Powell reflected that 'they are the jolliest and merriest comrades in arms on the face of the earth. Many and many a glass I have had with them on the French Hill at Balaklava,'[44]

Dr Frederick Robinson was equally grateful for French hospitality. On the march from Calamita Bay to the Alma, Robinson's first impression was one of envy. French soldiers were allowed to pillage for food, taking and eating what they liked from the local peasants, but the British had to make do with three days of cold salt pork and biscuit, issued on ship before landing.[45] But he soon came to cherish these foreign collaborators, learning fast

British and French soldiers enjoying each other's company. In the centre a highlander engages with a Frenchman over a game of chess. (Author's collection)

that little exceeded 'the kindness and even tenderness of the French soldiers'.[46] Having survived a serious case of diarrhoea which took on 'a choleraic form', leaving him dangerously sick throughout October, Robinson endured the harsh winter of 1854/55 in the misery of the trenches. On 16 January, having washed in water lumpy with ice, the surgeon complained that a portion of freshly made mustard froze within minutes. He grew tired of treating frostbite and illness, especially soldiers with 'mortification of the toes', and hoped his government would send no more men to die in the futile venture.[47]

The one comfort in this calamity was French food. Robinson was pleased to find by mid-January that 'Bread is now to be obtained at an enterprising French baker's' for the 'modest sum' of two shillings a loaf. French butter was to be had too. Here was a welcome alternative to the salt pork, potatoes, and preserved milk on offer in the British army.[48] Beyond bread and butter, the French had also tried to assist with treating sick and wounded British soldiers, but found the task overwhelming. Robinson appreciated the 'French charity, on which we have hitherto depended so much', but acknowledged that it had been 'overtaxed and exhausted'.[49] It was not the job of the French army to prop up the British indefinitely.

The problem, as Robinson saw it, was that unlike the French, the British army lacked any sense of 'system'. Many shared this view that the French were vastly better organised. Florence Nightingale, appalled at the lack of medical provisions encountered during the war, looked to the French army for a model of how to cope with casualties. Its hospital facilities were superior, as was the training of its medical orderlies. In June 1856 she expressed her envy of French medical statistics. Although the French had a poor ratio of medical officers to patients compared with the British, Nightingale lamented that they still managed to keep better records of medical treatment and patient observations.[50] Maintaining the army's health relied on keeping track of a patient's symptoms and condition, and of how they had been treated. Evidently this was a struggle for British doctors, but the French seemed far more competent.

Indeed, it was hard to review Britain's performance in the Crimea without reference to the French army. And it did not make for pretty reading. In a war in which the majority of casualties were from disease, exposure, and infection, Britain's healthcare was pathetic. During the awful winter of 1854/55, over 35 per cent of those admitted to British hospitals died. In French hospitals the rate was just 6 per cent. Throughout the winter almost of a quarter of British troops in the Crimea died, compared with 11 per cent of the French force. The sanitary reforms, in which Nightingale was so central, did much to improve this. By the following winter just under 2 per cent of British casualties died in hospital. Surprisingly, the French rate peaked during the same time, at 35 per cent.[51] But by then Sebastopol had fallen, the war was drawing to a close, and few cared so much about a conflict that had gone on too long. When it had really mattered, between 1854 and 1855, the British army had been a national embarrassment.

On the battlefield too, the French soldier was respected. William Russell informed his readers that 'The French are very good soldiers, and very kind and good natured. They will do any thing for the English. They fight to the last man for the English.'[52] Russell reported how, late one night, a force of Russian troops sallied forth from their defences to surprise a British encampment. He woke to find the French had foreseen the attack and plotted an ambush. The French valiantly defended their allies and deterred the Russians from venturing beyond Sebastopol again. Likewise, at Balaklava it had been French daring that had come to the partial rescue of the Light Brigade. Russell described how, on seeing the disaster unfold, 'the French cavalry made a most brilliant charge' to relieve pressure on Cardigan's cavalrymen who were, by this point, returning down the valley on foot.[53] This was in fact, a brigade of French-African chasseurs, without whom Bazancourt asserted the Light Brigade would have been annihilated altogether.[54]

Though unquestionably a tragedy, the Crimea did provide opportunities for Britain and France to show off their technological enterprise. The fleet that carried the expedition included several steamships, and the conflict was the first to be photographed. Never before had the bleakness of battle been so much on public display. Both Victoria and Napoléon acquired large photographic albums of the war. This was also the first time the railway appeared on the battlefield. In February 1855 a group of British engineering entrepreneurs constructed a 10-mile line from Balaklava to the front. At first, horses pulled trucks along the rails, replaced then with a stationary steam engine, and eventually steam locomotives brought in from Britain. With telegraphy the expedition was in daily communication with its political leaders in Paris and London. In April 1855 a submarine link from the Crimea to Varna, and then to Istanbul, connected up with an overland route to Paris. A message from Balaklava could reach London within five hours. British and French generals alike resented this communication system. The daily reporting this involved marked a significant loss of authority for the military command as politicians secured increased influence over the campaign. Victoria and Napoléon demanded a daily telegraph report from their generals, while Palmerston, who had replaced Aberdeen as Prime Minister in February 1855 at the head of a coalition government, complained of the lack of detail in despatches.[55] At the grand age of seventy, Palmerston ascended to the position of Prime Minister on 6 February 1855, very much the embodiment of an imperial statesman who understood Britain's global obligations. Unlike the peace-seeking Aberdeen, Palmerston was seen as a leader who knew how the war should be managed, but his ability to control Parliament through his hold on public opinion often drew comment that he was dictatorial. Telegraphy offered the new Prime Minister an unprecedented amount of influence over military affairs for a politician. In many ways the Crimean War, was the first industrial conflict. Machines, steam power, and electricity were all brought onto the battlefield. Added to the trench stalemate of Sebastopol, it is hard not to see this as a dark premonition of the twentieth-century horrors of the First World War.

Sebastopol would not finally fall until 8 September 1855. By then, Napoléon was eager for peace. In many respects, the war had been fought to secure popular support, but the shambles that unfolded had the opposite effect and the emperor recognised the prudence of an early ceasefire. The Russians, for their part, were in a hopeless position. Though only by the inches of siege warfare, they had undoubtedly lost in the Crimea, they had failed to beat the Turkish on the Danube, and it looked likely that the Austrian Empire would soon open hostilities. Ironically, by 1856 Britain, under Palmerston's aggressive premiership, had finally mobilised a large naval force, which was ready to sail for the Baltic to St Petersburg. This never happened, the war ending damply at the Peace of Paris, signed on 30 March. Along with pulling out of the Danube provinces and returning territory to Moldavia, Russia agreed to abandon its claims to protect Christians living within the Ottoman Empire, handing this responsibility over to France, while its battleships were prohibited from the Black Sea. However, Turkey remained unstable and the peace brought about no permanent solution to the problem of the 'Sick Man of Europe'. For a conflict that had cost 750,000 lives, including soldiers and civilians, this felt unsatisfactory.

Catastrophe and Collaboration: The Crimean War

Few thoughtful observers could deny that France had saved Britain in the Crimea. It was only French organisation and French numbers that had prevented this chaotic calamity descending into a total disaster. Back home, churchmen sought to determine the implications of the war for congregations across the British Isles. *The Times* might have held sway with the educated reading public, but a considerable majority of society looked to the pulpit for an interpretation of the conflict. And there was no shortage of religious, Biblically informed readings of the Crimea, delivered through hundreds of sermons. At the parish church of St Mary Abbots in Kensington, John Sinclair, the local vicar, preached a sermon in March 1855 on the true cost of the campaign. Accusing his congregation of hubris, he warned against the 'blind mistaken patriotism which exaggerates British prowess, and pronounces victory inseparable from the British standard'. The shambles that had ensued was God's punishment for this sin of pride. Since 1815, Britain's fleets and armies had acquired new 'engines of destruction', including bigger guns and steam-powered ships, enriching man's 'art of destroying human life'. But it was the cholera that had proven deadliest – providential wrath in the form of disease had trumped human technology. Sinclair grimly reflected that 'the pestilence that walketh in the darkness' is often still more desolating than 'the arrow that flieth by day'.[56]

On the same day that Kensington audiences took heed of Sinclair's challenging words, H. G. Merriman spoke in the Parish Church of Badger, in Shropshire. Again it was the nation's arrogance and confidence in its technological power that were the clergyman's targets. He reminded listeners of the euphoria of the outbreak of war back in 1854 and the belief in modern steam power and artillery. 'What was the sound that we heard on all sides? What was the note which the journals of the day sounded in our ears?' he asked, before answering that 'We were told that modern discoveries had made us independent of the winds and waves; that modern science would soon enable us to destroy, without risk to ourselves, the strongest works of our enemy.'[57] Armed with science, the public had abandoned faith, Merriman asserted. Religion had been 'but a useless revival of a worn-out superstition', now made redundant 'by the powers of steam'. But the moral lesson of the Crimea was that modern science had not placed man beyond God's judgement. The army was weak, sick, and starving. Like some Old Testament plague, cholera had ravaged the expedition, while Sebastopol's walls had not fallen, baffling all 'the resources of modern science' and shaking man's belief in his own ingenuity. At sea, ships still wrecked on rocky coasts, evidence of the tiny power of steam. On land and on water it was God, not man, and definitely not Britain, who determined events.[58]

The war with Russia shook national confidence and the tedious siege of Sebastopol sapped spirits at home. But it was not all doom and gloom. Many took comfort that Britain had at least been on the winning side. On 4 May 1856, the Sunday appointed for giving national thanks for the Peace of Paris, sermons throughout Britain announced victory in no uncertain terms. Between 1836 and 1860 architect Charles Barry designed and built the new Palace of Westminster, home to Britain's Houses of Parliament. In 1856 his son, Revd Alfred Barry, gave a sermon at Leeds Parish Church offering thanks for the end of the war. Although the nation had discovered its weaknesses, it had also demonstrated its strength. Barry asked the good people of Leeds if there had ever been such 'a great war which was so little felt directly or indirectly, by the country'. Before a collection for the Nightingale Fund, he declared that Britain had enjoyed 'all the blessings of peace, while our enemies suffered under the horrors of war'. The conflict had 'called out, instead of weakening, our material power, and our national spirit; so that it seems that we are the only nation in Europe, who could continue it without distress'.[59] For evidence, he invoked the noble charity of Britain's nurses, especially Nightingale.

True enough, the experience of the Crimea for most in Britain was through the comfort of *The Times* and sermons, rather than actual warfare. A cynic might have pointed out that Britain had only been able to weather the challenge by relying on France's large army. Naval and financial power was one thing, but someone had to do the fighting and it was not going to be the British army alone. But Barry's views were widely shared. Victorian Britain encountered the war as a novelty to be read about in the news. At Walbrook Church, George Croly echoed Barry's sentiments. The fault of the war was obviously Russia's and its defeat evidence of heaven's 'providential government'. Britain and France had little choice but to rescue Turkey. Croly agreed that while Russia was now ruined, the success and wealth God had granted Britain was sure proof that the country was now 'the substitute for Israel' and the English His chosen people. Victory had entailed French cooperation, but this merely showed that Britain was 'on a throne of influence', far greater than any 'throne of conquest'. Technology confirmed this moral superiority. God had seen fit to bestow 'the two greatest inventions of mankind – the railroad and the steam engine' on Britain, as well as the telegraph. 'England is the most opulent of nations,' Croly boasted; there was 'no country whose wealth is so exhaustless'. Like Barry, he thought the pressure of war but lightly felt. Such financial costs would have broken any other nation, but Britain could afford the huge debt, 'well and wisely incurred', to purchase peace. Though professing modesty, Croly announced that the colossal national debt of £700 million should be a source of pride: pride that Britain could finance it. In the name of peace, he declared that

Britain could equally manage a debt of £7,000 million. Financial power beyond counting was the nation's divine gift; its debt a symbol of patriotism. Even the colonies of India, Canada, the West Indies, and Australia were not conquests, but 'matters of divine benefaction and benediction, as plainly as if they had been offered to our hand by the Almighty'.[60]

As much as congregations might learn of a British triumph over Russia, above all else the Crimean War illustrated the importance of British and French collaboration. It is unlikely that either nation could have single-handedly sustained both the expedition to the Crimea and the blockades of the Baltic and Black seas. While Britain's Royal Navy ruled the seas, France was the only nation of the two capable of supplying the numbers of troops required to seize Sebastopol and convert naval control into results on land. Financially and economically Britain was undoubtedly the senior partner, but at times France's military organisation and numerical strength had carried the British army in the Crimea. Nevertheless, together the empires of Napoléon and Victoria proved irresistible and had dealt Tsarist Russia a heavy blow. Tsar Nicholas had died in March 1855, leaving an empire in political and economic turmoil to his heir, Alexander II.

3

PROJECTIONS OF GLOBAL POWER: CULTIVATION AND COMMERCE IN CHINA AND SUEZ

France saw two great departures in 1854. The first, an army, bound for the Crimea. The second, a man, destined for the Orient. Both passed east through the Mediterranean. Just a month after the Anglo-French expedition disembarked on the ominous beach of Calamita Bay, Ferdinand de Lesseps arrived in Egypt. And as British and French soldiers dug in before the walls of Sebastopol, Lesseps began work of a far greater historical significance. Throughout the winter of 1854/55, while French bakers gave bread to frozen British soldiers in the ice of the Crimea, Lesseps surveyed the rolling desert of the Isthmus of Suez, for he had arrived with a single purpose: to build a canal that would unite the oceans.

A canal linking the Red Sea with the Mediterranean would be of huge value to Britain because this would shorten the distance between the mother country and its empire in India and Australia. Lesseps, a Frenchman, could not fail to see the geopolitical significance of his project. While cutting the canal itself was important, so too was the cultivation of Anglo-French relations. As with their shared interest in restricting Russia to the Black Sea, the Mediterranean once again brought Britain and France together in 1854. Again they shared a mutual interest in managing this crucial trade link. But this time it would be an endeavour of shovels and shares, rather than military expeditions and naval blockades.

Lesseps was no engineer. He was a diplomat, having a career lasting twenty-nine years. After a government appointment to Rome in 1849, he purchased a farm in France's Berry district as a retreat, but amused himself reading of the Orient. Soon his attention turned to the Isthmus of Suez, which had first roused his interest in 1841. Surely this should be the route from France to India and, in this age of science and steam, the construction of a canal was within reach. Between 1849 and 1854 Lesseps became fixated on this idea, mixing great questions of geopolitics with the rearing of cattle on his farm.[1]

No engineer to be sure, but Lesseps was a promoter of engineering projects without equal. He knew an opportunity when he saw one and the more audacious the scale, the greater the relish. There was no bigger prize than Suez. A canal here was an old idea, certainly not original to Lesseps. On his ill-fated expedition to Egypt in 1798, Napoléon Bonaparte had thought the prospect tantalising. What would Britain say if France controlled a direct route to India and China? What indeed. This would cut weeks off the voyage between Europe and the subcontinent by way of the southern tip of Africa. Many before him had speculated on this vision, but Lesseps had an energy and determination bordering on monomania.

After diplomatic discussions with the Egyptian Viceroy, Lesseps began his investigation of the land through which he would cut a waterway. Between December 1854 and January 1855 Lesseps' expedition worked away in the desert heat, travelling by camel and living like Bedouin.[2] His conclusion was that, for £6.4 million and six years of digging, a canal 30 leagues long, 100 metres wide, and 8 metres deep could be excavated.[3]

Obviously this required financing on a grand scale. And obviously it involved immense engineering skill. But there were

PORTRAIT OF M. DE LESSEPS

Ferdinand de Lesseps, no engineer, but France's great champion of the Suez Canal project. (Author's collection)

also political difficulties. Lesseps had to get Egypt to support the scheme, as well as the world's leading naval power, which was Britain. By the end of 1854 he had the Egyptians on board. The Khedive of Egypt agreed that Lesseps could establish a company to build and operate a canal, open to all nations. With this authorisation, in 1855 Lesseps launched a charm offensive on

France's commercially minded allies. Within months of returning from Egypt, he sailed for London and a whistle-stop tour of Britain and Ireland to promote his venture. Lesseps' arguments were very simple. The canal would shorten the passage from India to Britain by 3,000 miles and as Britain conducted more trade than the rest of Europe combined, it was British merchants, financiers, and manufacturers who had the most to gain. For example, the round trip of cotton sent from Bombay to Liverpool, then processed in Manchester, before returning to India as cloth could be completed within seventy days, should Lesseps succeed.[4] He declared England to be 'interested more than any other power in the construction of a canal through the Isthmus of Suez' and resolved to 'ascertain the state of public opinion in England on this question'.[5] Above all, the Frenchman came to reassure British audiences that his vision would not injure their trade or their empire. He stressed the canal was not calculated to give France any strategic advantage over world affairs, but was a commercial project. And he was keen to show that Britain had the most to gain from the French endeavour.

The ensuing Lesseps tour was a masterpiece in public relations. Armed with a concession from the Egyptian Viceroy and an apparently credible plan, he began with London, visiting the directors of the East India Trading Company and several leading shipping lines. All seemed to be in favour. The chairman of the Peninsula and Oriental Steam Navigation Company (P&O) wrote a letter supporting the scheme. Emphasising the commercial gains up for grabs, Lesseps then visited Liverpool, Manchester, Dublin, Cork, Belfast, Glasgow, Edinburgh and Leith, Aberdeen, Newcastle, Hull, Birmingham, and Bristol, before returning to London. In these centres of industry and trade he canvassed support from bankers, merchants, and manufacturers. They had nothing to fear from France, Lesseps assured them. France's noble investment would enrich the British beyond all others. This was not about national rivalry, so much as 'the great principles of civilization and of free trade'.[6]

Lesseps pre-circulated a treatise, *The Isthmus of Suez Question*, to shipping and financial communities around the British Isles, setting out the case for the canal, before visiting them in person. He had this pamphlet published in Paris, before then having it translated into English. Lesseps found London's publishers far easier to work with. While the French publication entailed much state regulation, Lesseps appreciated the freedom of England's press.[7] And it was this free press that he mobilised throughout his tour. Here it paid to be the diplomat, rather than the engineer. In each town he visited, he invited journalists to his public meetings. When, the following day, local newspapers published their accounts of the popularity of Lesseps' scheme, the entrepreneurial diplomat had thousands of copies produced, which he took to the next city on his schedule, having these widely distributed. He never mentioned what he did with newspaper reports that were less favourable.

This was not just a charm offensive; it was outright spin. The Suez canal scheme was as much an exercise in propaganda as it was in engineering.[8] All in all, Lesseps held eighteen public meetings and reported almost unanimous approval. In that summer of 1855 he found Britain very much open for business. At meetings, he claimed his listeners were 'subordinating, with a magnanimity that does them honour, the interests of England to those of civilization and humanity'.[9] His loyal collaborator, Bathélemy St Hilaire, launched a Parisian journal which informed French readers of the publicity coup across the Channel. The canal was of such imperial value that 'the public spirit of England rose above all considerations of national interest, however legitimate such may have been, and the question was grasped in all its magnitude and in all its truth'.[10] Lesseps' propaganda conjured up success from the appearance of success.

It was hoped that Britain's politicians would follow the nation's capitalists on the Suez question and back the enterprise in the name of international commerce and cooperation. However, Lesseps found the British government less obliging. In the House of Commons, the MP and engineer Robert Stephenson cast doubt on the scheme's practicality.[11] Lesseps later recalled that during his propaganda assault in Britain, 'while finding sympathy in the commercial and lettered classes, I had found heads of wood among the politicians'.[12] Particularly problematic was that the Prime Minister, Palmerston, declared his personal opposition to Lesseps' project. A canal through Suez risked reordering the balance of international power. Despite British and French armies still allied in the Crimea, Lesseps was annoyed to find himself under direct attack from the Prime Minister. 'He had represented me as a species of pickpocket, wishing to take the shareholders money out of their pockets,' an insulted Lesseps recalled.[13]

The Times was also sceptical. French vanity had clearly got the better of Lesseps. He had been taken in by his own rhetoric. 'The Suez Canal scheme,' observed *The Times*, 'is a question of money, but, unhappily, it is a question that will never be answered. There might be an end, though a very remote one, to the money it would cost for making; but there would be no end to the money it would cost for keeping up.' With sand constantly refilling the excavation, the task would be akin to 'filling a sieve'. There could be no profit in Lesseps' hole in the sand, the newspaper concluded.[14]

Frustrated with what he saw as the British government's lack of vision, in 1858 Lesseps launched a public subscription. Having failed to secure foreign finance, French investors took all 220,000 shares, amounting to 110,000,000 francs at 5 per cent. Amusingly for Lesseps, patriotism and anti-English sentiments proved powerful inducers for subscribers. He found that soldiers and priests were especially eager to put their money in an endeavour 'so eminently French'. One old soldier, a bald-headed priest, arrived to purchase shares at Lesseps' office full of glee at the chance to get his own back for French defeats in the Peninsula War and at Waterloo. 'Oh, those English!' laughed the priest, 'I am glad to be able to be revenged on them by taking shares in the Suez Canal.' Another sharp investor turned up wanting to put his money into the 'Railway of the Island of Sweden'. When Lesseps told him the scheme was actually a canal through the Isthmus of Suez, the prudent financier replied 'That's all the same to me ... provided it be against the English, I subscribe.'[15]

It had taken years to build belief that his project could be realised, as well as to accrue the cash to enact it, but in June 1859 Lesseps finally announced that work had begun.[16] Ten years and millions of francs later, the canal was complete. On its opening in November 1869, *The Times* reported that two ships, one from the Mediterranean and the other from the Red Sea, had met at the lake harbour that connected the canal in the middle of the desert. Lesseps' triumph was certain. 'The antagonism of nature had been vanquished. The difficulties of mechanical science were overcome,' declared *The Times*, flexible as ever. It was not just the difficulties nature presented that had had to be overcome: Britain had also contributed its own fair share of trials. To complete the canal, Lesseps had employed forced Egyptian labour and slave workers from all over the world. About 1.5 million labourers toiled in the desert in woeful conditions, with thousands succumbing to frequent epidemics, especially cholera. Opposed to both the canal and slavery, the British government consistently condemned the French practice of forced labour, even going as far as to provoke unrest among the canal workers. Lesseps, however, was not to be deterred.

Awards and honours followed swiftly, including Queen Victoria appointing Lesseps, appropriately, an honorary Knight Grand Commander of the Order of the Star of India for his efforts to bring Britain and India closer together. While acknowledging the extent of Lesseps' monumental achievement, the British also apparently followed through on a trick of profound annoyance to the French, somewhat ruining the canal's opening ceremony. Marking this great project of Napoleonic internationalism, the Empress Eugenie sailed on *L'Aigle*, the French Imperial yacht, to complete the first official voyage through the canal on 17 November 1869. However, the night before another vessel made this historic passage. It was not a French ship, but HMS *Newport* of the Royal Navy that completed the first transit of the canal. Under Captain George Nares and the stealth of night, the *Newport* made its audacious way through the darkness, passing the massed line of waiting ships and taking a position in front of *L'Aigle*. On the morning of the opening ceremony, the *Newport* led the convoy through the canal, leaving the French horrified. Officially the Admiralty did not condone Nares' daring seamanship, but privately gave thanks for this very British coup. But nothing, not even the possibly apocryphal daring of the *Newport*, could detract from the fact that this was a very French success and the credit belonged to Lesseps. Under the management of the Suez Canal Company established in 1858, in which French shareholders held a majority, the Isthmus of Suez was elevated to the centre of world trade.[17]

Nature would have its revenge though, on Lesseps at least. Never content to rest on his laurels, he set his sights on an even greater prize: the Isthmus of Panama. Having already brought Europe nearer the Far East, in 1879 Lesseps established the Panama Canal Company, tasked with uniting the Atlantic and Pacific Oceans. But this engineering feat was beyond him. Facing the challenge of digging through a mountain range, in what became known as the Culebra Cut, amid torrential rains, and plagued by yellow fever, the French attempt to build a Panama canal was a complete disaster. Lesseps had turned from a canal digger to a gravedigger. In 1889, work was abandoned with the Panama Canal Company declared bankrupt. This failure knocked Lesseps, so famous around the world as 'Le Grand Français' into 'a state of stupor' from which he never recovered, being oblivious to all around him during the final years of his life.[18] He died in 1894, his ambitions costing some $287,000,000, virtually bankrupting France, and producing a death toll of over 22,000 to disease and work-related accidents. It would take the United States and a new century to finally construct the Panama Canal, which opened in 1914. Even then, Lesseps' plan of a sea-level cut canal had to be abandoned. Instead, it would take a system of lock gates to lift ships through the Culebra Cut. Panama was not Suez.

Nevertheless, Lesseps had been right about one thing: British shipping benefitted most from his canal through Suez. In 1874 he reported annual figures for maritime traffic travelling through the passage. British shipping accounted for a staggering 1,797,000 tonnes. In contrast, France was the next biggest user with 222,000 tonnes, then the Dutch with 103,000, Austria 84,000, Italy 63,000, Spain 50,000, Germany 39,000, and the rest of the world totalling 65,000.[19] But the fact remained that Suez was not British, it was French. Then, in 1875, a rare chance presented itself to Benjamin Disraeli, by now Prime Minister, to seize control of this vital imperial connection. Between 1862 and 1875 Egypt's debt boomed from £3 million to £60 million, mostly to French and British creditors. When the Ottoman Empire declared itself bankrupt, the Egyptian state's ability to borrow money was undermined, and the Khedive was forced to sell his country's shares in the canal to raise capital. Disraeli's Conservative government took swift action, securing a Rothschild loan to pay

Entente Imperial

£4 million for the Khedive's 176,602 canal shares, amounting to a 44 per cent stake in the Canal Company. Fearing that the French or Russians might purchase the Khedive's holdings, Disraeli's cabinet worked with impressive speed to make the purchase. Disraeli was rumoured to have announced the British triumph to Victoria with his customary cool charm. 'You have it, Madam,' he informed the enamoured queen of Britain's newest imperial acquisition.[20]

In the 1850s and 1860s, British influence over the canal was far from certain however, and even after 1875, French shareholders still commanded a majority holding in the Canal Company. France would have to be kept on good terms. Although many in Britain feared a French Suez Canal would risk the country's global dominance and threaten its subcontinental possessions, this was not the case. The canal turned out to be just one part of a broader expansion of Anglo-French influence throughout the world. They were rivals, it is true, but these two imperial powers did not operate in isolation. Rather, they collaborated to ensure that they ordered world affairs. A canal through Suez, the containment of Russia in the Baltic and Crimea, vast overseas territories with networks of steamships, railways, and telegraphy to connect them, and huge financial and industrial strength ensured the mid-nineteenth century was the high point of *entente cordiale* influence.[21]

*

In 1859 these global aspirations again united France and Britain. As with Suez, both nations looked East. Having seen off Russia in 1856, attention now turned to China. British and French consumers coveted few things as much as Chinese tea and silk. But China wanted little of European manufacture. Until the early nineteenth century, the purchase of Chinese goods required gold and silver, but this strained Europe's bullion reserves. Opium was the answer. This highly addictive drug, made from poppies that grew well in British India, reversed the flow of precious metals. China became increasingly hooked on opium, with its inhabitants debilitated and its gold and silver rapidly draining away. The celestial Xianfeng Emperor, Yizhu, tried to restrict this European exploitation, but succeeded only in provoking war. Between 1839 and 1842, Britain won a decisive victory in the First China War. The concluding Treaty of Nanking ceded Hong Kong to Britain and opened Canton and Shanghai to European merchants. By 1856 the Xianfeng Emperor's refusal to honour the treaty's trade obligations caused a second war. In October 1856 the Chinese seized the *Arrow*, a ship flying a British flag, using the pretext that its Hong Kong registration had expired. In response, Sir John Bowring, Governor of Hong Kong, ordered an attack of the port of Canton. Palmerston supported this action, defending the right of a governor to act with force as he saw fit, as was his customary practice in such matters. This had not been the first case of China ignoring the terms of the Treaty of Nanking. Palmerston took an aggressive line, with Canton seized on 1 January 1858. In June 1858 the belligerents signed the Treaty of Tientsin, in which China promised Britain and France increased trade rights and allowed each to send a Resident Minister to Peking, the Chinese capital.

Anglo-French success was short-lived. China in 1859 was in chaos. Xenophobia fuelled rebellion, with Taiping and Boxer rebels concentrated around the foreign trade hubs of Canton and Shanghai.[22] The Taiping rebels were challenging the Qing Dynasty's authority and the loss of face incurred from Emperor Yizhu's defeat by foreign powers threatened to undermine him altogether. At the same time, he doubted Britain and France had the ability or resolve to move beyond the coast and, through a mainland invasion, seize Peking. So in 1859 Yizhu again reneged on his treaty commitments, refusing entry to the two European ambassadors. At the mouth of the Pei-ho River, the gateway to Peking, the Taku forts denied access to a Royal Navy task force under the command of Admiral James Hope. Hope ordered an assault on the forts, but of 1,100 Royal Marines deployed, 430 were killed or wounded. It was an embarrassing defeat.[23] Back home in Britain, Palmerston's government could not fail to act. It was now apparent that nothing short of an invasion of China would do. Peking would have to be taken to ensure the emperor complied with the terms of Tientsin. Napoléon was only too pleased to provide support.

Having recently quashed a bloody rebellion in India between 1857 and 1858, the Indian Mutiny, or the First War of Independence, Britain assembled troops at Hong Kong. French soldiers gathered at Shanghai. James Bruce, 8th Earl of Elgin, took responsibility for the diplomatic side of the impending invasion. Elgin's father had been responsible for the earlier removal of the Parthenon Marbles, later known as the Elgin Marbles: James's own mission to China in 1860 would come to be remembered most for an even greater act of cultural brutality. Acting with the authority of the Foreign Office, Elgin would oversee the enforcement of China's treaty obligations and negotiate compensation. The British army of some 16,000 men was under the command of Lieutenant-General Sir Hope Grant. A lean Scottish cavalryman, Hope's only book was the Bible and his relaxation the cello. General Charles Cousin-Montauban, a future Prime Minister of France, commanded the French force, 7,600 strong. Together they were to enforce the Treaty of Tientsin, secure reparations for the war, and get an imperial apology for the Taku Fort incident of 1859. Partnership would be key, as Grant acknowledged, informing the Duke of Cambridge at the War Office that he was 'fully aware that the position in which I am placed with regard to the French force will be one of some difficulty, and as I strongly feel the necessity of keeping on cordial terms with our allies', he would work hard to cultivate a good understanding.[24] Nevertheless, the French were ultimately under Grant's authority and this was a sore point for Britain's partners. But Grant was determined to avoid repeating the mistakes of the Crimea.

With the war against Russia still fresh in public memory, the gradual escalation of hostilities with China provoked mixed responses. An anonymous foreign commentator was confident in the shared power of Britain and France's partnership. Against such might, having already seen off Russia, China had no chance of resistance. As the writer explained, 'We are on the point of seeing an armament by the two most powerful nations in Europe directed against a people as remarkable for their intelligence, in comparison with the other Eastern nations, as they have been heretofore for their helplessness in war against the Powers that they have unwittingly, and perhaps unintentionally aroused.'[25] Doubting that the war would yield financial gains, the commentator was sure the French motive was to secure its alliance with Britain. Nothing brought the rivals together like a fight.

Another anonymous observer, this time British, agreed. War in China would be expensive and any conquest ruinous. While the occupation of India had cost Britain £100 million in liabilities, the author declared that trade with China had made the nation rich. It had 'propped up the debilitating finance of India'. Warning against the acquisition of more territory and the formation of an 'Anglo-Chinese Empire', the one consolation appeared to be Anglo-French collaboration. 'France, it must be taken for granted, could have had no other object in acceding to our invitation to take a share in the expedition … than a desire to cement the alliance with this country,' the observer concluded.[26]

If it was generally assumed that France's reason for war was to preserve relations with Britain, then Britain's motives were usually taken to be economic. On the face of it, China was a protectionist state, taking gold and silver from tea-addicted Europeans, but rejecting competition in the shape of opium-peddling British merchants. War with China was a sort of free trade crusade. Except it was not quite so simple as this. Writing for the *New York Daily Tribune*, Karl Marx took a particular interest in events in the East. As early as 1857 he voiced doubts over Britain's ability to project military power into China. Only a 'decisive result' at Peking would do, and this, Marx calculated, would be difficult for a naval power. Peking, with its vast walls, was the size of London and over 100 miles inland. It would be hard to operate so far from the coast. Even with military success, he warned that the destruction of the Qing Dynasty would open China up to Russian influence and further political instability. Britain and France did not have enough troops to control the outcomes of any victory they might secure.[27]

Marx's grasp of military strategy was hardly strong, but his analysis of the economic implications of the war was far sharper. Britain might claim to be the champion of free trade, but in China it revealed itself a monopolist. Marx argued that British imperialism relied on the opium trade, as much as any addict. The loathsome product was worth £5 million of revenue to Britain's Indian government, which was about a sixth of its total income. To protect this, the government forced Bengal to grow poppies for opium, which was then sold to merchants at Calcutta. The government, having exclusive control over these sales, took most of the profits. Merchants had the job of 'poisoning an empire', but it was the government that orchestrated the trade. Lose opium and British rule in India would become unaffordable, was the Marxist interpretation. Although British politicians claimed to want China open to a free trade in opium, it was British India that grew the poppies. Merchants might compete with each other, but the produce itself had a single source. 'While openly preaching free trade in poison,' Marx claimed, Britain 'secretly defends the monopoly of its manufacture. Whenever we look closely into the nature of British free trade, monopoly is pretty generally found to lie at the bottom of its "freedom".' So much for Victorian liberalism. What really motivated the British, Marx informed American readers, was profit, not competition. In 1858 alone, Britain imported over £9 million of Chinese goods, exporting just £2,876,000. This deficit could only be balanced by Australian gold and American cotton. War would certainly follow. Here was shaming evidence of what Marx saw as the 'self-contradiction of the Christianity-canting and civilization-mongering British Government'.[28]

If Marx saw the rising tensions between Britain, France, and China as evidence of monopoly and hypocrisy, John Stuart Mill took a different view. The Utilitarian philosopher and champion of women's rights thought China provided evidence of the dangers of infringing on personal freedoms and individuality. *On Liberty* became one of the most important works of British political liberalism, but in 1859, with war looming in the East, Mill looked to China for a lesson on liberties. Arguing that individuality and differences among people were crucial to progress, Mill maintained that a nation in which everyone was the same would stagnate. 'We have a warning example in China,' he alleged, a nation that was once so advanced but that was now 'stationary'. Foreign intervention was required to bring about improvement. The problem, as Mill put it, was that China had succeeded 'in making a people all alike, all governing their thoughts and conduct by the same maxims, and rules'. Mill did not advocate an invasion, but he summed up the British perception that China's lack of competition and liberalism had retarded its development. Without individuality and freedoms, 'Europe, notwithstanding its noble antecedents and its professed Christianity, will tend to become another China.' Be the analysis liberal or Marxist, British-Chinese tensions were becoming increasingly ideological.[29]

Oblivious to the analysis of Mill and Marx, Grant departed Hong Kong on 11 June 1860, joining the French at Shanghai five days later. Here the city's merchants, nervous over the threat rebels posed to their property, provided rich hospitality. Grant, between cello recitals, met Montauban and they agreed to seize the Taku Forts. After a French shortage of horses caused some delays, the expeditionary force made for Talienwan, on the Manchurian Peninsula, to prepare for the invasion.[30]

At Talienwan there was mild panic, with echoes of the Crimea, when several soldiers displayed cholera-like symptoms. Two men died from the mystery illness. However, this was no Crimea. The British army was exceptionally well organised and equipped. The cholera turned out to be some dodgy local oysters. And though there were delays at Shanghai and Talienwan, it was not the British but the French who were at fault. 'If in our previous alliance in the Crimea the French cavilled at our want of preparation for war, the boot was certainly on the other foot now,' one satisfied British officer mused.[31] This was a fair point. The French contributed relatively few troops to the war in China and their cooperation appeared of little value beyond the political pressure on Napoléon and Palmerston to maintain healthy relations. Montauban was far from competent, a later commentator observing that the French army's lack of impact on proceedings was due to the incapacity of the general, 'who was a gasconading, self-opinionated man, without a particle of military talent'.[32]

In late July, the Anglo-French force landed on the Chinese coast about 20 miles south of the Pei-ho River. The armada that carried them was truly immense, composed of 173 British and thirty-three French ships. There could be no doubting Britain and

France's ability to project naval power wherever they chose. The young Captain Garnet Wolseley described the marvel: 'Looking around on the brilliant naval spectacle, I could scarce realise the fact of being some 16,000 miles from England. It was a sight well calculated to impress everyone with the greatness of our power ... The magnitude of our naval resources was brought forcibly home to the mind of everyone who saw such a vast fleet collected in the Gulf of Pechilli, without in any way interfering with our commerce elsewhere.'[33] Here was the might of two European empires presented to the world.

On 3 August the two armies moved on the Taku Forts. All the way, Grant, a strict disciplinarian, had his men pay the locals for food. The French preferred to loot. 'This dreadful alliance, what will it not have cost us before we are done with it? The French by their exactions and misconduct have already stirred to resistance the peaceful population of China,' a worried Elgin pondered.[34] Even gunboat diplomacy evidently required some sensitive handling of local inhabitants.

On the River Pei-ho there were four Taku Forts in all. Though the Chinese put up a determined fight, there could be little doubt over the result. Bringing to bear concentrated modern artillery, the Anglo-French bombardment wrought carnage within the forts. On storming them, the allies found a harrowing scene. The savagery of modern gunnery and all the terror of industrial warfare was striking. At a cost of 201 British and 158 French lives, the road to Peking was open.[35] It was much the same story during the allied advance on the capital. Against European guns, Chinese resistance disintegrated and in Peking the emperor fled the foreign invasion.

A plucky young officer, George Allgood, thought it a highly enjoyable affair. Having previously fought in the Indian Mutiny, he had travelled directly from Allahabad to China, via Hong Kong and Singapore on an opium clipper. Writing to his mother, he told her he found Hong Kong's climate preferable to Calcutta's and the Chinese a polite and hospitable people. On the march to Peking he informed her that the land was so comfortable the army would be happy to stay for years if required. It was overflowing 'with milk and honey', full of sheep, cattle, fruit, vegetables, and cheap ice. Even 'Jack Tar' would no longer take his grog without a lump of ice in it, the optimistic young officer marvelled. The one disappointment was the French, who Allgood thought poor allies. 'The French play quite second fiddle, as they have no Cavalry and their Artillery ponies are all done up. Ours is perfection,' he boasted.[36]

Nevertheless, Britain's military reputation from the Crimea lingered on. Keeping a close eye on Anglo-French movements in the East, the *New York Times* in July described, on the occupation of Chusan Island, just south of Shanghai, 'The French, alert as usual, taking advantage of the hesitating steps of their allies to seize upon the best portions of the island, and hoisting the Imperial tri-color over the stone walls which were painfully erected by the English for their own accommodation' during the previous conflict.[37] As in the Crimea, the French appeared the more agile of the European powers. Still, the American newspaper thought both nations absurdly committed to the humiliation of China. Demanding an apology from the celestial emperor for the 1859 Taku Fort incident, 'the Cabinet of St. James and the Cabinet of St. Cloud' had unfairly rejected China's account of the dispute.

Even with victory in battle, doubts persisted over the prudence of the venture. *The Examiner* thought the routing of Chinese troops deceptively easy. 'Thrashing those people is like thrashing water, which after the splash finds its level again.' China's huge population would be difficult to control. Advising that the Chinese Qing Dynasty be maintained and Britain and France content themselves with enforcing trade terms, the newspaper lamented that China had a 'superabundance of lives to squander. Indeed, they are as prodigal of life as we are of money.'[38] At all costs a war of conquest was to be avoided.

The *New York Times* was equally sceptical over the wisdom of the invasion. 'Armed with the latest inventions of science', the elite British and French armies had crushed all Chinese resistance. But what wisdom was there, the American newspaper wondered, in 'using force to compel an exclusive and barbarous people like the Chinese to abandon their policy, habits, and even instincts, for the benefit of commerce and civilization?'[39] The moment Anglo-French troops left China, the emperor would again ignore all his treaty obligations.

But if this was a war of 'civilization', then Britain and France were about to commit an act of barbaric vandalism, almost without parallel. On 6 October the allies arrived at the Summer Palace. Known as the Yuen-ming-yuen, this was the dreamlike home of the emperor and seat of power. First at the Summer Palace, the French found it poorly defended. 'Twenty badly-armed eunuchs' were easily disposed of. The British command arrived shortly after. Wolseley, who although only twenty-seven years old was already a veteran of the Crimean War and Indian Mutiny, guided Elgin and Grant to the palace to confer with Montauban. They entered the beautiful private rooms of the emperor, untouched since his flight.[40] From that moment a 'mine of wealth of everything curious in the empire lay as a prey before our French allies', Wolseley noted.[41]

The destruction and looting that followed shocked Wolseley, revealing the savage nature of soldiers. He explained that 3,000 Frenchmen were 'let loose into a city composed only of Museums', wreaking havoc beyond compare. The French camp at the palace was littered with silks and surrounded by soldiers 'decked out in the most ridiculous-looking costumes they could find, of which there was no lack as the well-stocked wardrobes of his Imperial Majesty abounded in curious raiment. Some had dressed themselves in the richly embroidered gowns of women, and almost all had substituted the turned-up Mandarin hat for their ordinary forage cap.'[42] Even French officers were seized with this 'insanity'.

One young captain in the Royal Engineers, a zealous Christian named Charles Gordon, witnessed the horror, but blamed the French entirely: 'You would scarcely conceive the magnificence of this residence or the tremendous devastation the French have committed ... the French have smashed everything in the most wanton way.'[43] Of course, the British soon joined in and, for good measure, razed the edifice. This disorder clearly shocked Gordon, and he was not the only one.

Back in France, a year before the publication of his celebrated *Les Misérables*, Victor Hugo penned a violent condemnation. A year after the barbaric act, Hugo lamented how the armies of Victoria and Napoléon had destroyed a wonder of the world. He explained how, 'One day two bandits entered the Summer Palace. One plundered, the other burned ... One of the two victors filled his pockets; when the other saw this he filled his coffers. And back they came to Europe, arm in arm, laughing away.' Britain and France were not so much allies, as partners in crime. Their cooperation had robbed the world of the Oriental equivalent of the Parthenon. But Hugo believed the loss was far greater even than this:

> Imagine some inexpressible construction, something like a lunar building, and you will have the Summer Palace. Build a dream with marble, jade, bronze and porcelain, frame it with cedar wood, cover it with precious stones, drape it with silk, make it here a sanctuary, there a harem, elsewhere a citadel, put gods there, and monsters, varnish it, enamel it, gild it, paint it, have architects who are poets build the thousand and one dreams of the thousand and

one nights, add gardens, basins, gushing water and foam, swans, ibis, peacocks, suppose in a word a sort of dazzling cavern of human fantasy with the face of a temple and palace, such was this building.

This was irretrievably lost in the name of European commerce. Hugo placed the Summer Palace alongside the Pyramids of Egypt, Notre-Dame in Paris, and the the Colosseum of Rome. European imperialism had shown its brutality. Whatever the cause of war or advantages of collaboration, the French author was unequivocal in his abhorrence of this act. He looked forward to the day when France and Britain would seek redemption and restore to China its stolen treasures. As Hugo put it, 'The French empire has pocketed half of this victory, and today with a kind of proprietorial naivety it displays the splendid bric-a-brac of the Summer Palace. I hope that a day will come when France, delivered and cleansed, will return this booty to despoiled China.'[44] Hugo would have a long wait. Ironically, given the immense destruction of China's historical relics during Mao's 'Cultural Revolution', the items stolen from the Summer Palace in 1860 have ended up being some of the very few antiquities to have survived into the twenty-first century. Perhaps Hugo might have here found a quantum of consolation.

As much as Hugo mourned the loss of a wonder of civilization, Wolseley was less than impressed with China's art. On entering the celebrated Audience Hall of Hienfung, he was sorely disappointed:

> Everything upon which the eye could rest was pretty and well designed, each little object being a gem of its kind, but there was nothing imposing in the *tout ensemble*. Chinese architecture can never be so; to produce such an effect is seemingly never attempted by the architects of that country. Both in landscape gardening and building, the Chinaman loses sight of grand or imposing effects, in

his endeavours to load everything with ornament; he forgets the fine in his search after the curious. In their thirst after decoration, and in their inherent love for minute embellishment, the artists and architects of China have failed to produce any great work capable of inspiring those sensations of awe or admiration which strike every one when first gazing upon the magnificent creations of European architects.[45]

Hugo never actually saw the Summer Palace, but Wolseley had, and it only confirmed his notions of European superiority. Unlike the Pyramids of Giza or works of Thebes, built to endure, the Audience Hall was merely rich in gilding and colour. It was only made of wood after all. Though the puzzle-like wooden roofing of Chinese architecture was curious, Wolseley thought such perishable structures far from the works of a great civilization. He was again disappointed with the Imperial Throne Room. The throne itself was beautiful but the architecture was found wanting.[46]

There's no knowing the value of what was looted from the Summer Palace. British officers handed over their share for public auction and this alone raised £50,000. Divided out, a private collected £3 and an officer £50. But many French soldiers walked away rich men.[47] Years later at a French government inquiry into the sacking, Montauban blamed the British entirely; his claim that there was no looting of the palace before his allies arrived was a blatant lie.[48]

When the plundering finally ended on 9 October, the allies marched on Peking itself. Remarkably, Wolseley confessed astonishment at how quickly the French army restored order. Concerning the crime of looting, he felt that it was not 'attended with such demoralizing effects in a French army as it is in ours. The Frenchman is naturally a more thrifty being than the careless Britisher, who squanders his money in drinking, and "standing drink" to his comrades. Three days afterwards when the French moved into their position before Pekin, they seemed to have regained their discipline ... as if nothing had occurred to disturb the ordinary routine of their lives.'[49] The allies took the walls of Peking on 12 October, without a fight, hoisting the Union Jack and Tricolour side by side over the entrance to the capital of the most populous nation on Earth.[50] The city surrendered the next day.[51] As Wolseley triumphantly concluded, 'The far-famed celestial capital, the pride of China, and hitherto esteemed impregnable by every soul in that empire', was now in Anglo-French hands.[52]

After forcing exacting terms on the imperial regime at Peking, instability followed the Anglo-French success. The allied armies left Peking, with a small force of Indian and British soldiers remaining in Shanghai to help the Chinese in quelling the Tai-ping Rebellion. This was a crucial centre of European trade but was constantly under threat from the rebels, who thrived off the Imperial regime's defeat at foreign hands. Imperial China's obvious weakness fuelled the idea of a political power vacuum and stoked up xenophobia, much of which was focused on Shanghai. Within a year of the sacking of the Summer Palace, the Xianfeng Emperor had died, leaving behind a regency that was soon ousted in a coup in which the Empress Dowager Cixi took power; she would govern for forty-seven years as a regent. Between 1860 and 1864 a Euro-American led force, which became known as 'The Ever Victorious Army', fought on behalf of the Qing Dynasty and in defence of European trade. The officers were drawn from Shanghai's merchants and bankers, including Americans, French, and British. In 1862 command fell to the mystic young engineer who had witnessed the horrors of the Summer Palace two years previous. Charles Gordon coordinated a tenacious campaign against the rebels. He became famous as 'Chinese' Gordon, and would be speared to death and beheaded by the Dervishes in

Khartoum twenty-three years later, the epitome of the Victorian adventurer.[53] But it was his handling of the fallout from the Second Anglo-Chinese War that secured him celebrity. Those commentators, including Marx, who had foreseen the disorder that would arise from a war on the celestial Chinese state were proven sadly prophetic.

*

China humbled and the Summer Palace in ruins, Britain and France had seen off yet another potential rival. 1860 might well be identified as the apex of this Anglo-French axis of power. With both Russia and China subdued, the only extra-European competitor of note was perhaps the United States, but its eventual economic and industrial boom was far from foreseeable in the 1850s. Indeed, between 1861 and 1865 the fledgling nation descended into a brutalizing civil war and was in no position to threaten Anglo-French hegemony. Without doubt this was a profound moment of European dominance. To contemporaries, the Second Anglo-Chinese War must have seemed a matter of preserving free trade, regardless of Marx's critique. Looked at more closely, this was the upholding of a world order built through the global ambitions of Britain and France.

4

PEACE SECURED: FREE TRADE AND THE COBDEN-CHEVALIER TREATY

At the newly expanded naval base in Cherbourg on 4 August 1858, Emperor Napoléon again hosted Victoria and Albert. The royal couple were en route to Prussia to see their daughter, Victoria, who was three months pregnant with the future Kaiser Wilhelm II. Although visiting their daughter, who had recently married Frederick, heir to the Prussian throne, their inspection of Cherbourg was not insignificant. The construction of this naval dockyard had fuelled talk of an impending French invasion. Though fond of Napoléon, the Queen privately noted her fears over France's growing naval power.[1]

Wars are often steep learning curves and the Crimean had been no exception. The importance of military organisation, sanitation, and professional officers all became clear. A high price was paid for this harrowing education. But arguably the most depressing lesson was the ephemeral nature of a military alliance. Between Russia's capitulation at the Peace of Paris in 1856 and the invasion of China in 1860 there was a temporary suspension of Anglo-French collaboration. The two partners went their separate ways. Suspicion and anxiety between the rival powers grew quickly and, by 1858, France was again seen as a military threat, as opposed to an ally. There had been invasion panics before, but few matched the hysteria of 1858–59.

Anglo-French relations took a turn for the worse at the start of 1858. In January the Italian revolutionary Felice Orsini's botched assassination attempt on Napoléon was the cause of a diplomatic crisis. It later turned out that Orsini's bomb had been made in Britain and it was likely that his plan had been too. Napoléon demanded that Palmerston, Liberal Prime Minister since 1855, take action to prevent a repeat. In February, Palmerston introduced a Conspiracy to Murder Bill into Parliament which would allow suspected terrorists to be imprisoned and extradited to France for trial.[2] Even the self-avowedly pro-French *The Spectator* found Palmerston's actions troubling. Britain was home to France's refugees, be they royalists or revolutionaries. They came in fear of persecution, but Palmerston's proposal to give France jurisdiction over these migrants would make Britain but an extension of the French empire. The bill would have the Home Office rounding up and extraditing exiles; it would become 'the auxiliary of the newly-organised French police'. It was as though Waterloo had never been fought.[3] Parliament rejected the bill, Palmerston resigned, and the Conservatives formed a brief administration under the Earl of Derby.

The Orsini affair was only the beginning. Cherbourg's development as a modern naval base was just one part of a broader French expansion in naval power. Its naval budget trebled during the 1850s, peaking at two-thirds of Britain's expenditure. By 1859 the French briefly appeared to be rivalling the Royal Navy's dominance of the sea. To Britain's ninety-five ships of the line and ninety-six frigates, France could boast fifty-one ships and ninety-seven frigates, though admittedly many of these were obsolete.[4] Worse still, Napoléon's navy had taken a brief technological lead.[5] It was not in the dockyards of Cherbourg that

France's greatest weapon was in progress, but in Toulon. It was here in the sun-baked Mediterranean port, throughout 1858 and 1859, that the *Gloire* took shape. The stuff of English nightmares, she was armed with cutting-edge guns, either rifled or firing explosive shells, and was the world's first ironclad warship. The *Gloire* still had a wooden hull, but this was clad in 12cm-thick iron plates, capable of resisting a shot from a British 68-pounder, the most powerful gun the Royal Navy had. Britain's immense fleet of wooden battleships suddenly looked rather vulnerable and nothing horrified the Victorians more than the prospect of losing their naval dominance. The island nation's supreme confidence at sea, dating back at least to Horatio Nelson's victory at Trafalgar in 1805, was shaken to say the least. The queen fretted and sought reassurances from the Admiralty. The Royal Navy responded with HMS *Warrior*, ordered in 1859 and launched in December 1860, the first armour-plated, iron-hulled warship and more than a match for the *Gloire*.[6]

The Earl of Derby knew just how to calm things down: 'What a store of powder they have in hand! Enough for six Crimean wars!' he exclaimed, reassuringly.[7] It had been a controversy with France that had brought the Conservatives into power in 1858, so it was fitting that Napoléon played a part in ending their administration less than a year later. Inadequate military spending and defensive measures had cost the Conservatives power in 1852 and now, seven years later, a repeat looked certain. In February 1859 the Conservative government tried to increase naval expenditure, but the flamboyant Chancellor, Benjamin Disraeli, again struggled to deliver a viable budget. Disraeli had the rhetoric and would one day be Prime Minister, but his Liberal rival Gladstone was by far the superior Chancellor. On fears of a French invasion, Palmerston returned as Prime Minister: only by an exuberant display of defence spending would he remain in office.

Appearing too close to Napoléon in 1858 had cost Palmerston his premiership. He would not make the same mistake twice, securing popular approval through a rigid anti-French stance. He used the threat of invasion to present himself as the patriotic defender of the nation, building up dockyard fortifications along the south coast of England and restoring Britain's naval supremacy. When Palmerston's Chancellor, Gladstone, attempted to rein in this spending, the Prime Minister suggested to the Queen that 'it would be better to lose Mr Gladstone than to run the risk of losing Portsmouth or Plymouth'.[8]

*

This was the panic-stricken Britain to which the radical MP and manufacturer Richard Cobden arrived. Cobden had long been an advocate of peace, campaigning for a reduction of defence spending throughout the 1840s and 1850s and promoting non-intervention in European affairs. In 1849 he had called for military expenditure to be cut back to the levels of the mid-1830s and, between 1849 and 1853, he sat on a series of parliamentary select committees in which he attempted to reign in the army's budget. This brought him into conflict with the Liberal Party, which, under Palmerston's influence, was largely in favour of a highly active foreign policy. Amid the rising tensions with Russia and France of the early 1850s, Cobden found his calls for reduced defence spending unpopular and he grew increasingly politically isolated. In the run-up to the Crimean War he opposed British intervention to prop up Turkey, a decaying Muslim state, at the cost of relations with Russia, which he thought wanted peaceful commercial relations. After the Crimean War, Cobden again found himself on the wrong end of Palmerston's foreign policy over China in 1857, opposing the British bombardment of the port of Canton in response to the illegal Chinese boarding of a British ship. When Palmerston called an election later that year, Cobden lost his seat in Parliament, as did many Liberal and radical MPs. Cobden's finances fared as poorly as his political career, with his speculative investment in the Illinois Railway Company forcing him to borrow heavily to keep up with the company's calls for cash from shareholders. In February 1859 he travelled to the United States to investigate the state of the Illinois Railway in person and he spent four months there, moving between New York, Washington, and Chicago. While abroad, Cobden was returned as MP for Rochdale, thanks largely to the efforts of his radical political allies.[9]

Fresh from his tour of the United States, Cobden landed in Liverpool late in the summer of 1859 to find the recent fall of Derby's short-lived Conservative government presenting a rare opportunity. Having a slender majority in the House of Commons, Palmerston was keen to have Cobden in his Cabinet to keep radical MPs onside. But Cobden refused to serve the 'warlike, intermeddling and quarrelsome' new Prime Minister.[10] Certainly Palmerston had profited from the growing hysteria that France was on the verge of invading. Yet he was a politician, if not an outright cynic. Publicly he lavishly armed Britain for war; privately he tried to improve relations with France. And Cobden was to play the pivotal part in this cunning manoeuvre that would see Palmerston, that most English of England's ministers, bring Britain and France back into partnership while simultaneously preparing for war.

Not long after arriving back in Britain, Cobden received an intriguing letter from Michel Chevalier, the celebrated French political economist, arguing that now was the moment for Anglo-French free trade. Chevalier had been France's leading liberal light for three decades. His *Système de la Méditerranée*, published in 1832, called on France to look to Africa and Asia

Britain's leading radical light and outspoken champion of free trade Richard Cobden in 1846. (Author's collection)

for new colonies and to exploit these through the technologies of telegraphy, railways, and steamships. Four years later, having completed a tour of the United States, Cuba, Canada, and Mexico, he championed further reforms. France's North American empire was long gone, while the 'Latin' colonies of France, Spain, and

Portugal, including Mexico and Cuba, were in a detestable state of poverty. In contrast, the 'Anglo-Saxon' colonies of Canada and the now independent United States were flourishing. Chevalier urged France to emulate Britain's colonial practices of liberalism and free trade. Indeed, he saw France as Britain's natural partner in upholding imperial power and spreading 'civilization' throughout the world, albeit as the junior partner. He even proposed a railway between London and Paris. Under Napoléon, Chevalier was a major influence behind French economic expansion. French exports rose from 10 per cent of the world's trade in 1850 to 15 per cent by the mid-1860s. Even more dramatic was the rise of its overseas investments, from just ¾ billion francs in 1850 to some 13.3 billion by 1870.[11]

Cobden and Chevalier had met before, first in Paris in 1846, and the Frenchman had initially floated the idea of a free trade treaty to Cobden in 1856 at the Peace of Paris which concluded the Crimean War.[12] At the time, Cobden had no political influence and so the suggestion went no further. But in 1859 Cobden had a Prime Minister who was eager to please. Meanwhile, the new Chancellor of the Exchequer, Gladstone, had the luxury of a budget surplus on his hands. The moment was, as Chevalier observed, ripe.

Cobden responded to Chevalier with qualified enthusiasm. Britain did not need the trade. He was emphatic on this point. His country wanted 'no extension of our foreign trade' having as much to do as it was. Indeed, British trade and manufacturing was booming to the point of exhaustion. So much so that Cobden thought it 'very difficult to manage ... the working classes owing to the great demand for their labor. - I am afraid we shall have "strikes" in all directions, & if we were to have any sudden & great expansion of demand from abroad it would probably throw the relations of Capital & labor into great confusion.'[13] Like many a solid radical, Cobden was eager to 'manage' the working classes. But the fact was that Britain did not want any more trade having too much to do as it was. He echoed this sentiment to Gladstone, asserting that 'we have no necessity to seek for customers for our manufacturers, that we have quite as much demand for our products as we can supply, & that the main difficulty with our manufactures is how to produce the raw material & the *labor* to supply the wants of the markets already open to us'.[14]

Despite the irritation of too much economic prosperity, Cobden thought Chevalier's treaty a capital notion. But he did not support Chevalier's proposed treaty for commerce: he supported it for peace. Cobden sorely lamented the tensions between Britain and France and thought little of military collaboration. It was something of a Victorian article of faith that free trade was a harbinger of political liberalism. And only by bringing nations closer to British liberalism could peace be secured. Most Victorians were confident that countries who embraced free trade did not go to war with each other. If Napoléon would sign up for free trade, then this was the clearest indication that he did not intend to invade Britain. Cobden certainly subscribed to this assumption. Free trade was his only hope 'for any permanent improvement in the *political* relations of France & England'. Governments, generals, and diplomats could do little to make or preserve peace. Only by bringing peoples of each nation 'into mutual dependence by the supply of each others wants' would war be avoided; it was, according to Cobden, 'God's own method of producing an *entente cordiale*'.[15]

Cobden voiced his abhorrence of Anglo-French military collaboration consistently throughout the wars in China. In 1859 he predicted the 'eventual occupation of Pekin', fearing his country was 'destined to cover all Asia with our crimes'. Apocalyptically, he warned that if there was any truth in the idea of 'a Divine Providence governing the earth on principles of retributive justice', then Britain would one day 'find its chastisement if not its executioner in the East'.[16] It would be some time before China ascended to an economic position of 'retributive justice'. For Cobden the military expedition to China was pointless, given that Britain spent most of 1859 plagued by fears of French invasion. As he put it, what was the 'value of an alliance in China or any other pretended *entente cordiale* whilst we were keeping up 26 millions of armaments principally as a defense against France'.[17] Cobden genuinely despaired at the irrational paranoia of his fellow countrymen: the imagined threat of a foreign invasion seemed to have driven them senseless. He simply did not see any danger from Napoléon, but instead thought the invasion fears 'a hoax' by those in political power to distract the public from more important problems at home. The government's naval spending secured it popularity, so it was in its interests to fuel the scaremongering that France was preparing to invade at any moment. The 'English people have gone mad,' Cobden proclaimed.[18]

Cobden knew France's dockyards well. He had visited Toulon and thought it 'a *slow* place compared with Portsmouth or Plymouth'. There was no secret shipbuilding programme and Napoléon had no schemes for war. If the British government and middle classes were 'less absurdly conservative', Cobden was sure they could 'carry on a close alliance with Louis Napoléon'.[19] Unlike the ruling elites, Cobden explained that the 'manufacturers of England do not want customers at present. – What they want is a guarantee that their present well-being is not likely to be disturbed by the warlike or ambitious policy of the French ruler.'[20]

Cobden visited Gladstone at his country seat, Hawarden Castle in Flintshire, spending 12 and 13 September walking the grounds and discussing the reduction of trade tariffs on French imports with the chancellor.[21] With the authority to negotiate the treaty virtually single-handedly, Cobden left for Paris.[22] If he had doubts over the intellectual calibre of his own countrymen, a few days in Paris convinced him the French were little better. 'Ignorant' and 'vain' beyond 'even our own masses', Cobden again complained of the damage of Anglo-French 'warlike alliances'. These did 'more harm than good even in the relations of the two Countries which they are intended to unite'. Just as the British seemed obsessed with the prospect of a Napoleonic invasion, the French appeared convinced that Britain was interested in peace with France simply to take advantage of its manpower. The people of France seemed to think 'we *come* to them for help, in Crimean & China wars, *because we have no soldiers of our own*'.[23] Frustrated with Anglo-French relations existing purely in militaristic terms, Cobden envisaged the free trade treaty as the start of something more idealistic. Liberal free trade would usher in a new age in which nations did not value each other for their military potential in times of war. This utopian future was one in which peoples of all countries depended on each other's products to such an extent that war would be inconceivable. However, despite the support of Chevalier, Cobden found free trade a hard sell in the French capital.

Between the 1820s and 1840s British free traders had waged a relentless war on trade barriers, the climax of which had been the repeal of the Corn Laws in 1846. The removal of tariffs on corn, intended to protect Britain's landowning agriculturalists, promised a new era of cheap bread made from imported grain. In France things were different. Here the watchword was protection, a reputation that, rightly or wrongly, has persisted until today. Britain during the 1830s and 1840s was a place where the words 'free trade' won you elections, especially after the 1832 Great Reform Act, which expanded the electorate from 500,000 to 813,000 voters. Few had the vote, but nothing stirred up the middle classes quite like the prospect of an abolished tax. In France, still under the monarchy of King Louis Philippe, liberal trade ideas flourished but lacked the popular backing encountered in England.[24] When, in 1846, the free trader Frédéric Bastiat tried to copy Britain's popular campaign to abolish the Corn Laws, it ended miserably. Protectionists thrived off fears that France had to be sheltered from cheap English imports.[25]

In 1860, though the monarchy had long been consigned to history, France's protectionists were still politically powerful. Ever uneasy over the stability of his regime, Napoléon took care not to antagonise this influential group. But Napoléon was desperate to improve relations with Britain, despite being no free trader himself. It was not Britain he sought conflict with, but Austria. His hope was to rid Italy of Austrian rule and in April 1859 he went to war over Italian independence. Despite military success, he abruptly ceased hostilities when Prussia mobilised troops on the Rhine in support of the weakened Austrians. Going into 1860, Napoléon was still committed to encouraging Italian independence, but wanted to avoid war against an Austro-Prussian alliance. In this context, it was crucial to keep Britain, if not an ally, at least neutral. Prussia would think twice about riding to Austria's rescue over the Italian Question if Napoléon had British support.[26] For all the fears of a French invasion, quite the reverse was true: Napoléon wanted Britain as a friend. Cobden's arrival in Paris provided just the opportunity he was looking for.

Having secured an audience with Napoléon, Cobden gave the French emperor a patronising crash course in free trade, advising him to target duties on iron, just as Britain had focused its own efforts on corn back in 1846.[27] But Napoléon had doubts: he feared the protectionists at court. Worried that the emperor would flee the negotiating table, Cobden wrote to Gladstone requesting all duties on French manufactures be dropped and that tax on brandy and wine be dramatically cut. Such measures would secure Napoléon sympathy with manufacturers in Paris and Lyon, as well as from the wine regions. An early British concession of this nature would give the beleaguered emperor leverage with his own people; he would be capable of doing 'any thing he liked in the way of reductions' without risking his own position.[28]

Though Napoléon was concerned about cheap British industrial manufacturers, especially iron, Cobden warned the emperor that without a treaty, war between France and Britain was likely. Napoléon would rather have had a diplomatic treaty respecting Italian independence, but quickly recognised that Cobden would accept nothing less than a free trade treaty.[29]

Cobden returned to London in November, reporting to the Cabinet that Napoléon was ready to adopt free trade measures. By 28 December the radical MP was back in Paris, negotiating the treaty's specifics with the backing of Gladstone and Palmerston. Despite continued French proposals for a political alliance instead of a trade treaty, Cobden pressed ahead, driving Napoléon and his ministers reluctantly towards free trade.[30] Back home, *The Times* had mixed feelings about the treaty. The organ of Britain's Conservative conscience was clearly uneasy at a measure so obviously radical in political origins. One contributor worried that Napoléon was too changeable to be trusted. Self-styled 'Economist', the anonymous author feared that Cobden did not value public revenue and had such an aversion to indirect taxation that he would have agreed to any terms. The loss of tax on French imports might well be regretted.[31]

On 23 January 1860 the treaty was signed after impressively swift discussions. Both Cobden and Lord Cowley, the British ambassador, signed on behalf of Britain. France promptly annexed Nice and Savoy, confident that British neutrality had been secured. On learning that the treaty had been signed, *The Times* congratulated France on finally taking steps towards free trade after forty years of protectionism. The autocratic system of government of Napoléon would make the implementation of the treaty relatively easy compared with the checks and balances of parliamentary Britain. But the newspaper laced its praise with mild condemnation of French attitudes towards British free trade. Although Britain would do well to 'look a little more to foreign systems of administration, and foreign canons of taste', *The Times* implored foreign powers to stop thinking that England's commitment to free trade was some Machiavellian policy to ruin her rivals. This misconception was at the root of France's protectionism: that free trade was English because it benefitted only England. It was a deeply ingrained belief dating back to Napoléon Bonaparte. Apocryphally he had damned Britain as a 'nation of shopkeepers' and, sure that all its wealth derived from trade, had attempted to beat the country into submission through his 'Continental System'. Bonaparte had, through this economic blockade, isolated Britain from European trade but, ironically, this policy brought about his own destruction. Both Portugal and Russia continued trading with Britain, provoking Bonaparte to invade both. In the Iberian Peninsula from 1808 and then in the freezing snow of Russia in 1812, the once glorious armies of France wasted away and, by 1814, Bonaparte was in exile on the tiny Mediterranean island of Elba. The French preoccupation with English trade had already brought down one emperor. In 1860 the obsession persisted with another. But, *The Times* asserted, France was mistaken. Britain was not wealthy because of its trade alone and never had been. Rather, it was to Britain's industry, agriculture, and, above all, 'English mining, with its enormous weight of coal, iron, lead, and tin every year brought to the surface of the earth', that *The Times* credited the nation's prosperity.[32]

*

Despite the treaty's signing, there remained the precise tariff schedules to be negotiated, and Cobden returned to Paris to conduct these talks in April 1860, remaining there until November. Along with setting new tariff rates, France and Britain agreed to abolish passports and improve postal facilities. In the end, despite Britain agreeing to terminate most duties on imports from France, the French government merely reduced existing duties or replaced prohibitions with 25–30 per cent tariffs on British goods. And while Gladstone would announce the reductions in his next budget, France would take several years to adjust their taxes.[33] This was by no means insignificant, but it was not quite free trade. Nevertheless, to put it in perspective, countries affected by the Cobden-Chevalier treaty saw their average tariffs fall by about 48 per cent in the decade that followed.[34] Cobden was certainly pleased. 'The effect of the treaty will be felt all over the world,' he boasted; it 'will raise the topic of "international tariffs" into practical importance with all the Governments of Europe'.[35]

Back home in Britain, honours for Cobden abounded, bestowed by grateful cities, manufacturer's associations, and chambers of commerce. Palmerston tried to get Cobden to accept a baronetcy or position as privy councillor, but he refused and returned to his customary criticism of the Prime Minister's aggressive foreign policy. In early 1860 Palmerston had agreed to invest in new coastal fortifications, ignoring Cobden's appeal for this to be delayed until the treaty was completed. Back in Parliament, Cobden continued to oppose British foreign intervention and the naval arms race between Britain and France.[36]

It is worth emphasising just what an article of Victorian faith free trade presented. Arguably, there was no policy more likely to convince British liberal audiences of Napoléon's peaceful intentions than by bringing down the barriers of protectionism. Overtly about commerce, the Cobden-Chevalier treaty was really about peace. To become mutually dependent on each other through free trade meant, theoretically, that Britain and France would not go to war. Economic integration was, in fact, taken to be an inducer of political integration and this unifying of societies would sustain international harmony. At least this was Cobden and Chevalier's conviction, and it was a conviction that, in 1859, many Victorians shared and the governments of Palmerston and Napoléon readily bought into.

5

THE MEASURE OF NATIONS: LIBERALISM AND THE METRIC SYSTEM

Along the River Thames at Millwall a fearful sight loomed over London. Between 1854 and 1858 a vast iron leviathan emerged from the mud of the Isle of Dogs. The *Great Eastern* steamship was a monster. The brainchild of the enigmatic engineer Isambard Kingdom Brunel, she was the largest manmade moving object ever constructed and would not be surpassed in length until the White Star Line's *Oceanic* in 1899. At 692 feet long, she took more than four painful years to build. Perhaps the one thing that dwarfed the ship was the ambition of her designer. Brunel's career had been spectacular, if chequered. The son of a French émigré and himself educated at the University of Caen in Normandy, the engineer earned fame for his work on the Thames Tunnel and construction of the Great Western Railway, linking London with Bristol and eventually the south-west of England. His bridges at Saltash, Clifton, and Maidenhead are still eye-catching wonders today. Not content with connecting London and Bristol, his first two steamships, the *Great Western* and *Great Britain*, were conceived of as an extension of his railway. Through steam power, Brunel's vision was of a route from London to New York.

When in 2002 the BBC conducted a nationwide poll to determine the '100 Greatest Britons', Brunel came second, beaten only by Winston Churchill. Amid the surrealism of the opening ceremony of the London Olympics in 2012, it was Brunel who kicked off proceedings. Portrayed by Kenneth Branagh, Brunel's recital from Shakespeare's *The Tempest* put in motion an elaborate display of industry. 'When I waked, I cried to dream again,' declared Brunel, seeming at a stroke to initiate an entire industrial revolution, glowing with red-hot iron and spewing steam. The rest of the world looked on, mystified and amused at this eccentric choreography, but British audiences would have needed little reminding that here was a 'great man'.

Except had you been a Victorian, or worse still, a shareholder in one of Brunel's schemes, you might not have thought him so great. Brunel's projects usually went wrong, or at the very least, ruined their investors. And the *Great Eastern* was no different, bedevilled by a concatenation of calamities. Costing more than £640,000 to build, she was grossly over the contract price of £332,295. Once finished, she was too heavy to launch and, after a humiliating ceremony in November 1857 ended in just a few inches of movement, three months of pulling and pushing followed. This cost another £170,000, which bankrupted her owners, the Eastern Steam Navigation Company. Brunel's collaborator, the naval architect John Scott Russell, stood accused of stealing iron from the project to pay off his personal debts and would never build another vessel. Brunel's engineering epic turned into an embarrassment. Once at sea, an on-board explosion on her maiden sea trial off Hastings injured a dozen crew, with several fatalities, fuelling suspicion that the ship was cursed. Her maiden voyage to New York in June 1860 attracted only thirty-five fee-paying passengers. Built to carry 4,000, there was never enough demand to fill even half this number. Her career was miserable, completing only nine voyages to North

America before being retired from passenger-carrying in 1863 with the liquidation of her new owners. In 1861 she was disabled in an Atlantic storm and was holed by a rock in Long Island Sound on a later voyage. The *Great Eastern* ended up being used as a giant advertising billboard before she was sold for scrap in 1888. Aged just fifty-three, Brunel died in 1859, with rumours abounding that the stress of building the leviathan had killed its designer.[1]

Commercially out of touch and ruinously expensive, the *Great Eastern* was a complete disaster. Why then had she been built at all? In a word, 'coal'. The *Great Eastern* was intended to have the capacity to steam from Britain to Calcutta and Australia, around the Cape of Good Hope and across the Indian Ocean, without having to stop for coal. In 1851 a ton of coal cost about fifteen shillings in Britain, but the Peninsular and Oriental Steam Navigation Company (P&O) was paying forty-two shillings a ton for coal in Hong Kong, while the Royal Mail Steam Packet Company (RMSP) paid £3 a ton at coaling stations in the West Indies. The *Great Eastern*'s promoters thus claimed that, by carrying all the coal required to get from Britain to Australia and back, the ship would save £9,000 on fuel per voyage. The problem was that it took an immense amount of coal to feed her hungry boilers during this mammoth voyage. In January 1859 *The Engineer*, a specialist journal in technological matters, calculated that the giant ship would consume 900 tons a day, meaning that it would hardly be able to carry enough coal to get to New York and back, let alone Calcutta. In the end, the *Great Eastern* never made it to India or Australia. There was never the demand.[2]

Nevertheless, Brunel's monster ship revealed much about 1850s Britain and its anxieties. As the world's foremost trading nation, the country relied on a colossal network of ships to sustain its commerce and imperialism. Cunard, P&O, RMSP, and the Pacific Steam Navigation Company (PSNC) were just some of the liner companies that kept the arteries of empire open with fleets of steamships connecting trade centres around the world. While Cunard operated a reliable transatlantic route, RMSP endeavoured to connect Britain to the West Indies, and P&O offered services to Hong Kong, Singapore, and Shanghai by way of Suez. All three secured the financially crucial government mail contracts, effectively operating official networks of communication.[3] This is to say nothing of Britain's informal empire. Though not outright colonial possessions, British influence in South America was considerable, including great financial and commercial interests, especially beef exports. It was here that PSNC established a line of ships between Britain and Peru, Rio, Montevideo, Punta Arenas, and Valparaiso.[4] But as sailing ships were in increasing competition with the apparent punctuality that new steamships provided, the need for coaling stations became pressing. Wherever you found the British, you would probably find coal stacks, from Madeira and Cape Verde to Aden, to Cape Town, Georgetown, Bombay, Valparaiso, and Ceylon. Fleets of sailing ships kept trade posts like these stocked with coal. The *Great Eastern* was Brunel's solution to this question of fuel.

Imperial trade involved coaling stations and efficient steam engines. It was operated through shipping, railways, and telegraphic communication. It also took a large navy to protect it. This was a global expansion forged through the enterprise of commercial adventurers, setting up businesses in the lonely corners of empire. The exploitation and subjection of indigenous peoples was equally inseparable from this rampant capitalism. But, unseen and uncelebrated, Britain's globalisation was also a matter of measurement, and not just in terms of the amount of coal required to get to Australia. Accurate standards became an important part of this global system. Weights, distance, volume, fuel consumption, and electrical resistance were just some of the measures that underpinned Britain's imperial expansion. In the mid-nineteenth century, standardised measurements were critical concerns. And there was no measurement matter quite so urgent as those in use between the two most eminent nation's on Earth: Britain and France. Both had different systems of weights and measures and both had very different ways of enforcing them. In the context of the Great Exhibition and the Cobden-Chevalier free trade treaty, these differences became increasingly apparent.

The metre was the ultimate symbol of French reason. Before the Revolution of 1789 France allegedly had some 250,000 different measurements in use, under 700 to 800 different names employed throughout the country. In August 1793, having guillotined King Louis XVI in January, the revolutionary government vowed to introduce a single system of weights and measures within eleven years. This 'metric system' would be based on the principle of decimalisation and its fundamental unit, the 'metre', was defined as one ten-millionth part of the distance from the equator to the North Pole, which had been calculated by measuring the meridian arc between Dunkirk and Barcelona. Measures for weight and volume were based on the metre, with the millilitre equal to one cubic centimetre of water and the gram the weight of a cubic centimetre of ice at melting point. With all units in this way derived from the Earth's dimensions, this was a system which France proudly proclaimed to be both rational and based on nature itself.[5] Accompanying the metre was a new Republican Calendar of twelve months, decimalised into three ten-day periods. The metric eventually secured support as an international system of measurements but the calendar did not last long: Napoléon Bonaparte got rid of it in 1806.

Of course, in Britain, where the occasionally mad King George III still ruled, the metric system carried dangerous connotations. Such rationalisation was often seen as a fundamentally revolutionary obsession. One moment, the French were reinventing standards, the next they were guillotining aristocrats. Reorganising a nation's measures appeared inseparable from reorganising its society. In Britain it was not the metre but the yard that regulated trade. Merchants and traders could consult copies of pounds, yards, and inches at their local town halls, but these units varied throughout the country. A yard in Newcastle was certainly not the same as a yard in Exeter, let alone York. To end this chaos, in 1824, Parliament passed the Weights and Measures Act, stipulating a fixed length of 36 inches for the yard. This new legal standard was held in the vaults of the Houses of Parliament at Westminster until a terrible fire in 1834 destroyed the building, and with it, the nation's yard. Following this calamity, the government appointed a commission to recalculate and agree on a replacement national measure, which passed into law as the Imperial Yard in 1855 after some two decades of tedious inquiry. Sitting on the commission, the eminent mathematician John Herschel emphasised that the new yard, like the metre, had its reference in nature. Claiming that the measure was almost the same length as a pendulum calibrated to beat a perfect second of time at Greenwich, Herschel boasted that the yard was natural in origin 'as much as if it had dropped from the clouds'.[6] Herschel's mind was not what it had been in younger days, it is true, but as the nation's leading astronomer and son of the discoverer of the planet Uranus, William Herschel, few possessed so much influence on scientific matters.

Despite the new yard's credentials, it quickly became controversial. The problematic relationship between trading internationally and measurement had become very clear in 1851 at the Great Exhibition. One of the biggest challenges judges faced in awarding prizes was the array of various weights and measures which different nations used. This lack of international standards alarmed economists, engineers, merchants, and scientists alike. While Britain was still waiting for its new imperial standards, the French exhibited a set of metric weights and measures which drew much interest, particularly from London's Society of Arts, charged with encouraging British arts, commerce, and manufacturing. In the decade that followed, campaigners lobbied for Britain to adopt internationally agreed standards, with the first International Statistical Congress held in Brussels in 1853, which led to the formation of the catchily named International Association for Obtaining a Uniform Decimal System of Measures, Weights, and Coins. In 1859 this organisation declared metric to be the best possible system for international use.[7]

Amid this growing support for the metre, the Cobden-Chevalier treaty of 1860 added further urgency to the question of measurement. It rapidly became obvious that for free trade to flourish, shared weights and measures were crucial. Economic integration could not be secured without some structural unification. For a start, more trade would involve increased post between the two nations, which was difficult to manage without agreed prices and units of weight. But what really brought the importance of international cooperation in standards home to British politicians was, of course, alcohol. Naturally there was little, if any, point to having free trade with France if this did not result in cheaper wine and brandy. The problem, however, was that Britain and France had different standards for calculating alcoholic content. During the treaty negotiations in late 1859, Cobden wrote to William Gladstone of the trouble. Different wines had to be taxed at varying rates relative to their level of alcohol, but to do this you had to be capable of calculating proof with accuracy. The French used the alcoholometer of Joseph Louis Gay-Lussac. Since the seventeenth century it had been known that alcoholic content could be worked out by determining the specific gravity of alcohol. During the late eighteenth century, hydrometers for this purpose came into use in France and Britain, but these were not very refined, often giving the same percentage for brandies that were clearly of differing strengths. In 1821 the French government commissioned Gay-Lussac, a chemist, to revise this method of proofing, which he did by producing an increasingly precise measure of alcohol's specific gravity at 15°C. This standard became law in France in 1824, after Gay-Lussac brought out his own alcoholometer for sale in 1822 which became the official device for determining alcoholic content.[8] This new alcoholometer had a scale of 100 parts which, when plunged into a spirituous liquid at 15°C, gave a reading of alcoholic strength to the nearest degree, at least in theory. Today in France, alcohol by volume is often still referred to as 'degrees Gay-Lussac'.[9]

Mid-treaty negotiations, Chevalier sent a set of French instruments to Gladstone to convince him of the French measure's practicality. However, Cobden expressed doubts to Gladstone over the accuracy of Gay-Lussac's device. He alleged that if Gladstone was happy with knowing the content to the nearest 10 per cent, France's measure would suffice, but warned that the French were certain greater precision was secured through their methods.[10] Here then, the task of measuring was inseparable from taxing and, more importantly, trading. Cobden recommended wines under 10 per cent proof be taxed at 9d per gallon, 11–20 per cent at a shilling and 6d, 21 per cent and above at two shillings and 6d. Believing most French wine was under 10 per cent, Cobden asserted such rates amounted to a large reduction in tax. In contrast, Chevalier favoured a tax of 1d per degree of alcohol, relying on French instruments to measure the strength with accuracy.[11] Both the British and the French were united in their desire to trade wine, but measuring proved troublesome, and without international collaboration through political negotiation, free trade would remain but a dream.

Following the experience of negotiating the Free Trade Treaty, British politicians seriously contemplated the introduction of the metric system throughout the empire. Adopting the metre was, for radical politicians like Cobden, the next logical step after securing Anglo-French trade. As he put it, metrication was effectively 'free trade in arithmetic'.[12] Predictably, the idea of Britain converting to French standards raised much opposition, which was exacerbated by the fact that it was radical MPs who were the most vocal supporters of the metric. While Edwin Chadwick was most famous for leading public health reforms during the 1840s, John Bright, Cobden, and William Ewart all had a reputation for challenging traditional ruling elites.[13] Nevertheless, the growing enthusiasm for measurement reform was hard to ignore, especially as it did not just come from Cobden. In 1860, Prince Albert voiced his support for the metric system at the London meeting of the International Statistical Congress. Metrication brought royal and radical together, while the advantages to international trade of integration were tantalising. In the United States there was talk of similar reforms from 1859 and by 1862 most of Europe, including Portugal, France, Belgium, the Netherlands, and the Kingdom of Italy, had gone metric. In the same year Uruguay, Chile, Brazil, Peru, and Argentina followed, as did Germany in 1871.[14]

Under mounting pressure, Parliament appointed a Select Committee to investigate how Britain should proceed. Its chair, Ewart, had been the liberal radical for Dumfries Burghs since 1841, constantly championing free trade, international cooperation, and the repeal of the protectionist Corn Laws. An industrious investigation of Britain's weights and measures followed throughout 1862, which found the country in a complete mess. Different regions used yards of different lengths and varying weights for different objects, such as wool, coal, gold, straw, and diamonds. For capacity there were at least twenty competing bushels and there were no fewer than ten different stones.[15] The committee agreed on the propriety of introducing the metric system, observing that countries the world over were 'yearly becoming more and more mutually connected and mutually dependent; most of them composing the Great European family of nations, and many of them near our own shores'.[16] However, Ewart's committee also came to realise how difficult any unification of weights and measures would be to implement because of Britain's parliamentary political system.

The big difficulty was that enforcing any unifying steps would involve political reform. Integrating trade with France could not be achieved without some degree of political alignment. The French state was capable of enforcing measurement standards on its population because it was autocratic and had no qualms about interfering in the lives of its people. But Britain thought itself different. Its parliamentary tradition and constitutional monarchy emphasised the rights of individuals. In this *laissez-faire* style of government, the state interfered as little as possible in the country's economic and social affairs. Minimal government was the cornerstone of Victorian liberalism and it was this preservation of liberties that, according to most Victorian commentators, set Britain apart from the rest of the world. Its prosperity was thought to be the result of socio-economic freedoms; France's interventionist state was the very antithesis of this.

But avoiding government interference meant that enforcing the metre on an unwilling society would be virtually impossible. Aligning with France's metric system would mean aligning, at least to some extent, with France's political system. Parliament would have to pass laws and tamper with the personal liberties of individuals. George Biddell Airy, the Astronomer Royal and autocratic director of the Royal Observatory at Greenwich, recognised the dilemma. Knowing that most of Britain's standards were localised and inaccurate, he wanted an effective national system of weights and measures, but also knew that this would infringe on 'local liberties'. It would require 'the creation of a Department' to instigate the new system, just as there was one in France. Other countries had done this too, such as Belgium, Portugal, and Switzerland. Though incompatible with British political values of liberalism, Airy recommended to the 1862 select committee that the government, 'instead of being passive, ought to be active' and appoint a department with a capable chief. Above all, the metric system had to be made the legal national set of standards. Airy explained that 'There is no country which interferes so little as this country does with the education of the people, and with their internal affairs. The rule in this country is that the people should act for themselves; but the rule in the foreign countries … is that the Government should act for the people.' As a result, 'our Government interferes less in the private concerns of the people than is the case anywhere else'.[17] Though apparently desirable, unifying standards risked undermining British liberalism.

In May 1863, armed with the report of his select committee, Ewart introduced a bill into the House of Commons for decimalising Britain's system of weights and measures and bringing them into line with 'those of foreign countries'. Kilograms, metres, and litres were all included, but most radically of all the proposed legislation specified that within three years 'the Imperial and all local or customary Weights and Measures shall be abolished'.[18] This was a revolution. It amounted to nothing less than the complete implementation of a French rationalisation of British trade and commerce at a moment when Britain was at the zenith of its imperial and industrial pomp.

If Ewart was hoping for a fight, the House of Commons did not disappoint. His Metric System Bill provoked a bitter argument in

PUNCH'S FANCY PORTRAITS.—No. 134.

SIR GEORGE B. AIRY, K.C.B., F.R.S.,

Punch's satirical depiction of George Biddell Airy, his head attached to Greenwich Observatory's time ball apparatus for displaying accurate time signals to ships waiting on the Thames. (Author's collection) the chamber. Ewart began by emphasising that railways, steamships, increasing postage, and electric telegraphy were all hastening international commerce. He was sure that this demanded integration to function. The metric should be implemented in Britain because this was now 'the general European system'. The clincher though, was that Britain exported just £24 million of goods to non-metric nations, compared to £55 million to those on the French system.[19]

Conservative MP Joseph Henley was the first to object, full of Biblical wrath. He wanted to know how Parliament could prevent the people using the weights and measures they had always used. France had only managed it through the disorder and chaos of the 1789 Revolution. Henley declared uniformity to be irreligious: 'If it had pleased God that there should never have been a Tower of Babel.' He was sure international merchants would be delighted, but God had not made the world a place of unity and convenience.[20] Henley disliked the idea of having to consult Paris to check the length of a metre. Britain seemed to him to be in the grip of some sort of 'Gallo-mania'.[21]

John Hubbard, Conservative MP for Buckingham, also opposed the bill, this time on the grounds that when the French had attempted to decimalise time, 'nature itself declared against them'. As the day, month, and year could not be made to conform with the metric system, he thought it clear that there was no naturalistic argument to be made for the reform. Nature did not work according to tens, hundreds, and thousands. Equally, it was impossible to see how the measure could be enforced without harming the liberties of the people.[22] Other critics argued that the metric only benefitted financiers and merchants. The common man would be robbed: introducing the litre would mean the labourer would effectively lose an eighth of his pint.[23]

As Chancellor of the Exchequer, Gladstone weighed in, prophetically warning that as no government could make a new system compulsory, decimalisation and the metric were doomed to fail.[24] But Ewart did not have to look far for friends in the House. Cobden, champion of Anglo-French free trade, spoke up. He claimed to have been embarrassed when in Paris at the superiority of the French system. He also recalled that when the revolutionary state created the metre in the 1790s, it had actually invited Fellows of London's Royal Society to France to help calculate the unit. It had always been envisaged as 'a system of weights and measures for the world', rather than a French plot to control her rival's commerce. The British government had rejected the French invitation.[25] Furthermore, as the metre was one ten-millionth part of a quarter of the globe's circumference, it was not special to France or a 'concession to French ideas', but a universal measure taken directly from nature.[26] Cobden finished with a flourish aimed at riling the more patriotic MPs within the House. 'The French are generally considered a more logical people than the English,' he declared, and this was a view largely derived from the fact that the French employed a decimalised system of weights and measures.[27]

Privately, Cobden doubted the British people would ever see the inherent reason of French decimalization. When Richard Rickard, a Cornish mathematics teacher, sent Cobden a copy of his recently published *Anglo-French Ready Reckoner*, he found little enthusiasm from the radical MP. This book, intended to 'familiarise the public with the French system' of measurement, offered simple instruction and conversions between imperial and metric. Cobden liked it but was skeptical as to its commercial value, reflecting how he sometimes thought 'with dismay of the precedent of the Gregorian Calendar which required nearly a century & a half to surmount the somewhat Chinese conservatism of these good Islanders!'[28] Britain was not a place for rapid change.

Nevertheless, stuck between embracing the French metre or the reputation of being less logical than their nearest rivals, the Commons passed Ewart's bill 110 votes to 75. The following year, Ewart and his pro-metric allies revised their bill, changing the reform from a compulsory to a permissive measure. Instead of instantly reorganising Britain's weights and measures, this thin end of the wedge would hopefully be more likely to become law. Although opposed again on the grounds that the metre was a 'revolutionary measure', a majority of thirty-eight votes was secured.[29] Yet the success of the bill was limited. Despite the metre now being a legal standard, this meant little practical change and the use of imperial persisted.

It might seem today that Britain had a straight choice between the yard and the metre. But this was not the case in the 1860s. There was a third, thankfully now forgotten, system of measurement rivalling both: Pyramidology. The basic idea of Pyramidology was that Britain should use a system of measurement with divine origins and that God had bestowed His own sacred measurement on His chosen people, the Israelites. According to leading scholars of Ancient Egypt, this unit, which was apparently equal to twenty-five imperial inches, had been used to build the Great Pyramid at Giza. The lead spokesman for Pyramidology was the eccentric Astronomer Royal of Scotland, Charles Piazzi Smyth. He argued that Britain's inch was in fact very close to the 'Pyramid Inch'; this was hardly surprising for many Victorians, confident that they were obviously, by the 1860s, God's chosen people. But the great virtue of Pyramidology was that it was a religiously grounded measurement system and, therefore, the very opposite of France's atheist, revolutionary metre.[30]

Unfortunately for enthusiasts of Ancient Egypt, radical MPs remained committed to the metric system and failed to see the merits of Pyramidology. In 1868, a bill for the compulsory use of the metric system again passed in the House of Commons and for a while it seemed inevitable that Britain would adopt the metre. But in 1869 the Royal Standards Commission, which the Cabinet had recently appointed, surprised everyone in judging Britain unready for the metric to become law. A later bill to make the metric compulsory was defeated by five votes in 1871. It would take decades for the metric to again secure parliamentary support.[31]

*

It was not just weights and measures that raised questions over the political differences between Britain and France. In the early nineteenth century different orchestras across Europe used musical notes of varying frequencies. The note of C at the Paris Opera was not the same as a C in Lyon, or Vienna, or at the Royal Opera House in Covent Garden. In fact, rarely did musicians in the same city use notes of the same number of vibrations, so wherever you went, music always sounded just a little bit different. At the same time, there was a prevailing belief that to play notes at a slightly higher pitch would make music sound better. The result of this was that by the 1850s, not only was there no uniformity among musicians, but some eighteenth-century compositions, such as Handel's, were being played at such a high pitch that they no longer sounded the way composers had originally intended.

In 1858 Napoléon III took action. He launched an investigation to resolve this musical chaos. In February 1859 he issued an *arrêté* (decree) establishing the *diapason normal* as France's official musical standard, specifying that an A above middle C should be played at 435 vibrations per second. Obviously musicians could not actually count vibrations this accurately, but the new standard was supposed to be enforced with tuning forks calibrated to sound the *diapason normal*.³² As with the metre, Britain looked to France for a musical standard. On learning that Napoléon was planning to regulate musical notes, leading musicians, composers, and critics across Britain proposed the Society of Arts take similar steps. *The Spectator* praised Napoléon's intervention but wondered how, without the power of a 'gracious Emperor', Britain could do the same. The newspaper wanted to see the state take a more active role in British social and economic life and thought that adopting the *diapason normal* as a legal musical standard would be an ideal place to start.³³

Throughout late 1859 and early 1860, at the very moment that in Paris Cobden was overseeing his free trade negotiations, in London a specially appointed Society of Arts committee discussed how Britain could musically emulate France. But, yet again, adopting French-style regulation and achieving musical unification was impossible without political integration. Yet again the problem was that within a liberal framework, Britain was trying to replicate a measure that in France had the support of an autocratic emperor. In many ways this musical unification provided a rehearsal for the later debates over the metric system.

In mid-1860 the committee reported, actually rejecting France's *diapason normal*. It felt that the French standard was too different to the higher pitches in use in Britain and would mean ruinous costs for musicians and instrument makers as they adapted their instruments to this lower frequency. Instead of an A at 435, the Society of Arts recommended a C above middle C of 528, which worked out at A at about 440, so slightly higher than the French pitch. It was Britain's political culture that shaped this variation. Choose a pitch too low and no musician would voluntarily agree to use it. Enforce a lower pitch with parliamentary legislation and you risked appearing to compromise the principles of liberalism.

So the only option was a compromise pitch that musicians might freely choose to play.

The committee was very well aware of this political dilemma. John Hullah, an authority on music, explained that were the committee 'a parliament, and could force the country to adopt this view [that a lower pitch was preferable], the case would be different'.[34] The committee's instigator, Harry Chester, agreed and recognised that in Britain the most that could be done to regulate music was to establish 'a voluntary law' and hope musicians followed it.[35] The committee itself reported that in France there had been 'considerable difficulties ... in enforcing the new musical diapason' and this was with Napoleonic state power 'such as would never be sought for, or obtained, in this country'.[36] Indeed, many were sure that a voluntary standard would place Britain, by virtue of its liberalism, 'in a position superior to their French neighbours under compulsory legislation'.[37] Unsurprisingly, British musicians took little notice of the Society of Arts' suggested pitch and went on playing much as they had done before. As with the metric system, there was much discussion over the French *diapason normal*. There was much discussion, much good will, and much desire to integrate with France but, ultimately, there was not much achieved.

*

Regardless of the limited success in bringing Britain's musical pitch, weights, and measures into line with those in use on the Continent, it is revealing that the metric system attracted such serious consideration. Given that imperial standards could be said to be the system of a global empire, this was not just a case of a parochial set of British weights and measures competing with a universally accepted metric regime. To be pro imperial in the 1850s and 1860s was by no means the mark of a 'little Englander', inherently hostile to Europe and external regulation. In the mid-nineteenth century it could fairly be asked why Europe should not integrate with the British system. But British free traders believed that there were rich rewards in adopting France's standards. Many were happy to see the government's *laissez-faire* principles suspended and for Parliament to impose metric reforms on liberal Britain in a manner more akin to Napoléon's state interventionism. If anything, having a huge empire and a dominance of global trade seemed to imbue politicians like Cobden and Ewart with the confidence to promote Anglo-French political, as well as economic, integration.

6

ENTENTE DIMINISHED: THE FALL OF PALMERSTON AND NAPOLÉON

Punch never really knew what to make of Napoléon III's relationship with Palmerston. After the various war scares of the 1850s, the remarkable flexibility and endurance of Anglo-French relations mystified the satirical journal. Or at least, it liked to appear bemused. On learning of the Cobden-Chevalier Free Trade Treaty in early 1860, *Punch* pushed the wordplay on entente cordiale to breaking point and beyond. The implications of the treaty were uncertain, but it specified that 'this celebrated Anglo-French "Cordiale" is likely to be affected much by the remission of the duties on French wines and spirits'. The consumption of these would surely increase and, with it, 'the strength and purity of this "Cordiale". Not only is it stronger in spirit, but it is likewise freer from the slight tendency to acidity, which, at the smallest turn of politics, was apt to vitiate all its good qualities.'[1] The anonymous authors of *Punch* evidently had a lot of time on their hands.

Two years later, the same publication was pleased to report that the entente was progressing healthily, learning from the Paris correspondent of *The Times* that there was talk in Normandy of organising English-style fox hunting. This was surely brilliant news to all who delighted in 'every step made towards Anglicising Frenchmen and Frenchifying English', *Punch* declared. Yet the canny journal was cautious, warning that 'Knowing somewhat how *la chasse* is pursued across the Channel, we can picture to our mind the ludicrous absurdities French "sportsmen" will commit, in the way of hands and horseflesh, customs and costume, ere they succeed in hunting foxes à la mode anglaise.' How absurd the French would look in hunting pink, joked *Punch*: how would they translate 'view holloa' and 'tally ho'? And did anyone know the French for 'yoicks'? 'These and other questions of like national importance are suggested to the mind of the meditative reader.'[2]

Punch was often obscure, but equally unclear was the precise nature of the entente in the 1860s, which had much to do with the French emperor himself. His rule consisted, broadly, of two acts. In the first, the 1850s, he appeared an autocrat, exerting a tight grip on the French state. The second, the 1860s, saw a more liberal Napoléon, ceding political powers through a series of reforms. Up to 1860 Napoléon read most government reports, but the final decade saw his energy decline and the rising influence of his ministers. As sharp and agile as he had been in the 1850s, Napoléon seemed to lose a sense of strategy after 1860, both at home and internationally. Since 1853 Napoléon had promised eventual reforms, looking to British institutions with admiration. Liberalisation came in 1860 and 1861, followed by much less voluntary concessions in 1867. By the end of the 1860s it was clear that Napoléon's political strategy had become muddled. Even his charmed friend Queen Victoria began to view him as increasingly unpredictable.[3]

Napoléon's misguided attempt to establish a Mexican monarchy under French protection, orchestrating the crowning of Maximilian, younger brother to Emperor Franz Joseph of the Austro-Hungarian Empire, as Emperor of Mexico in 1864, ended badly. Hoping to secure French financiers control over Mexico's silver mines, promote a regime committed to free trade, and check American influence in the region, Napoléon's designs rapidly unravelled, despite British marines landing with the French army in 1861, once again demonstrating the shared interests of Britain and France. A Mexican rebellion saw French influence implode and the pro-French Maximilian executed in 1867.[4]

In Britain, the days of Palmerston were also numbered. Ailing and decrepit, the grandmaster of foreign policy was rapidly losing his grip on world affairs. Without a reliable ally on the Continent between 1860 and 1870, Britain was to find that its ability to influence international affairs was actually quite limited. For all its economic, industrial, naval, and imperial strength, without the agile cooperation of France, British policymakers found it far harder to determine European affairs than it had done during the 1850s. The Anglo-French order, so laboriously crafted between Palmerston and Napoléon III, was to disintegrate as the partners failed to work together. With British policymakers lacking decisiveness and unwilling to commit themselves on the Continent, and the French Emperor lumbering from one international fiasco to another, the entente lost all direction. In its place, a new Continental rival grew increasingly powerful: the German Empire.

*

The first signs of the waning of Anglo-French influence in Europe became apparent in 1863. In Russian Poland a rebellion had broken out, only to be cruelly subdued. Appalled, Britain did little more than deliver a protest to the Tsar. Worse was to come, this time over the escalating tensions between Denmark and the German states, under Prussia's lead, surrounding the duchies of Schleswig and Holstein. This marked the first serious lack of coordination between Palmerston and Napoléon.

Holstein had been a dependency of the Danish crown since 1489, but in 1848 it had, along with the Duchy of Schleswig, revolted against the rule of King Frederick VII of Denmark. With German military support, the two duchies secured autonomy.[5] As part of the Treaty of London that concluded this Dano-German war, signed in 1852, Frederick agreed not to try to incorporate Schleswig within his lands. Spurred on by Danish nationalists, this is exactly what his successor, Christian IX, tried to do on ascending the throne in November 1863, signing a constitution that reasserted control over Schleswig.

This was a golden opportunity for Prussia and Otto von Bismarck (1815–98). As Minister President of Prussia from 1862, Bismarck orchestrated European affairs for almost three decades with unrivalled skill and finesse. His object was clear: to unify the Germanic states into a German Empire under Prussian leadership. Nationalistic, Lutheran, a solid member of his country's governing Junker class, and loyal to his king, Wilhelm I, Bismarck looked to use the Danish question to bring the German-speaking lands under Berlin's authority. Since the Congress of Vienna in 1815, these states formed the German Confederation. As the dominant powers within this alliance, Prussia and Austria-Hungary vied for influence, seeking to bring greater direction to the confederation.

The German Confederation issued an ultimatum demanding the Danish king's November constitution be revoked and Schleswig autonomy returned. Instead, the Danes occupied Holstein too. With the German states incensed and Bismarck eager to add the duchies of Schleswig and Holstein to Prussia's territories, the Austro-German allies and Denmark edged closer to war.[6] All the while, British and French politicians kept a close eye on this rapidly escalating Schleswig-Holstein crisis. This was a potentially embarrassing diplomatic incident for Palmerston's government. After all, Queen Victoria's son and heir had married the Danish

Prussia's maverick Minister President and builder of the German Empire, Otto Bismarck. (Author's collection)

Princess Alexandra in 1863, following the 1858 marriage of Victoria's daughter to Crown Prince Frederick of Prussia. With children in both the Prussian and Danish royal families, the Schleswig-Holstein crisis was something the British government could not easily ignore.

In September 1863, the Foreign Secretary, Lord Russell, had reports that the Quai d'Orsay could not allow Denmark to remain unprotected, fearing a disturbance to the balance of European power.⁷ Both the Foreign Office and Quai d'Orsay recognised that they had to cooperate to restrain German aggression, but these aspirations came to nothing. In late January 1864, the French ambassador to London made it very clear that as much as France wanted to contain Prussia, war was out of the question, informing Russell that while it 'may be comparatively easy for England to carry on a war which can never go beyond maritime operations ... a war between France and Germany would be one of the most burthensome and one of the most hazardous in which the French Empire could engage'.⁸ As one cynical American observer put it, Napoléon III would only risk war if it was it popular with the French people and if it helped erase memories of his Mexican debacle.⁹

In London, the indecision was exacerbated by a confrontation between the Crown and the Cabinet. Queen Victoria had very different views as to who was at fault to those of her Prime Minister and Foreign Secretary. Palmerston and Russell both regarded Prussia as a danger that needed restraining, but Victoria was sympathetic to the Germans, believing the Danes had acted recklessly. She had, after all, been married to a German and was still mourning the death of Albert, a victim of typhoid fever and the drains of Windsor Castle in 1861. If the people of Holstein and Schleswig did not want a Danish king, surely this was their prerogative? Victoria remained committed to peace, finding Russell's determination to call Prussia's bluff distasteful. When the Foreign Secretary warned Prussia not to violate the 1852 Treaty of London, she thought this too strong, provoking a stand-off between the queen and her government.¹⁰ In January 1864, she reminded Palmerston that the Germans were 'our *natural* old allies'.¹¹

On 1 February 1864, Prussian and Austrian troops marched into Schleswig-Holstein. Copenhagen requested aid from Britain, France, and Russia, but to no effect. On 15 February, German troops invaded Denmark proper, while the Austrian navy sailed towards the Prussian fleet in the North Sea. Alarmed and enraged, Palmerston and Russell wanted to despatch ships to the Baltic to prevent the Germanic fleets from bombarding Copenhagen, but the Cabinet opposed this action, as did the queen. Together, this resistance pushed the interventionist duo close to resignation. Without the Cabinet or the Crown on side, Britain's leading statesmen were left exposed on the international scene.[12]

Throughout the summer, Anglo-French arbitration efforts failed too. In late June, Napoléon proposed French aid to the Danes, but only if Britain provided support. This Victoria rejected altogether. Palmerston was increasingly bed-ridden by gout. Amid a total breakdown of relations between the Crown, Cabinet, Prime Minister, and Foreign Secretary, the entente's international clout collapsed.[13] By October, the unopposed German armies had seized the Duchies of Schleswig, Holstein, and Saxe-Lauenburg, condemning Denmark to a humiliating defeat.

Although the British public was firmly opposed to Prussian aggression and Napoléon had proposed both a peace conference and a war to stop Prussia, Palmerston had never really been committed to either measure. For all his blustering, he was never likely to intervene and Prussia, calling the aged Prime Minister's bluff, pursued its hostilities. The British cabinet took no action, resolving by a single vote that they would only intervene should the Danish capital, Copenhagen, be threatened directly. Reflecting on the Schleswig-Holstein question, Palmerston weakly lamented that 'Ships sailing on the sea cannot stop armies on land.'[14]

Britain was isolated in Europe, even if its politicians did not fully appreciate this new reality. Palmerston died in 1865, marking the end of a career defined by foreign policy and 'gun-boat diplomacy'. Few British ministers were so shrewd and aggressive on the international scene. Yet the days of Palmerstonian threats were over and with it, the Franco-British supremacy of the 1850s.

Domestic commentators in Britain, though alarmed at the outbreak of the Schleswig-Holstein War, thought the idea of an Imperial German Empire some way off, given its unpopularity with many of the smaller German states. For all the Prussian ambitions of a united Germany, in 1864 this seemed no nearer to being forged 'than is the Cathedral of Cologne to being completed'.[15] But then, few counted on Bismarck's remarkable strategic resolve. With Denmark subdued, the Prussian maverick turned on Austria-Hungary, looking to settle the question of influence over the German Confederation once and for all. A brief war resulted in a thumping Prussian victory in 1866. At the Battle of Königgrätz, Helmuth von Moltke's army smashed the Austrian forces, inflicting some 44,000 casualties. Bismarck looked on from Moltke's side, before forcing Emperor Franz Joseph to surrender all Austrian influence in the German lands.

In place of the German Confederation, Bismarck established a new North German Confederation in 1867, appointing himself Chancellor. At the Peace of Prague, Prussia took control over Schleswig, Holstein, Frankfurt, Hanover, Nassau, and Hesse-Kassel. Along with twenty-one German states, this new Prussian-led northern alliance was firmly under Bismarck's sway. All the while, Britain and France looked on at this Germanic reorganisation, incapable of restraining Prussia's ambitions. Napoléon urged restraint, calling for the German borders to return to those established in 1815. But with his troops spread out across the globe, in Mexico, Algeria, and Rome, there was little the Emperor could do to restore the pre-1866 status quo.[16]

*

It was not just diplomatically that Britain and France drifted apart during the 1870s. Social differences between the two countries continued to be prominent: nowhere was this more apparent than in each society's perceptions of the political regimes of their cross-Channel rivals. One divisive question was how the governments of each country dealt with the great pandemic of the day: the spread of venereal diseases through the business of prostitution. Few controversies demonstrated British anxieties over French-style regulation quite so revealingly as the opposition to the Contagious Diseases Acts of the 1860s. At stake here were concerns over the role of the state in controlling the spread of disease: should governments intervene and attempt to prevent infection from spreading, or should individuals be trusted to protect themselves?

In France and Prussia, prostitution had long been state regulated. To protect soldiers from sexually transmitted diseases, primarily syphilis, scabies, and gonorrhoea, it was customary on the Continent for prostitutes to undergo regular medical examinations. From the 1830s, French specialists increasingly relied on the use of the speculum, a horribly invasive metal device, for internal examinations. In Britain, this quite literal state intervention into women's bodies not only seemed indecent and degrading, but appeared indicative of France's lack of respect for personal liberties. Polite British audiences were confident that this official sanctioning of prostitution reflected the nation's moral decay.[17] It was not just that France's government seemed autocratic, but it was construed to be actively promoting immoral behaviour.

While British statesmen could never officially approve of prostitution, they were happy to turn a blind eye to it. There was something of a consensus that sexual desire, while clearly odd in a woman, was perfectly normal in a healthy male. But pre-marital sex was a problem: promiscuity raised troubling questions over paternity and, therefore, matters of inheritance. The solution was a sex trade on the sly: Victorians endeavoured to ignore the corrupting practice. However, following the lamentable showing of the British army in the Crimean War, the government appointed a Royal Commission in 1857 to investigate the health of the nation's armed forces. In 1860 it was reported that 37 per cent of army hospital admissions were for venereal diseases, equating to about 586 a day out of a domestic establishment of 60,000 troops. For all the rigour Britain's army had lacked in the Crimean, it was very far from lethargic when it came to carnal affairs.

Under the guidance of Florence Nightingale, an 1862 parliamentary committee sought to resolve this dire state of affairs. It was Sir John Liddell who took a lead in the ensuing investigation, and it was to France that he looked for inspiration. Since 1802, the French state had regulated prostitution through compulsory medical examinations. Liddell recommended the same was essential for Britain, which had up to half a million women working in the industry, almost half of which were also employed in domestic service, despite the official figure being just 30,000. In 1864, Parliament passed the Contagious Diseases Act, giving the police in ports and garrison towns powers to arrest suspected prostitutes and subject them to medical inspection. A second act followed in 1866 that introduced compulsory checks every three months, and then a third act in 1869 extended this regulation to all garrison towns throughout Britain. Potential prostitutes could be held for up to five days without trial, and if found to be infected, would be hospitalised until cured.

The legislation found much support among Britain's medical professions, who were all men of course, aside from Elizabeth Garrett Anderson (1836–1917), the first qualified British female doctor. But then even Anderson, having taken her MD from the University of Paris, favoured the French-style regulation of women's health. A subsequent Royal Commission in 1871 found that the system of medical checks and issuing of certificates to healthy prostitutes had reduced the rate of venereal disease among soldiers from 194 to 37 per 1,000, while increasing the life expectancy of those engaged in prostitution. The medical press, especially *The Lancet*, heralded this French system as a triumph. Fans of the laws even went so far as to establish the imaginatively named 'Association for Promoting the Extension of the Contagious Diseases Act of 1866 to the Civilian Population'. Few parliamentary acts would, however, spark so much anger.

While the first few acts passed peacefully, the 1869 legislation galvanised polite, middle-class society and initiated the first large-scale female political organisation in British history.[18] Not only did the government's apparent approval of prostitution appear corrupt, not helped by the fact that Parliament was exclusively male, as were the medical professions and the electorate, but the new police powers meant that any woman could be arrested, even if only suspected of prostitution. All this was made even more blatantly unfair by the passing of the 1867 Reform Act, extending the vote to all male heads of households, giving many working-class men the right to vote, while all upper- and middle-class women remained unrepresented. The speculum was especially notorious, with rumours abounding of brutalising and embarrassing examinations. At Devonport these were done in a room with clear-glass windows near where the dockers worked. There was panic that the invasive speculum could ruin a virgin, encourage sexual fetishes, and corrupt the pure minds of innocent women.

Enough was enough. In October 1869, Elizabeth Wolstenholme took action, inviting Josephine Butler (1828–1906) to lead a campaign against the state's tyranny.[19] Two months later, on New Year's Eve, over 120 women, including Nightingale, signed a declaration opposing the acts and announcing the formation of the Ladies' National Association for the Repeal of the Contagious Diseases Acts (LNA). Escalating rapidly to over 2,000 members, this organisation would campaign for the repeal of the acts for the next sixteen years. As much as the intervention of respectable women into a controversy over prostitution might have struck Victorian audiences as rather risqué, Butler proved the ideal leader for the LNA, keen to proclaim the movement's Christian morality and political liberalism. As a devout mother and wife to an Anglican evangelical church minister, she had impeccable social credentials. But for all that this was a cause about women's rights, it also involved profound questions over what it was to be English, as opposed to being French.

In every sense, this was a crusade against Frenchness, both in terms of liberties and morality. Detailing her first act as leader of the LNA, Butler later summed up the implicit Francophobia at the heart of the campaign. On visiting Crewe, she delivered a speech to a small group of working-class labourers. She recalled how, in response, they 'surprised me by saying, "We understand you perfectly. We in this group served an apprenticeship in Paris, and we have seen and know for ourselves the truth of what you say. We have said to each other that it would be the death-knell of the moral life of England were she to copy France in this matter."'[20] The degree to which the labourers of Crewe had experienced these particular Parisian transactions is unclear, as is the accuracy of Butler's recollections. Nevertheless, the association between French immorality and prostitution provided a powerful resource with which to unite liberal middle-class English women and working-class labouring men. Both shared fears that, unless repealed, the Contagious Diseases Acts would undermine all English decency and corrupt the nation's political freedoms. After all, how would helpless English men be able to restrain themselves if prostitution was to be officially legislated for? They would surely become more French. As novelist Wilkie Collins put it, 'The morality of England is firmly based on the immorality of France.'[21]

The subsequent LNA campaign was a publicity masterpiece. With powerful rhetoric, Butler's charismatic leadership, and a range of well-crafted tactics, the acts were suspended in 1883 and repealed altogether in 1886. James Stansfeld (1820–98) and Henry J. Wilson (1833–1914) provided crucial support for the movement in Parliament, while outside, the LNA targeted Liberal MPs who supported the acts, such as at the Pontefract by-election in 1872, where the movement worked to drastically reduce Hugh Childers' majority. He had, as First Lord of the Admiralty, zealously endorsed the Contagious Diseases Acts, but this almost cost him his seat. The LNA was significant not only in that it was Britain's first organisation of women for a political cause, but also in that its strategy and practices would be replicated well into the twentieth century as women fought for greater political rights.[22] The Contagious Diseases Acts and state efforts to regulate prostitution according to France's example would prove the catalyst for the subsequent women's suffrage campaign which successfully won the vote in 1918.

*

As much as British audiences liked to vilify France and its lack of morality, the truth was that their once able ally and conduit for European influence was weak: Napoléon's star was waning.[23] Prussia was in the ascendant. Bismarck's triumph over the Austrians in 1866 had remained a constant sore point in France, with the public eager for the restoration of French influence in the German lands that Bismarck had so effectively undermined. Germany's unification was troubling for the French emperor. In 1820 Prussia had a third of the population of France, but by 1860 the united German states were nearing parity, and after 1866 its armies were a third larger than France's. Prussian and Saxon coal produce was treble that of France's mines, and German industry was expanding at an astonishing rate. All this was quite alarming for French audiences: in less than a decade, an almighty power had risen up along France's eastern border.[24]

Fat, old, and lethargic, plagued by gout, gallstones, and haemorrhoids, Napoléon III now ruled over a corrupt, repressive regime. Even his English mistress, Miss Harriet Howard, collected a salary of 700,000 francs.[25] His popularity lost, his authoritarian empire resented by all but the country's agricultural peasants, and increasingly weak internationally, the Napoleonic state was frail. The end was in sight. Prussia's success in 1866 marked a real insult to French prestige, sweeping away all memory of France's Germanic influence, which had culminated in Bonaparte's 1806 founding of the 'Confederation of the Rhine'. To restore confidence in the empire, Napoléon III desperately wanted a popular military victory.[26] Ideally, the blow would be landed on Prussia, but even the annexation of the Rhinelands, Belgium, or Luxembourg would do. In 1867 he offered to buy the latter, but failed.

France's aggression was invaluable ammunition for Bismarck. With Napoléon so desperate to expand eastward, the German states felt threatened. Bismarck saw yet another chance to mobilise German nationalism under Prussian direction and move the Confederation towards an all-out German empire. In 1868 he negotiated several treaties with the Southern German states of Bavaria, Württemberg, and Baden, establishing a *zollparlament*, a sort of 'customs parliament'. This was seen as yet another snub to French prestige in the region. Napoléon responded by demanding that Bismarck stay out of these three states sitting close to France.[27] Such sabre-rattling was music to the Chancellor's ears.

It was a domestic crisis that finally tipped Napoléon over the edge, with the French public and press demanding a war with Prussia to save the Second Empire and its influence in the German lands. In 1869, Napoléon called an election. Usually a formality, this effectively resulted in a defeat for the empire, as urban republicanism held sway. Three-quarters of Parisians voted against Napoléon, with his support confined to the rural provinces. Over half of the votes cast were for candidates opposed to the Second Empire.[28] Then in January 1870, Napoléon's cousin, Prince Pierre-Napoléon Bonaparte, shot and killed a republican journalist who had surprised him on his doorstep for a spontaneous interview. This bizarre incident sparked riots. Up went the barricades in Paris. Luckily for Napoléon, Haussmann's redevelopment of the capital and careful open-space planning meant that the unrest was easily subdued. Nevertheless, the emperor agreed to relax police powers and sack some of the more reactionary members of his government.[29] Fearing a *coup d'état*, Napoléon acknowledged that his only solution was a war to galvanise public support: a victory over Prussia was the one thing that might unite France through a wave of nationalism.

In Berlin, Bismarck was equally keen on a war with France, hoping to push the German states together. But he recognised that it was crucial France be seen as the aggressor, to convince the southern states of the urgency of closer German integration. While Bavaria and Württemberg both wanted defensive treatises with Prussia, they were determined to remain independent: a French invasion might just change this. The 'Iron Chancellor', Bismarck, resolved to provoke France's ailing emperor into an act of aggression. First, he declared that King Wilhelm should be made 'Kaiser', emperor of Germany. Bismarck then financed a German railway through Switzerland, raising concerns in Paris that Prussia was interested in exerting influence in Italy. Napoléon did nothing. So Bismarck then announced Prussia's support of the candidacy of Leopold of Hohenzollern-Sigmaringen to the Spanish throne. This promotion of a Prussian prince was outrageous to French audiences. Napoléon could not ignore the provocation and demanded Bismarck withdraw his support of Leopold's claims. When this was rejected, France was enraged. The Parisian crowds expected war and, on 14 July 1870, Napoléon obliged, mobilising his armies.[30]

What followed was a catastrophe. The German states united and Prussia's powerful armies, well equipped with modern artillery, inflicted a series of crippling defeats on Napoléon's forces. At the Battle of Sedan on 1 and 2 September, the German armies encircled Napoléon's forces. Of some 130,000 troops, 122,000 were killed, captured, or wounded. It was a devastating blow, with the emperor himself taken prisoner. Two days later, his empire capitulated, with France declaring itself a Republic.

From 19 September, Paris itself was besieged. In 1814 and 1815 the capital had not been fortified – an oversight that Napoléon Bonaparte long regretted during his exile on St Helena, musing 'what influence would that have not had on the events of the world', if only the city could have held out for eight days.[31] But in 1870 things were quite different: Paris was ready for a fight. For four gruelling months, more than 47,000 civilians perished amid the chronic food shortages. Reduced to living off rats, dogs, horses, and even the zoo animals of the Jardin des Plantes – including both of Paris's elephants – this was a harrowing experience that would haunt Parisian memories for decades to come.[32] The Prussians seized Versailles in October, turning the comfortable palace into the German headquarters from which to orchestrate the siege.

Throughout all of this, Britain had remained remarkably inactive. In London, William Gladstone's Liberal ministry was mocked for its 'hesitating impotence'. To all, it seemed that Bismarck had taken a complete grip on European politics. The *Pall Mall Gazette* presented British readers with a desperate picture. With two million citizens in Paris and more German guns and shells arriving each day, the French were gambling 'on the effects of disease in the investing army brought on by exposure to cold'. The problem was that the countryside around Paris was so full of cosy little villages and country houses, that the besiegers were living in great comfort, many enjoying better food and quarters than they did in their own homes. The *Pall Mall Gazette's* correspondent in Versailles assessed France's position to be hopeless.[33]

Some in Britain were delighted to see this Gallic humiliation, but others lamented the absence of a Palmerstonian figure, believing Gladstone to have lacked initiative. In early January 1871, *The Times* demanded intervention, but by the end of the month Paris had capitulated and calls for military assistance turned to relief efforts. Within two days of the surrender of Paris on 28 January, the Mayor of London began sending food supplies to the beleaguered city, with the British government following suit. About £52,000 worth of perishables were included in the first delivery. With their failure to aid France during the war, Parisian attitudes to the British were hostile in January, but had softened by February. Nevertheless, the new provisional government remained firm in its political convictions: among the food packages were luxury goods, including pheasants, that were politely returned to Britain.[34]

With the new Third Republic of France having moved its capital to Tours, Paris erupted into a centre of radical socialism, with a revolutionary government taking control in March, establishing what became known as the Paris Commune. Two months would pass before the Republic suppressed this movement during 'La semaine sanglante', the Bloody Week, of late May. It marked the completion of a dramatic fall from Napoleonic empire to chaotic republic as France awaited Bismarck's peace terms.

Though aggressive, Bismarck was careful, eager not to extract so much from France that it would turn towards radical republicanism or remain bent on revenge. He settled on the annexation of Alsace and Lorraine to subdue French industry, an indemnity of 5 billion francs to keep the new Republic in check, and a victory parade through Paris to remind the French of the totality of their defeat.[35] During the peace talks at Versailles, French diplomats insisted they could not pay the demanded reparations. Bismarck coolly replied that if this was the case, Germany would occupy France and then 'we will see if we can get 5 billion from it.'[36] It proved a persuasive argument: France agreed to pay up.

*

In 1871, in the Palace of Versailles's mesmerising Hall of Mirrors, so long the seat of French royal authority, Bismarck announced an end to the North German Confederation and the creation of the German Empire. As Chancellor of this new global power, he declared King Wilhelm I of Prussia emperor, or Kaiser, of the German lands. In Britain, Benjamin Disraeli asserted in the House of Commons that the war, effectively completing 'the German

Revolution', marked a far greater shift in European power relations than even the French Revolution of 1789.[37] In April 1871 the publication of a pamphlet, *The Fall of England or the Battle of Dorking*, sparked further public fears, with its narrative of an imagined German invasion of Britain. By December it had sold over 200,000 copies.[38] It had not taken long for Germany to replace France as the focus of British invasion anxieties.

As for Napoléon, he settled down to the life of an English gentleman. After his capture at Sedan and subsequent abdication, the ex-French Emperor was exiled to England. He had always feared this would happen, keeping a permanent account of £1 million with Barings Bank in London.[39] On his arrival in Britain, the deposed emperor visited a consoling Queen Victoria at Windsor before retiring to Chislehurst in Kent, where he died in 1873. His son joined the British army only to be killed in 1879 on campaign in South Africa. Aged just twenty-three, the last of the Bonaparte dynasty met his grisly end at the hands of the Zulus, ironically while in the uniform of a British officer.[40]

Napoléon gone, France defeated, and Britain's influence in Europe greatly diminished; Prussia's victory made Britain's isolation extremely clear. While France lost Alsace and Lorraine to Germany and Russia reasserted itself in the Black Sea, Gladstone's government never lifted a finger. Unlike the days of Palmerston and Napoléon, where alliance ensured action, Britain alone was a much-reduced power and dared not risk a second Crimea.[41] The Anglo-French world order of the 1850s was well and truly over.

7

IMPERIAL RIVALS: THE ANGLO-FRENCH DIVERGENCE, 1871–98

For all its trade, industry, naval power, and colonial territories, there was no greater symbol of Victorian Britain's ordering of global affairs than its regulating of the world's time. In October 1884, the International Meridian Conference, held in Washington, agreed on a global system of standardised time in which the Greenwich Meridian would be the line of longitude at zero degrees. In other words, the universal day was internationally acknowledged to commence at midnight in London and the world's time would conform to the governance of the Royal Observatory at Greenwich. The Observatory's transit telescope, used to calculate time in reference to the stars, was to be at the centre of a global system of regulation. British time would, from 1884, order the business of the world. How and why this came about not only revealed Britain's immense international influence but also France's relative decline since the 1860s.

Greenwich had been at the forefront of nineteenth-century efforts to standardise time. Traditionally, time was taken locally in reference to the sun. Different towns and cities would each record their own measurements using solar dials, which were then propagated through the clocks and bells of churches and town halls. But geographical differences meant that no two locations could observe the same time in reference to the sun. These regional variations were acceptable during the early nineteenth century, but with the rise of railways during the 1830s and 1840s, such inconsistencies caused confusion. Oxford was five minutes behind London, Bristol ten, and Plymouth about fifteen. For the management of railway travel and production of accurate timetables, a single shared time, set in a fixed location, was essential. By 1847 the Great Western Railway began running trains according to time taken at Greenwich, a practice soon adopted throughout Britain's growing railway network. As other countries followed this example, building railways of their own, so the question of standardised time became an international concern. German railways, for example, originally had five different time zones, set respectively in Berlin, Munich, Stuttgart, Ludwigshafen, and Karlsruhe. These would eventually be merged into a single zone, conforming to Berlin time, on the urging of Count Helmuth von Moltke. With typical Prussian military precision, he stressed that standardised time was crucial to army planning and timetables for mobilisation. When, in 1914, Germany invaded France at the outbreak of the First World War, it did so according to a well-regulated system of time.[1]

For the United States, with its vast territorial expanses, the problem was even more acute and it was this American desire for regulation that provided the impetus for the Washington Conference.[2] Here it was resolved that the globe should conform to a single ordering system of twenty-four time zones and a prime meridian appointed from which each new day would begin. As the most accurate time was measured not by the sun, but astronomically using fixed celestial bodies, the meridian would have to be appointed in accordance with an observatory. In 1884 the leading candidates for this prestigious role were the observatories of

Berlin, Washington, Paris, and Greenwich.³ While the conference delegates unanimously agreed on the desirability of appointing a prime meridian, of the twenty-six participating nations represented, twenty-two endorsed Greenwich as the first longitude. Only San Domingo voted against. The Danish delegate never turned up, and Brazil and France both abstained.⁴

The key argument supporting Greenwich's claims was that most of the world's shipping already conformed to the Royal Observatory's time and worked to Greenwich as the longitude of zero degrees for navigation. Accurate time was essential to calculating a ship's location at sea: if you knew what time it was in a fixed position, and then took the local time using the sun, it was possible to calculate the relative longitude of a ship. In 1884 the most common fixed position for such navigational practices was Greenwich, with vessels carrying highly accurate marine chronometers set to Greenwich time. The British delegate for Canada, Sandford Fleming, made this point explicitly at the Washington conference. In total, 37,663 ships worked to Greenwich time, being about 65 per cent of the world's shipping. In tonnage, this figure was even more staggering, with Greenwich regulating some 14,600,972 tonnes, or 72 per cent of the world's trade. By comparison, Paris Observatory regulated 5,914, this being about 10 per cent of global shipping, or roughly 8 per cent in tonnage. The remaining carrying capacity was registered to nine rival meridians.⁵ The consensus reached in Washington was, therefore, hardly surprising. As *The Graphic* smugly observed, 'The adoption of Greenwich as the Prime Meridian is, we believe, satisfactorily received in all countries, except France, whose leading astronomers desire the adoption of a neutral meridian, which desire will, we have no doubt, be waived in view of the fact that the scientists of other nations are unanimous on the point.'⁶ Clearly, the journal did not understand French determination.

France's delegation had done all it could to undermine the Washington consensus, observing that as Britain still refused to implement the metric system, it was in no position to orchestrate an international system of regulation. To this the American delegate pointed out that for all scientific works of significance, British scientists did employ metric weights and measures.[7] Despite French resistance, Greenwich time was the only practical international standard: shipping carried the day. Belgium and Holland implemented the conference's recommendations in 1892, followed a year later by Germany, Italy, and the Austro-Hungarian Empire.

Predictably, France refused altogether. Indeed, as the rest of the world subscribed to the disciplining order of Greenwich, French time remained anarchic. Each region of the country maintained up to four separate local time zones, all set to solar measurements. Cities continued to take their time from the sun, but complemented these readings with astronomical time set by the stars, this being about four minutes behind solar time. French railways took Paris time, which became France's legal standard in 1891. However, railway stations projected time five minutes behind Paris time, so passengers had extra minutes to get to their trains. While the clocks inside railway stations were five minutes behind Paris time, those on the outside of the stations conformed to local time, creating immense confusion between what became known as *l'heure de la gare* and *l'heure de la ville*.[8] Until new legislation in 1911, trains remained on time zones five minutes behind the stations through which they passed. Although perhaps convenient for a polite citizen running a few minutes late, France's time system appeared chaotic in contrast to Greenwich's global order. The act of boarding a train effectively meant passing through three time zones: that of the local town, that of the station, and that of Paris. Even when Paris time did become the nation's single standard in 1911, the Anglophobic wording of the new law rejected any deference to London, specifying that 'the legal time in France and Algeria is the mean Paris time slowed nine minutes and twenty-one seconds.'[9] This was Greenwich Mean Time in all but name, but France would never formally agree to such a standard, opting instead for a 'Paris Mean Time'. In 1978 France finally adopted the international time standard, but saved face thanks to its tactful redefinition as 'Coordinated Universal Time'.

Throughout the nineteenth century, however, French time appeared to British audiences as symbolic of French disorder. Perhaps the most powerful indictment of the importance of Greenwich time to Britain's imperial hubris appeared twenty-three years after the Washington Conference in Joseph Conrad's (1857–1924) *The Secret Agent* (1907). An aristocratic Polish émigré and master of English prose, Conrad played on British anxieties over its control of international time by setting the Royal Observatory at Greenwich as the target of a fiendish terrorist plot. Despairing of Britain's obsession with liberalism and tolerance of politically radical troublemakers, the mysterious diplomat Vladimir hopes such an outrage will provoke the British government into a spate of repressive measures against the European anarchists and revolutionaries taking refuge in the liberal nation. Vladimir observes that while the English care nothing for their politicians or art galleries, the great middle-class 'fetish' of the day was science, musing that 'It would be really telling if one could throw a bomb into pure mathematics.' As this was impossible, Vladmir demands 'the blowing up of the first meridian', as the 'whole civilized world has heard of Greenwich. The very boot-blacks in the basement of Charing Cross Station know something of it.'[10] Ultimately the attempt fails, with the bomb detonating prematurely in Greenwich Park. Conrad's identification of the prime meridian as the one thing that might shock liberal England out of her *laissez-faire*

Imperial Rivals: The Anglo-French Divergence, 1871–98

mentality and political tolerance is nevertheless telling of the centrality of Greenwich time to imperial prestige. Above the arts, trade, wealth, and overseas territories, time was the real gem in the British Empire's crown.

Conrad was not the first to think this. *The Secret Agent* in fact made use of a very real act of terrorism. In 1894 the Royal Observatory was indeed the target of a revolutionary attack of a very French character. Late in the afternoon of Thursday 15 February, an explosion echoed across Greenwich. Two of the Observatory's staff rushed outside to find the remains of Martial Bourdin (1868–94), a twenty-six-year-old French anarchist, splattered across the park. His left hand missing and stomach ripped open, he would be dead within thirty minutes, never revealing what his precise intentions had been. Given his location, however, the observatory's destruction was almost certainly his objective. A member of the popular London club for exiled anarchists, the Club Autonomies, Bourdin's bomb had exploded too soon to damage the observatory, but offered rich inspiration for Conrad.[11]

Bourdin did succeed in closing the observatory early that Thursday afternoon, with the two traumatised staff members sent home to recover. Although an anarchist, his plan of destroying the prime meridian, however absurd, would have found much sympathy back home in France. While many resented Britain's eminence in ordering global affairs, British society was equally touchy over any threat to its position as the world's timekeeper. Nevertheless, there would be consolation for the French. From 1910 the Eiffel Tower commenced the wireless transmission of Parisian time. Compared to Greenwich's reliance on its international network of telegraphic cables to distribute its regulating signal, Paris had taken a radical step, which by 1912 had been extended to Nancy, Charleville, and Langres. France had effectively established the world's first wireless national time signal. Eager not to lose out to Greenwich again, President Raymond Poincaré (1860–1934) promoted the holding of an International Conference on time in Paris that same year and, from 1 July 1913 the world's first truly global time signal was transmitted from the Eiffel Tower. While Greenwich remained the world's prime meridian, Paris could also boast of being a time centre, having become 'the watch of the universe'.[12]

Despite this eventual sharing of spoils, Britain's early triumph at Washington and France's continuing hostility to Greenwich's dominance was in fact part of a much wider deterioration in Anglo-French relations. The demise of cross-Channel collaboration after 1871 was initially gradual, but after collapsing completely in the early 1880s, it would remain in tatters until the twentieth century. Yet it was not the French rout over the prime meridian that was to cause this disintegration, but a rivalry between the two expanding empires that would span the globe.

*

Britain and France took very different paths after 1871. The limited influence of British diplomacy on the Continent, without French support, had become starkly apparent with the German occupation of Alsace and Lorraine, as well as with the unchecked growth of Russia's naval presence in the Black Sea. The Franco-British order established in the Crimean War was unravelling. At home, Benjamin Disraeli's aggressive imperialism presented Liberal audiences with a new Napoleonesque character. A master of popular rhetoric and easygoing jingoism, Disraeli's flashy foreign policy echoed the expansionism of France's last emperor. In true Napoleonic fashion, the Conservative Prime Minister sought military glory between 1877 and 1879 in Afghanistan and South Africa, and managed secret deals with the Ottoman Empire to snatch Cyprus at the

1878 Congress of Berlin. Apparently lacking moral principles, Disraeli cut the figure of a 'conspirator' and adventurer, driven by a French-like thirst for popular support through territorial expansion. His Jewish heritage made easy material for anti-Semitic portrayals of the Prime Minister as money-orientated and corrupt, especially when, in 1875, he commissioned the purchase of shares in the Suez Canal to his old friends, the Rothschilds. A payment of £150,000 to the Jewish banking dynasty for a three-month loan of £4 million to finance the transaction struck many as typical of the patronage that had been so endemic to Napoléon III's regime.[13] Disraeli's premiership between 1874 and 1880, imperialistic and populist as it might have been, was framed by the more restrained Liberal ministries of William Ewart Gladstone. Disraeli's great rival, less flamboyant, was ever eager to avoid unnecessary overseas commitments: keeping government spending low and taxes to a minimum were the core values of his brand of liberalism. They would shape no fewer than four tenures as Prime Minister for the bulwark of Liberal Britain, stretching from 1868–74, 1880–85, 1886, and 1892–94.

France cut a very different figure. The newly established Third Republic, which would govern until the German invasion of 1940, laboured under the shadows of Germany's continuing military and economic growth. The new regime, comprising of a Chamber of Deputies and Senate, with an elected President, would oversee a reconstruction of a French global empire, securing the new territorial possessions of Indochina, French Polynesia, Madagascar, and more land in West Africa. But imperial adventure was not the chief concern of late nineteenth-century French foreign policy. Rather, it was her rivalry with Germany and constant fear of a rematch of the Franco-Prussian War.

It proved almost impossible for France to get over its defeat in 1871. Convinced that Germany owed its military success to the relatively good education of its soldiers, the Third Republic instigated radical reforms of the nation's education system. With the state introducing free and compulsory education throughout France, history was introduced as a mandatory subject for all children aged between five and thirteen in 1872. This was a highly politicised syllabus that focused purely on French history. New textbooks, state-regulated from 1890, accompanied this nationalistic indoctrination of France's youth. This was a history curriculum aimed at cultivating a love of domestic culture and instilling patriotism among future generations. Above all, it was taught that the children of 'civilized' republican France had a duty to one day reclaim Alsace and Lorraine from 'barbarian' Prussia. The Third Republic was fashioned as the end product of a historical progress through feudalism, monarchy, revolution, and empire, towards political representation within a democratic system of government.[14] France's universities were central to this pedagogical transformation, with the discipline of history increasingly professionalised within higher education. Under the leadership of academics Ernest Lavisse, Alfred Rambaud, and Charles Seignobos, French historians attempted to redefine their subject as a science, establishing the premier journal, *Revue historique*, in 1876 as part of this project. The objective of all this was, above all, to explain France's failure in the Franco-Prussian War and to ensure such a calamity would never again be endured. Through school textbooks and university history departments, republican France would restore its national prestige.[15]

In 1875 this restoration was put to the test as France neared a second German war. To keep France weak, Bismarck had allied with the Russian and Austro-Hungarian Empires to form the *Dreikaiserbund*, the Three Emperors' League, in 1873. The Russian chancellor, Prince Aleksandr Mikhailovich, however,

Imperial Rivals: The Anglo-French Divergence, 1871–98

engineered a rapprochement with France the following year. Combined with a new French law for increasing the size of its army, this Franco-Russian alignment encouraged Bismarck to act, informing the French ambassador in Berlin that France's armaments programme, if continued, would provoke war.

Recognising that France was effectively a second-rate power and too weak to risk another invasion, Foreign Minister Louis-Charles duc Décazes looked to Britain and Russia for help. There was some sympathy in London. Queen Victoria felt 'eager to do something', while Disraeli and his Foreign Secretary, Derby, were concerned that France should not be so diminished as to unsettle the European balance of power. Décazes's appeals fell on unresponsive ears. Derby was more concerned with France's post-Napoleonic political instability than German threats of war, while Lord Odo Russell, Britain's Berlin Ambassador, continually denied that Bismarck was seriously considering war. Publicly, Derby tried to persuade Russia that it had no interest in seeing France defeated and Germany in total control of Continental Europe. Britain's response to what became known as the 'War-in-Sight' crisis was a letter from Victoria to Tsar Alexander II, encouraging Russian mediation efforts. Derby privately noted his annoyance at Décazes's attempts 'to make it appear in the eyes of Europe that we have taken the side of France ... instead of simply intervening to keep the peace, as is the fact'.[16] After failing to help France in the Franco-Prussian War, Britain's continued apparent indifference marked a further divergence between London and Paris.

Outside of Europe, Britain and France continued to cooperate in imperial affairs, but with nothing like the intensity witnessed between Napoléon and Palmerston. At the Congress of Berlin, held during the summer of 1878, Anglo-French relations appeared stable. Under Bismarck's orchestration, this international conference divided the Balkan peninsula up in the wake of the recent Russo-Turkish War, reducing the Ottoman Empire's presence in Europe. Bulgaria and Romania established independence, as did Serbia and Montenegro, while the Austrians occupied the Sandžak region, as well as Bosnia and Herzegovina. In the background, Britain's new Foreign Secretary, Robert Gascoyne-Cecil, Third Marquess of Salisbury (1830-1903) and the chief French delegate, William Henry Waddington, worked well together. Salisbury secured Waddington's support over Britain's seizure of Cyprus and encouraged French ambitions over Tunis. Ceding influence over the North African Coast to France, Salisbury casually advised the French delegation to 'Do what you like there ... You will be obliged to take it; you cannot leave Carthage in the hands of the barbarians.'[17] Franco-British imperial aspirations still seemed compatible, but it helped that Waddington was the sort of Frenchman Salisbury could trust. The son of an English claret merchant, Waddington had been educated at Rugby and Cambridge, earning a rowing blue at university. Salisbury was an Oxford man, having taken a fourth in mathematics from Christ Church College in 1847, but this did not prevent a gentlemanly understanding: Waddington was a Frenchman he could do business with.[18] Salisbury would go on to dominate British foreign policy for the final two decades of the nineteenth century, serving as Foreign Secretary four times during 1878–80, 1885–86, 1887–92, and 1895–1900. His grip on diplomacy was demonstrated by his simultaneous occupation of the office alongside his position as Conservative Prime Minister during 1885–86, 1886–92, and 1895–1902.

But the really big imperial question in the 1870s was Egypt. And it was this growing concern that would complete the post-1850s demise of Anglo-French relations. Initially, the Foreign Office and Quai D'Orsay again saw common interests in the region. As

Egyptian Khedive from 1863 until 1879, Isma'il Pasha (1830–95) had been determined to modernise his country along European lines. He saw Egypt's future as one of industrialisation and social change, rather than African subservience to imperial powers. By 1873 Egypt was virtually independent of the crumbling Ottoman Empire, giving the Khedive considerable autonomy. He oversaw the construction of some 900 miles of railway, 5,000 miles of telegraphy cables, a huge network of canals and irrigation, the development of Alexandria's harbour, a National Library in 1871, schools, and a grand new district in Cairo modelled on Paris. Yet funding these schemes was ruinous, relying on finances raised on European markets, especially those of London and Paris. Egypt's national debt in 1863 had stood at just £3 million, with an annual income of about £8 million. But by 1875 Isma'il's visionary projects had bankrupted his country, lumbering the ailing state with debts of over £100 million.

In 1875 this financial crisis had forced the Khedive's sale of his Suez Canal shares to Britain, but this proved to nowhere near enough to prevent a complete collapse in credit the following year. In April 1876 he had to suspend the payment of treasury bills, having been offering creditors up to 30 per cent interest on Egyptian bonds. In May, the French, Italian, and Austro-Hungarian governments established the Caisse de la Dette Publique, an emergency commission tasked with protecting European holders of Egyptian debt. Foreign Secretary Lord Derby initially refused to participate. Egypt's creditors had been accepting a huge degree of risk in exchange for the large interest payments. As a stalwart of *laissez-faire* economics, Derby believed it was not for the state to intervene, but a matter of private negotiation between bondholders and borrower: if lenders lost out, this was a fair result of a free market.[19]

French policymakers, however, felt quite differently: they wanted to protect the interests of their country's lenders. When the French government despatched R. Joubert as a financial advisor to Egypt, Britain could hardly afford to lose influence in the region, given the presence of the canal. Together, Britain and France forced a system of dual financial control on the Khedive, who in 1876 appointed both a British and a French Controller-General. With Major Evelyn Baring the British representative, this Franco-British power axis would force a stringent programme of debt consolidation on the Khedive.[20] An ardent free trader with strong Christian values, Baring was vehemently opposed to high taxes and state expansion. At Cairo, he sought to stabilise the country's finances, reduce the Khedive's spending, and enhance the conditions of Egypt's impoverished *fellahin* class. Although something of a Francophile, Baring grew increasingly despondent over the exacting policy of his French partners. In contrast to Baring's commitment to combining liberal financial responsibility with constitutional reform, the French Controller-General's instructions were to extract ruthless debt repayments at all costs.[21]

Eager to limit French influence in Egypt, at the Congress of Berlin Salisbury managed to reject Waddington's proposals for expanding the 1876 system of dual control into something politically influential. But then in 1879 the Khedive's efforts to oust the Anglo-French presence from his country by means of a nationalistic revolt drew the two European powers further into Egyptian politics. Taking greater control over Egypt, Britain and France forced the abdication of Isma'il in favour of his more controllable son, Tewfik Pasha (1852–92). The 1879 revolt was very much a response to European control, but the replacement of Isma'il with Tewfik precipitated a new system of dual control, with even greater political power and an equally rigorous commitment to debt repayments. Britain and France established a new Commission of Liquidation, which demanded two-thirds of Egypt's predicted revenue, along with any surplus, be paid to bondholders. Baring objected to this, believing it would certainly provoke further unrest; he left Egypt for a post in India in 1880.[22] His fears were soon confirmed when a second wave of nationalism engulfed the country. In 1881 Egyptian army officer Ahmed 'Urabi (d. 1897), himself from the *fellahin*, led a mutiny against the Khedive. In a brilliant coup, 'Urabi took power from Egypt's Anglo-French masters. Even for Gladstone's Liberal administration, it was clear that British interests in Egypt were at risk: the safety of the canal, the vital link to India, would have to be protected.

At first, Gladstone and his best friend and Secretary of State for Foreign Affairs, Granville Leveson-Gower, second Earl Granville (1815–91), both hoped to collaborate with France should military intervention be required, but it became increasingly clear that the French were in no position to help. In the grip of yet another ministerial crisis, the French government was unable to aid Britain in an Egyptian invasion. With escalating turmoil in Egypt, Granville could wait no longer, convinced that 'anarchy, or some attack on the Canal' would force Britain to act.[23] As Foreign Secretary in 1851–52, 1870–74, and 1880–85, Granville was well accustomed to the difficulties of maintaining the Gladstonian policy of non-intervention. In contrast to the more active foreign policy of Disraeli and Salisbury's Conservative administrations, Granville worked to keep Britain out of wars and foreign adventure, avoiding embroilment in the American Civil War and Franco-Prussian War. But in 1882, Granville and Gladstone seemed unable to avoid being dragged into Egypt's internal chaos.

British and French warships steamed off the coast of Alexandria in May, sparking anti-European riots in the city. 'Urabis's army fortified the town, before the British delivered a crushing ten-and-a-half-hour bombardment of Alexandria on 11 July, preceding a landing of Royal Marines. With the port in hand, Gladstone ordered an army of some 40,000 troops under General Wolseley to invade the Suez Canal zone the following month. After slaughtering the Egyptian army at the Battle of Tell-El-Kebir on 13 September, Wolseley captured Cairo and restored the Khedive's regime. A small detachment of British soldiers remained to prop up Tewfik's shaky new government.[24]

What all this meant was that by the autumn of 1882 Britain had effectively taken sole control of Egypt. Much to the annoyance and embarrassment of the journalist-turned-politician Charles Théodore Eugène Duclerc (1812–88), France's Prime Minister between 1882 and 1883, Britain had acted without consulting her French partners. In September 1882 Granville instructed the British ambassador in Paris, Viscount Lyons, to reassure the French government that 'in the Egyptian, and in all other questions about which there may be discussion between the two Governments, England is and will continue to be desirous to act in a conciliatory and friendly spirit'.[25] But when a telegraph from Cairo arrived informing Granville that the Egyptian government would agree to end the system of Anglo-French dual financial control, replacing this with a single English Financial Controller, there could be no reconciliation. The Khedive warned that the system established in 1879 to protect the interest of international creditors was no longer sustainable in the face of continued anti-European popular unrest. Franco-British financial control had, he observed, become 'an institution bearing almost a political character'.[26] This was, despite all pretence, just what it was.

The alternative plan of appointing a single British advisor was, of course, just as 'political', but Granville was eager to stress that the arrangement would be temporary. On 23 October he wrote to Lyons, outlining the new plan for Egyptian administration. The British government, he explained, had thought that the dual system of control had 'worked well for the material prosperity of Egypt, and that both the English and French Controllers have laboured ably and conscientiously to that end. But recent events have shown that the system is not free from serious defects and dangers.' Basically, the system of dual control was untenable without British troops on the ground to maintain the Khedive's regime. A new system was essential, with the Khedive appointing 'a single European financial advisor' who would guide Egyptian policy towards economic development and debt repayment. Such an arrangement, Granville assured Lyons, would last no more than ten years, possibly even only five.[27]

Not only had Britain despatched an army to Egypt, but now the Foreign Office was working to eradicate French influence from the country altogether. Duclerc reacted furiously, with the French Prime Minister observing that the new system of control offered no compensation to the Third Republic: why could the Khedive not appoint both a French and a British adviser? On inspecting Granville's proposals, Lyons reported that Duclerc 'could really find in them nothing more than a simple exclusion of the French Controller. He denied that there was any essential difference between the functions which it was proposed to assign to a single new Financial Controller, and those of the two present Controllers.' Virtually the only change would, he surmised, 'be that, instead of an English and a French Controller, acting conjointly, there would be a single English Controller acting alone'.[28] Duclerc could never accept this: no government of the Third Republic could.

Suspicious that France would want to exert indefinite control over Egyptian finance, Granville emphasised that Britain was committed to the swift return of autonomy to the Khedive. It seemed clear though, that he could not 'rely wholly on Egyptian advice in regard to finance, or to lose the advantage which he would derive from announcing to the world at once his intention to profit by foreign aid'.[29] Granville denied any desire for British influence; what he proposed was simply a matter of propping up the Khedive through military and financial support. Duclerc resolved that he could not 'shut his eyes to the predominant prestige and influence which recent events had conferred upon England in Egypt', placing France in an unacceptably inferior position.[30]

Arguments between the Foreign Office and the Quai D'Orsay raged throughout the winter, well into 1883. It nonetheless remained the case that Britain had military control over Egypt and too great an interest in the Suez Canal to concede to French sensibilities. At the same time, with its interventionist tradition of government and domestic political instability, France was an increasingly unreliable partner. There is no doubt, however, that 1882 represented a considerable betrayal on the part of Gladstone's government. Long allies in Egypt, France was ruthlessly abandoned and humiliated as Britain manoeuvred itself into a position as the single power in the troubled country.

Duclerc publicly accused Britain of scheming, lambasting the aggressive 'all or nothing' policy of Gladstone's government and demanding France be allowed to share in the control of Egypt, which still had immense financial obligations to French investors.[31] When the fervent imperialist Jules Ferry (1832–93), replaced Duclerc as Prime Minister in 1883, Egypt provided an invaluable cause through which to build political support. As Prime Minister for 1880–81 and 1883–85, and President of the Senate in 1893, Ferry sought to expand France's colonial possessions in Indochina, Madagascar, Polynesia, and Western and Central Africa. But few causes secured so much unanimity within France's two debating chambers as the Egypt question. With the Chamber of Deputies still unhappy with Britain's arrogant assumption of control, the *République Française* reported in June 1884 that any criticism of Britain's position could only strengthen Ferry's administration.[32] Having so long cooperated, Britain and France had been torn apart over Egypt in 1882.

*

Franco-British relations would not recover from the breakdown of 1882 until the early twentieth century. Egypt was a constant sore point with French audiences for over two decades. In 1886, four years after Britain invaded Egypt, the *Daily News* reported how little had changed in Paris. While the city's public regretted the error of not joining Britain's initial military intervention, the mood was firmly set against their Anglo-Saxon rivals. Assessing the attitudes of the Chamber of Deputies and Chamber of Representatives, the *Journal des Débats* warned that if 'a permanent British occupation of Egypt should become an accomplished fact in spite of us, it would call forth in France such protests both in the Chambers and elsewhere, and would leave behind such strong and lasting resentment, that all idea of a good understanding between England and France would be rendered impossible for a lengthened period'.[33] Egypt was a festering sore that would continually plague late Victorian Anglo-French diplomacy.

Yet Gladstone and Granville had been sincere when they assured the French that they did not want to permanently occupy Egypt. This was not just appeasing rhetoric. Taking control of an independent state by military force to extract debt repayments was inconsistent with Liberal free-trade values and *laissez-faire* government. Gladstone in particular was opposed to expensive imperial annexations, believing the defence of the canal to be little justification for asserting authority over a country of some 2,000 square miles. Equally, he thought the advantage of Britain's empire in India to be minimal, being costly to garrison.[34] Gladstone's hope of a 'moral empire', run on the cheap with little governance, was completely at odds with the occupation of Egypt. Sir Louis Mallet, the leading free-trade disciple of the now deceased Richard Cobden, made these points explicitly. Egypt, he felt, would be a drain on the British economy. The government already spent £45 million a year on defence, of which £30 million came from taxes on alcohol. Mallet, who had worked alongside Cobden on the 1860 Free Trade Treaty with France and was, by 1874, Permanent Undersecretary of the India Office, argued that this funding of empire through the intoxication of the working classes was inhibiting the moral and social progress of the British people. Imperial expansion thus appeared incompatible with domestic reform and the extension of freedoms and democracy.[35] After all, how could Britain be liberal at home while acting despotically abroad?

Yet for all Gladstone's hopes that Britain's control over Egypt would be brief, throughout the 1880s Britain became increasingly entrenched in the country. Baring took the position of Consul-General in 1883 and, despite his reforming zeal, was soon convinced that without British administration and military support, the Khedive's government would collapse.[36] In the end, Duclerc had been correct in his observation that Britain had taken complete control. By January 1884, Granville ordered that the Egyptian government should consult London on all matters of policy, effectively reducing Egypt to a British protectorate. France attempted to exert what little influence it could at a conference on Egyptian finances later that year, refusing any diminution of debt repayments. At a second conference in 1885, France agreed to allow the Egyptian government to retain all surplus over its predicted tax revenue in exchange for Britain promising to withdraw within three-and-a-half years. Although by 1887 Egypt was declared solvent, Gladstone's Liberal administration had lost power to Salisbury's Conservative government. And Salisbury was not a man who would give up Egypt only to see French influence return to the strategically crucial region. He was content to leave the Egyptian question unresolved while the country was increasingly subsumed into Britain's booming empire.[37]

Hostilities between France and Britain grew rapidly after 1882. On the face of it, between 1871 and 1890, Britain's imperial expansion was impressive, adding Kenya, Uganda, Rhodesia, Zanzibar, Transvaal, Orange Free State, Nigeria, Burma, Malaya, and a string of Pacific islands to its already colossal empire. Along with some £4,000 million of overseas investments by 1913, this growth saw a quarter of a million square miles of land and 66 million people added to Britain's dominions.[38] Throughout, France was very much an aspirational thorn in Britain's imperial side. Britain's age of relatively cheap global dominance came to an abrupt end in 1884 when France and Russia established an alliance. Together, their two navies could match the Royal Navy in terms of first-class battleships. With a potential Franco-Russian fleet in the Mediterranean and the threat of a cross-Channel invasion on England's south coast, British sea power would be overwhelmed in the event of a war. Salisbury's panic-stricken government launched its 'Two-Power Standard', by which the Royal Navy would be kept a strength equal or above the combined fleets of its nearest two rivals. The Naval Defence Act of March 1889 established this policy with a huge construction programme of ten new battleships and an unprecedented budget of £21.5 million.[39] Sparking a naval race with France and Russia, this spending commitment ripped apart Gladstone's liberal consensus of low taxes and minimised spending. In 1892, Earl Spencer, First Lord of the Admiralty, warned that by 1896 France and Russia would 'have more ships and we shall only be about equal to them in power'.[40] In 1894 these fears were exacerbated when France and Russia formalised their alliance.

The Egyptian affair had alienated France, turning Britain's greatest European partner into a global competitor. When France eyed up a move into Burma, signing a Franco-Burmese treaty and encouraging King Thibaw Min's confiscation of the property of a British trading company, Britain responded by annexing Burma in January 1886. Throughout the 1880s, the British and French press continued to stir up xenophobia, with French papers riling against Britain's aggressive imperialism and the extravagant wealth of the City of London, while Britain's journalists stoked up Anglo-Saxon fears of Gallic Catholicism. British politicians grew particularly anxious over the rising French nationalism of the late 1880s under the leadership of George Ernest Boulanger (1837–91). Galvanising the working-class districts of Paris, as well as rural Catholics and Royalists, with demands to avenge the Franco-Prussian War, this anti-German nationalism, known as 'Revanchism', took Boulanger close to power before defeat in the 1889 elections. French right-wing nationalism would not recover until 1940, but as War Minister between 1886 and 1887, Boulanger's aggressive rearmaments programme sparked another war scare. Indeed, Salisbury wrote to Lyons in Paris, expressing his conviction that a second Franco-Prussian war would offer a helpful solution to the French problem. Even considering allowing Germany to violate Belgian neutrality in such a conflict, the Prime Minister remarked that 'For the present ... the enemy is France.'[41]

Things worsened in 1890, with Britain's agreement to exchange Heligoland for German-held Zanzibar, provoking fears in Paris of a British alignment with the Triple Alliance of Germany, Italy, and Austria-Hungry. In the same year, France withdrew from its free trade commitments, undoing the work of Cobden and Chevalier. Little now remained of the entente of the 1850s. Three years later, in 1893, France expanded into Siam, moving into a territory that had long acted as a buffer between British India and French Indochina. After a gunboat stand-off in Bangkok harbour, the Anglo-French convention of 1896 secured new territories for France in the Mekong Valley, but preserved Siamese neutrality, dividing the region into 'spheres of influence'.[42]

France enjoyed greater success in Madagascar. Britain had been committed to the territory's independence since 1862, but in 1882 France invaded despite Granville's warnings that his government recognised 'the Queen of Madagascar as the absolute monarch of the whole Island'.[43] After France agreed to a peace treaty with Queen Ranavalona III in December 1885 in exchange for Madagascar ceding control over its foreign policy to the European invader, Britain refused to recognise the new arrangement. But France here saw a chance to negotiate a deal over the island, later agreeing to acknowledge Zanzibar as a British protectorate in return for British support of French control of Madagascar.[44] Madagascar was certainly of less importance to British foreign policy than Suez, but for France such productive negotiations helped satisfy the national hunger for imperial prestige. In May 1895, France finally seized the entire island by force, removing the queen and her government.

From Africa to the Far East, Britain and France divided up an increasingly imperial world. There seemed no limit to the ambitions of the rivals. By the mid-1890s it was clear that the two empires were on a collision course. In 1898, at the tiny Sudanese village of Fashoda, Britain and France's imperial aspirations came to a head, almost sparking what would have been a global war.

Entente Imperial

Having taken control of Egypt in 1882, Britain failed to seize the Khedive's lands in full. As part of his Egyptian territories, the Sudan was now an area of British interest, but a fundamentalist Islamic revolt under the charismatic leadership of Muhammad Ahmad bin Abd Allah (1844–85), the Mahdi, had established Sudanese independence from Egypt between 1884 and 1885. Gladstone's hesitating government's response had been to send another religious fanatic, the evangelical General Charles Gordon, to shore up resistance to the growing Mahdist regime. The task clearly beyond him, Gordon died in the defence of the Sudanese capital of Khartoum, with a British expeditionary force despatched too late to save him. After Gordon's death, British politicians lost interest in the Sudan (for a time), which was of little economic or strategic value.

With Britain firmly entrenched in Egypt, but the Sudan unoccupied, France saw an opportunity to complete the vision of an unbroken west-to-east African empire from the Atlantic coast at Senegal through Mali, Niger, Chad, and across to the Red Sea outpost of Djibouti in French Somaliland. The great obstacle to this dream was the Nile Valley, which cut down through France's African territories. In comparison, British imperialists like Cecil Rhodes (1853–1902) planned to carve out an uninterrupted empire from Cairo to Cape Town, running from north to south by way of the Nile Valley. At Fashoda, these two monstrously imperialistic ambitions collided.

Lloyd's Illustrated Newspaper thought Fashoda worth little in itself, describing it in 1898 as a 'town of mud huts, forts, and prisons, where everything that is vilest in Eastern character may be found; for it is the place of transportation for criminals under life sentences'.[45] A place of unhealthy, pestilential airs, from which few prisoners returned, the village was in fact crucial to controlling the region known as the Bahr-el-Ghazal, which lay

Imperial Rivals: The Anglo-French Divergence, 1871–98

Lloyd's Illustrated Newspaper's depiction of Fashoda in 1898, a 'town of mud huts, forts, and prisons'. (Author's collection)

between the Congo and Nile valleys. It was, therefore, crucial to the French idea of 'spanning Africa from west to east'.[46] This was a dream that Théophile Delcassé (1852–1923) eagerly embraced on becoming undersecretary of the colonies in 1893. Along with Foreign Minister Gabriel Hanotaux, Delcassé hatched a cunning plan to occupy the Bahr-el-Ghazal and then descend on the Nile.[47] Following François Delonde's address to the Chamber of Deputies in 1895, in which the ardent imperialist argued that France had to move quickly into the Sudan, Edward Grey, as undersecretary of the Foreign Office, informed the House of Commons that 'the Egyptian and British spheres together cover the whole course of the Nile.'[48] But this did not deter French imperialists.

Under the command of Captain Jean-Baptiste Marchand (1863–1934), a small French expedition landed on the West Coast of Africa at Gabon in June 1896. Its objective? To steam up the Ubangi River through central Africa, then march overland through jungle and Sudanese desert and establish a French outpost at the isolated fort of Fashoda. On 10 July 1898, after a gruelling fourteen-month trek, Marchand finally arrived. His triumph was, however, to be short-lived.[49]

Although British politicians had no interest in adding the Sudan to the empire's growing commitments, the news that the French had despatched Marchand's expedition was provocative. Salisbury was convinced the Sudan belonged to the Khedive and, therefore, was a British concern. Any loss of control over the upper Nile Valley, the source of the water on which Egypt depended, was a loss of authority over Egypt itself. Salisbury took decisive action, opting for military intervention.[50]

In 1898 a British army invaded the Sudan, retaking Khartoum and avenging Gordon's death. Its commander, General Herbert Kitchener (1850–1916) had been part of the failed Gordon relief expedition thirteen years previously, having also served in a French field ambulance unit during the Franco-Prussian War. He had in this way earned a reprimand from his senior officers for participating in a foreign conflict and his overtly pro-French sentiments, but in 1898 he was only too well aware of the urgency of capturing the Sudan before Marchand could advance France's claims over the territory.[51] Kitchener's troops met the Mahdist forces just outside Khartoum, delivering a crushing blow at the Battle of Omdurman on 2 September, inflicting some 30,000 casualties for the loss of forty-seven or forty-eight British fatalities, thanks to the almost incredible effectiveness of modern artillery and machine guns.

Within days of the victory, word that Marchand had reached Fashoda reached Khartoum. In 1914, Kitchener would be appointed Secretary of State for War and would do much to build Britain's volunteer army – a force that would provide valuable relief to France during the dark days of 1916. However, throughout the autumn of 1898 he was faced with the delicate task of preventing any hostilities breaking out with France's expeditionary force in the Sudan. On 18 September, five British gunboats arrived at Fashoda, carrying 1,500 British and Egyptian-Sudanese soldiers. The following day Kitchener, fluent in French, met Marchand, where things remained amicable. Uncertain how to proceed, both commanders waited on the deliberations of their political masters back in London and Paris.

At home in Britain things were far less placid, with the press demanding France be made to back down. The *Evening News*, *Star*, and *Daily Mail* were all unrelenting in their calls for Marchand to be thrown out of Fashoda. Even the *Spectator* was unequivocal, declaring that 'It is quite clear that Fashoda must be retained, even at the cost of war.'[52] France's newspapers were calmer, eager to avoid war, but without losing face. At the end of October, Reuter's Special Correspondent in Paris reported that although Marchand had departed Fashoda for Cairo, President Félix Faure was a worried man at the Élysée Palace, warning that no settlement had been reached.[53] Little would be agreed. France's pragmatic new Foreign Minister, Delcassé, saw the hopelessness of the situation. As Kitchener's army outnumbered Marchand by ten to one, and the British public were apparently up for a fight, he had little choice but to back down. He did not want to alienate Britain as a potential ally should there ever be another war with Germany and, for all France's imperial ambitions, it was its land border with the powerful German Empire that was the priority of foreign policy. With the *Morning Post* asserting that Britain had 'set its heart on the Nile Valley from end to end' and the Royal Navy mobilising, the French government capitulated. On 3 November, the Third Republic agreed to abandon the Sudan altogether.[54]

Eager to calm his American cousins, a young Lieutenant Winston Spencer-Churchill (1874–1965) provided a defence of Britain's policy during the crisis. The future wartime Prime

Minister had served under Kitchener throughout the Sudanese conquest, charging with the 21st Lancers at Omdurman, and knew the political state of affairs in the region first-hand. Writing in December 1898 for the *North American Review*, Churchill felt it a 'duty for a citizen of the Great Empire to speak freely and fairly to the citizens of the Great Republic' and explain Britain's position. At the root of Britain's seizure of Khartoum was the desire to avenge General Gordon's death in 1885. The British people, Churchill declared, had ever remained angry at his murder 'at the hands of infidel savages' which had 'transformed him into something like a martyr'. This religious demand for revenge revealed, Churchill continued, how 'Even Western Civilization is not free from fanaticism.'[55]

It was true that it had only been news of the French expedition in 1896 that had sparked Salisbury into action, but this did not mean that Britain's claims over the Sudan were diminished, argued Churchill. France's subsequent withdrawal was only fitting of a dignified imperial power:

> France is a great nation; a nation of brave and brilliant men; of witty and beautiful women. She has long filled a splendid place in history. She is one of the Great Powers of the earth. If she had desired to prevent the British occupation of the Nile Valley, it was easy for her to protest against that occupation and to make it, if she thought it worth while, a *casus belli*.[56]

It was, he assured American readers, beneath her dignity to quarrel over what Churchill was confident was a British sphere of influence, while he reminded the entrepreneurial citizens of the flourishing United States that Britain was ever a friend of free trade, including on the Nile. 'We do not mind how much French merchandise passes up the Nile,' he observed, 'provided that the

French will recognise that that river flows between banks in which the Union Jack is firmly planted.'[57]

Churchill certainly knew how to put a positive spin on Fashoda. But across the Channel it had been a bruising encounter. Well into the twentieth century, 'Fashoda syndrome' became a common term among French officials and journalists for describing anxiety-driven French foreign policy aimed at asserting influence over areas which might otherwise fall into British hands. Within the Quai D'Orsay there was a fear of a repeat of the humiliation of 1898. Although Britain and France de-escalated tensions throughout late 1898 and 1899, marking out clear spheres of influence throughout Africa along the frontiers between the Nile and Congo Rivers and in Northern Nigeria, the Nile Valley remained an exclusively British concern.[58] Salisbury offered France no face-saving compensation. Fashoda was yet another imperial humiliation for the Third Republic.

*

There was no doubt that by Fashoda, the Franco-British entente of the 1850s had long passed. In his terrifying *The War of the Worlds* (1898), H. G. Wells aptly summed up these tensions. Although the story of a Martian invasion, Wells' science-fiction epic in fact revealed the genuine anxieties late Victorian Britons held over the possibility of a foreign invasion, be it from France or Germany. He played on readers' fears that the nation's overextended naval strength might not, after all, be invulnerable. It would have been lost on few contemporaries that Britain's final hope against the alien invaders, armed with their giant mechanised tripod machines and powerful heat-rays, was the arrival of the 'ironclads of the Channel Fleet'. The sinking of the Royal Navy's torpedo-ram, the *Thunder Child*, was hugely significant: with the navy useless, Britain and all human civilization was defeated. Yet equally important was Wells' account of the fleeing English refugees, desperately trying to escape to France and Belgium. One woman, on seeing the sea, 'gave way to panic. She had never been out of England before, she would rather die than trust herself friendless in a foreign country, and so forth. She seemed to imagine that the French and the Martians might prove very similar.'[59]

Despite these tensions, British and French societies were not alien cultures, but in fact highly integrated. Wells' Martian-fleeing refugees might have had qualms over French hospitality, but France was also a place of economic opportunity for many, especially those with engineering skills and industrial experience. Cornwall's miners illustrated this. Just as there were strong links between the steam engineering cultures of France and Cornwall in the 1820s, so these connections continued throughout the century. The formation of the Pontgibaud Silver-Lead Mining and Smelting Company, established in 1852, provided a good example of what could be achieved through collaboration. The brainchild of French industrialist Alphonse Pallu (1808–80), this enterprise extracted ore from several mines around Pontgibaud, along the banks of the River Sioule in the Puy-de-Dôme. With its head office in Paris, Pallu floated the company in London in December 1852, selling 4,000 shares at £20 each. Pallu had visited Cornwall in 1845, striking up a relationship with several local mine captains, including the eminently powerful mining entrepreneur John Taylor. Armed with these business contacts and a wealth of Cornish mining expertise, Pallu's mines went into production in 1853, with the company boasting four French and four British directors, including Taylor.[60] Along with British capital and management, Pontgibaud was itself turned into a small enclave of Cornwall. Most of the winding and pumping machinery and engines came straight from Cornwall, along with the workforce. Taylor recruited Cornish miners, especially from the Illogan district, who moved to France with their families. Of a workforce of sixty-three, thirty-four were Cornish and the remainder from other parts of Britain. Share prices boomed throughout the 1860s and 1870s, and by the time Pontgibaud's mines were in decline, some £378,000 of dividends had been paid out over forty years.[61]

A small example, but such ventures demonstrated the continuing commercial cooperation between Britain and France, with the latter mobilising British industrial technology and skills for economic growth. But it was not just business that united the nations. Mutual exchanges in art, music, fashion, architecture, and food brought them closer together. While Cornwall might have offered instruction to France in the art of mining, France returned the favour by providing a model for Cornwall's leading artistic movement.

Between the 1880s and the early twentieth century, the little fishing village of Newlyn, near Penzance, was home to an art colony dedicated to natural light and the daily lives of working communities. What became known as the 'Newlyn School' owed much to its French connections. Although Walter Langley (1852–1922) had initiated the movement, relocating to Newlyn in 1881 to capture working-class Cornish life, most famously in his 1901 *Between the Tides*, the Newlyn School's leading light was undoubtedly Stanhope Forbes (1857–1947). The son of William Forbes, an English railway manager, and his French wife, Juliette de Guise, young Forbes studied in Paris between 1880 and 1882, making several trips to Brittany. Here he developed skill painting *en plein air* at Cancale, making use of the region's country scenes and excellent light. At the Royal Academy's 1882 summer exhibition, Forbes made a name for himself with his *A Street in Brittany*, before following this up with his charming *Breton Children in an Orchard – Quimperlé*, painted in 1883.[62]

When Forbes moved to Cornwall in 1884, it was very much because of the county's similarity in culture and aesthetics to Brittany. Both offered cheap living, traditional working-class muses, natural beauty, and superb light. As Forbes later recalled,

> I had come from France and, wandering down into Cornwall, came one spring morning along that dusty road by which Newlyn is approached from Penzance. Little did I think that the cluster of grey-roofed houses which I saw before me against the hillside would be my home for many years. What lode-stone of artistic metal the place contains, I know not; but its effects were strongly felt in the studios of Paris and Antwerp particularly, by a number of young English painters studying there, who just about then, by some common impulse, seemed drawn towards this centre of their native land.[63]

With his wife Elizabeth Forbes (1859–1912), a Canadian artist, Forbes would spend decades capturing Cornwall in oil, founding the Newlyn Art School in 1899. However, this work contributed to a very French tradition of outdoor painting, centred on the village of Barbizon, near the Forest of Fontainebleau.

The Barbizon School looked to the natural landscape, as opposed to dramatic events, for inspiration. Some of its artists had been inspired by the exhibition of the English artist John Constable's rural scenes at the Salon de Paris in 1824. This preference for natural inspiration developed slowly in response to Constable's paintings throughout the 1820s and 1830s, until in the midst of the Revolution of 1848, a group of artists gathered at Barbizon to fully embrace this vision and take inspiration from the French landscape. Under the leadership of Théodore Rousseau, Jean-François Millet, and Charles-François Daubigny, the Barbizon school would be one of the most influential artistic movements of the century, with its calls for the truthful depiction of daily working life, rural settings, and natural light felt as strongly in Brittany as in Cornwall.[64]

Food provided perhaps the most visible exchange between France and Britain in the second half of the nineteenth century. Unlike the schools of little Barbizon and Newlyn, this was to be a very urban affair. Between 1850 and 1914, London and Paris were at the centre of a revolution in eating habits. The two imperial capitals witnessed an explosion in high-end dining, with a rapid expansion of luxury hotels, restaurants, and elite gentlemen's clubs. Overtly, London and Paris had quite different culinary traditions, with France's complex sauce-based dishes a stark contrast to the English penchant for joints of meat with condiments. Along with this great condiment-sauce divide, after the grim experiences of the 1870–71 siege, Parisians were accustomed to eating a more diverse selection of animals.[65]

Nevertheless, London and Paris became a shared culinary market, epitomised most famously by the great Ritz-Escoffier partnership. When the Swiss hotelier César Ritz (1850–1918) employed Georges Auguste Escoffier (1846–1935), a chef from near Nice, to work at his new Grand Hotel at Monte Carlo in 1884, it was to prove a defining moment. In 1890 the two entrepreneurs moved to London to revive the fading Savoy Hotel, which the impresario Richard D'Oyly had founded the year before. With an army of French cooks, they reorganised the hotel's kitchens and transformed it into the pinnacle of the London dining scene. With Ritz as manager, Escoffier here created a string of new dishes, including Melba toast in 1897. Dismissed the following year amid charges of corruption and bribery, the duo established the Ritz in Paris in 1898 and the Carlton Hotel in London a year later, before adding the Ritz in London to this empire in 1906. As the manager of the Carlton's kitchens until 1920, Escoffier delivered high-end French haute cuisine for London's elite clientele and set new standards for fine dining in the capital for decades.[66]

Along with food, few things brought French and British consumers together as much as alcohol and there was no better example of such well-lubricated integration than champagne. More than any other product, this luxurious beverage demonstrated the close socio-economic connections between the two countries: by the end of the nineteenth century, the form this wine had taken was a very Franco-British creation. Up until the 1860s, Britain imported 70 per cent of its wine from Portugal and Spain, favouring port, Madeira, and sherry since the Napoleonic Wars that had cemented the Iberian Peninsula's dominance of the British market. Following the 1860 Cobden-Chevalier free trade treaty, William Gladstone, as Chancellor of the Exchequer, had slashed wine tariffs through his budgets of 1860, 1861, and 1862. Committed to free trade, he reorganised taxation on spirits and wines so that the rate was based not on geographical region, but alcoholic percentage. At once, this opened the British market to France's lighter wines. From just 5 per cent in 1843, French wine accounted for 35 per cent of all wine consumed in England by 1898. In 1861 there was an immediate 60 per cent jump in the nation's wine consumption.[67] Over the next fifteen years champagne sales expanded three-fold, as it became the wine of choice for London's elite gentlemen's clubs and increasingly affluent middle classes, eager to emulate their social superiors.[68] London, especially the fashionable West End, was soon the world's premier champagne market. Veuve Clicquot's exports to Britain, for example, increased from just 1 per cent of its global sales in 1860, to 30 per cent by 1869. By the 1890s, the United Kingdom accounted for a quarter of all champagne exports.[69]

Gladstone's tax reforms, a blossoming middle class, and its symbolic image as a mark of prestige ensured champagne's popularity in late Victorian London, but this increasingly lucrative market was not merely a passive consumer of the wine: it actively shaped a revolution in the character of the drink. In the 1800s champagne was as often still as it was sparkling. And when it was sparkling, it was usually a sweet, amber- or grey-coloured fluid, unsuited to accompanying food. But by 1900 it had been radically transformed. Gone was most of the sugar. Instead, champagne had become the golden, pale, dry sparkling wine that we know today. And while 'champagne' was from the 1820s a generic term for all sparkling wines, by the end of the century it was a product inherently associated with the specific region of Champagne and the powerful branding of its houses, like Veuve Clicquot, Perrier-Jouët, Pol Roger, Laurent-Perrier, and Pommery. These houses were very focused on the British market, responding attentively to London's tastes.[70]

After a short-lived mid-century fashion first for pink, and then for amber-coloured champagne of considerable alcoholic strength from added cognac, the trend was firmly set towards increasingly dry, fine wines. As London wrested the champagne trade away from its traditional export markets in Germany and Russia, French producers paid growing attention to British tastes. In this process, it was London-based agents, rather than producers, who called the tune and character of the wine. It was agents who negotiated the 'dosage', or amount of sugar and spirit added, knowing best what would sell. Often this caused frustration with producers. As one manufacturer for Pommery & Greno complained to his London agent in 1871, 'Le champagne, on ne le prepare pas comme une omelette.'

Gladstone's move towards lighter wines found favour with the nation's increasingly temperate middle classes; champagne was compatible with a society eager to show restraint and avoid the displays of drunkenness so associated with the heavier spirits of 1820s Regency Britain.[71] Champagne was traditionally the tipple of choice for Britain's aristocracy, but with middle-class merchants and shopkeepers, the *nouveau riche*, craving the status the elite wine offered, British aristocrats turned to dryer variants. Believing that it was harder to attain a liking for dryer champagne and assuming that those new to the drink would prefer sweeter wines, Britain's old-money gentry demanded increasingly low dosages of sugar in order to maintain social exclusivity: to be sweet was to be common. The effect was dramatic. From an average dosage of sugar of 8–10 per cent in the mid-1860s, this had dropped to 2–6 per cent by the 1880s. Reduced sugar also suggested greater quality, as the wine itself was under scrutiny and imperfections could not be distorted by sweetness. Taste was inseparable from class and the upper classes were, above all, dry and refined. With an empire governed by gentlemen, France's global exports followed this trend, with champagnes destined for India set to a dosage of 1–2 per cent.[72] Such claims were supported by the champagne houses' own figures. Perrier-Jouët's British sales in 1859 ranged from a dosage of 10–14 per cent, compared to 16–18 per cent for France and Belgium, but by 1864 British sales were down to 5–9 per cent, while France and Belgian tastes had remained constant.[73] As the *Saturday Review* noted in 1876, 3 per cent dosage was for England, 18–20 per cent for Russia, America, and France.[74] This was a very British divergence in taste, but one that would, thanks to London's share of the market, dominate champagne's evolution. As champagne historian Robert Harding concluded, 'Champagne was, in essence, a wine made new in nineteenth-century Britain.'[75]

Whether it was Cornish miners extracting French silver, English artists taking inspiration from French painters, French chefs finding fame with London's elites, or London's elites dictating the taste of champagne, the economic, social, and cultural exchanges between Britain and France remained extensive. From Egypt to Fashoda, between 1882 and 1898, Anglo-French political relations were fraught, but for all the diplomatic tension, the societies of the two imperial rivals grew increasingly close back home in Europe. Such cultural connections and shared tastes were to prove vital to reviving the *entente cordiale* in the twentieth century.

*

The gradual drifting apart of the 1870s had descended into blatant hostility over Egypt by 1882. This British belligerence at the expense of its long-term partner in imperial concerns alienated France to the extent that by 1898, the two nations came closer to war than at any moment since Waterloo. The Fashoda Crisis was certainly a low point, but it was symptomatic of two decades of Franco-British strife. The real problem was that Britain's imperial expansion was coinciding with an unmistakable decline in France's international influence. While the Third Republic undoubtedly enhanced its overseas territories, a cynic could be forgiven for regarding these acquisitions as being little more than the bits of the globe that Britain did not want: the crumbs of empire. France's resistance to the global system of time reflected the nation's growing anxiety over its place in the world. Above all though, it was the fear of German militarism that dominated France's foreign policy and sense of national prestige, from politicians to Parisians with bitter memories of life under siege, to champagne makers and schoolchildren in the French countryside.

France's decline, exacerbated by its continued internal political instability, was fundamental to what can be seen as the total unravelling of the Anglo-French order of the 1850s. For all Britain's obvious expansion, a closer look confirms that its moment of unrivalled global dominance had passed. By the 1890s, Britain's greatest exports, textiles, were in decline in comparison with the booming industry of Germany and the United States.

Their economies employed modern technologies, taking the lead in the vital chemical and electrical industries, while Britain struggled to develop new products and lacked the innovation it had shown during the first half of the nineteenth century. Its economic lead was crumbling, with the growth of its industrial produce falling from 3 per cent p.a. between 1840 and 1870 to just 1.5 per cent between 1875 and 1895. Britain's share of the world's trade fell from 25.2 per cent in 1860 to 17.1 per cent by 1898. Of the world's manufacturing, 31.8 per cent was British in 1870, but this stood at just 14.7 per cent by 1910, compared to Germany with 15.9 per cent and the United States with 35.3 per cent. France, too, felt the pinch, seeing its share of world trade fall falling from 11.2 per cent to 8.4 per cent between 1860 and 1898.[76] Naval spending was also out of control with the Royal Navy's budget almost quadrupling to £40.4 million by 1910, having been just £11 million in 1883.[77]

At the end of the nineteenth century, the British might well have felt rather more complacent than their Gallic neighbours over their international prominence. But the two Old World powers were some way past the hegemonic days of Palmerston and Napoléon III. At the very moment that France and Britain abandoned each other over the Egyptian question, the United States and Germany sought to cast a new world order for the twentieth century.

Above: 1. Charles Barry's Gothic Palace of Westminster, home to Britain's brand new Houses of Parliament. (Image in author's possession, 2020)

Right: 2. George Gilbert Scott's Foreign Office, a Roman palace for Palmerston's imperial Britain. (Image by the author, 2020)

Below right: 3. Built between 1845 and 1855, Napoleon's beautiful new Quai D'Orsay made a fitting home for the French foreign office. (Image by permission of Harry Mace, 2020)

4. Haussmann's rebuilt Rue de Rivoli in 1877, with the Louvre on the left. (In public domain. Bibliothèque nationale de France)

5. The façade of Haussmann's stunning new railway terminus for Paris, the Gare du Nord, built between 1861 and 1865. (Image in author's possession, 2020)

6. Queen Victoria, who was thoroughly pleased with the Great Exhibition and awarded her husband Albert full credit. (In public domain. Birmingham Museums Trust)

Right: 7. With Prince Albert (left) and Napoleon III (right) on horseback and Victoria and Eugenie in carriage, the royal couples made a glamourous set for the crowds of Paris in the hot summer of 1855. (In author's possession, 2020)

Below: 8. Europe's power unleashed, with Britain's Royal Navy providing transportation for the huge French army. (In author's possession, 2019)

9. The Suez Canal works at El Girsh in 1863, displaying the application of industrial machinery to the excavation through the desert. (In author's possession, 2020)

10. The Suez Canal, after its turbulent history, still in operation today. (Image by the author, 2020)

11. The ruins of the Summer Palace today, a testament to an act of Anglo-French barbarism. (In author's possession, 2020)

12. Brunel's monstrous *Great Eastern* steamship taking shape on the banks of the River Thames at Millwall, towering over the terraced houses of London's East End. (In author's possession, 2020)

Above right: 13. A French depiction from around 1830 of syphilis concealed under the guise of a prostitute. (Image in author's possession, 2020)

Middle right: 14. Bismarck confers with the captured Napoleon III, just after his abdication following the Battle of Sedan in 1870. (Image in author's possession, 2020)

Below right: 15. A popular portrayal of the Eiffel Tower's radio signaling of time across the world at 11 p.m. every night. It was timekeeper of the world from 1913. (Image in author's possession)

Below left: 16. Stanhope Forbe's *A Street in Brittany*, painted in 1881 and exhibited the following year. (In public domain. Walker Art Gallery)

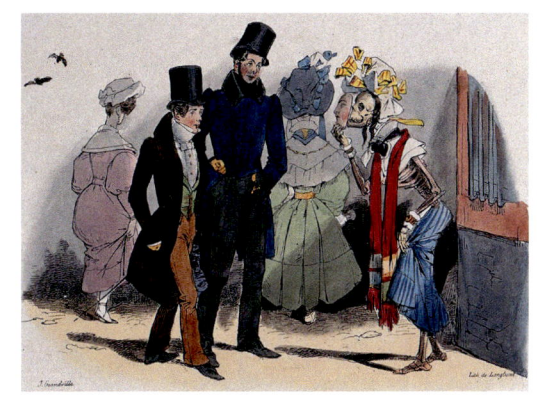

Left: 17. Amiens Cathedral's beautifully carved façade and elaborate rose window: the 'Parthenon of Gothic Architecture'. (Image by the author, 2020)

Below left: 18. The craftsmanship of the medieval artisans of Picardy on display in Amiens Cathedral, exhibiting the intensely white chalk of the surrounding Somme Valley. It is especially worth noting how effectively light is thrown into the building, something that Ruskin emphasized was a priority for medieval architects. (Image by the author, 2020)

Below right: 19. The slender chalk apse, high vaulting, and lofty nave of Amiens Cathedral's interior. (Image by the author, 2020)

20 & 21. The exterior and interior of the beautiful thirteenth-century Royal Chapel of Sainte-Chapelle, that Ruskin was so concerned was at risk during the Prussian siege of Paris in 1871. (Images by the author, 2018)

Above: 22. The British General Post Office's cable-laying ship the *Alert* in 1915. A year earlier, she had cut Germany's undersea telegraph cables following Britain's declaration of war on 5 August 1914. (Image in author's possession, 2020)

Left: 23. German wartime propaganda from 1915, depicting Britain as a spider, tying up its allies and Uncle Sam in its web. Its legs stride Britain's overseas territories in Malta, Gibraltar, and Egypt, as well as the recently invaded Dardanelles in Turkey, while it consumes its French partner. This was a bitter reflection on Britain's imperialism and its reputation as an ally. All the while, the German eagle looks on. (Image in author's possession, 2020)

Below left: 24. Away from the squabbles of the general staffs, British and French soldiers enjoy a rare quiet moment on the Western Front in March 1915. (In public domain. Bibliothèque nationale de France)

8

ENTENTE RENEWED: THE DRIFT TO GLOBAL WAR

Folkestone in 1887 was the setting of a pitiful scene. Arriving from London, a sixty-eight-year-old gentleman checked into the most fashionable hotel the Kentish seaside town could boast. An ostentatious shopping spree ensued, as the bearded gentleman proceeded to order two new coats and a series of fancy waistcoats, before purchasing a toy boat and some 'guards' to adorn his window. All the while, his valet looked on in confused wonder. A stylish haircut followed. Impressed with the hotel's champagne selection, the gentleman requested three bottles, just to 'study the labels'. Two of these he gave to the maids, along with half a sovereign each. Sherry went to the cook and a servant, and a new set of clothes to a lucky housemaid. This was eccentric behaviour, even by Victorian standards. But given the identity of the big spender, it was nothing short of a personal calamity. So long the anti-capitalist critic of commercial materialism and industrial mechanised labour, as well as Victorian Britain's leading advocate of a return to a simpler life, Folkestone had just witnessed the mental breakdown of John Ruskin.[1]

For thirty years, Ruskin's warnings over the moral and social corruption of coal-powered, machine-driven industry at the expense of honest craft and skill had marked him out as one of the nation's most influential figures, both in politics and in art. But in the years preceding his Folkestone calamity, his attention had very much fallen on the beautiful thirteenth-century Gothic architecture of northern France. Ruskin was eager that British audiences understand French Gothic and appreciate that this was a mutual, even transnational, inheritance. England and France shared a common architectural history. Both boasted splendid cathedrals from Rheims and Lincoln to Chartres and Canterbury. The origins of these mighty works was, Ruskin taught, to be found at Amiens. Although Chartres Cathedral was older, Ruskin agreed with French architect Eugène Viollet-le-Duc's (1814–79) declaration that Amiens Cathedral was 'The Parthenon of Gothic Architecture'.[2] In other words, it was the first work of pure Gothic, from which the medieval architects and stonemasons of France and England had taken their inspiration. Between 1880 and 1885, Ruskin brought the significance of Amiens to British readers through his popular *The Bible of Amiens*, which was an appeal for travellers to France to visit the cathedral, as well as serving as a visitor's handbook to the building.

For those with time on their hands, Ruskin advised approaching Amiens via the chalk hills from which the cathedral's stone was quarried, but for those *en route* to Paris, with only an hour to spare, he recommended a walk from the railway station. He strongly endorsed the purchase of a few bonbons or tarts from the charming patisseries along the way. Once at the cathedral, he directed visitors inside to see the woodwork of the choir. Here, sweet and young grained wood could be found, which under the skill of Picardy's medieval craftsmen seemed 'cut like clay, to fold like silk, to grow like living branches, to leap like living flame'. Indeed, there was 'nothing else so beautiful out of the godly trees of the world' that Ruskin knew of.[3] This was a virtuous building, displaying the moral values of medieval France, combining austerity, skill, and magnificence. With its richly carved façade, rose windows, and lofty knave, it was built to 'admit as much light into the building as was consistent with the comfort of it', but also without exhausting the city's finances. Ruskin drew particular attention to the soft, pale stone of the cathedral's interior, 'chalk from the cliffs of the Somme'.[4] The slender chalk apse was in itself fundamental to the Gothic style, being 'not only the best, but the very *first* thing done *perfectly* in its manner, by Northern Christendom'.[5] To understand the English Gothic and its centrality to the nation's Christian faith, France's thirteenth-century cathedral architecture had to be witnessed. With flying buttresses, traceries, tall narrow choirs, and fine vaulting, French cathedrals were threaded together as vast works to invoke nature.[6]

Victorian Britain's leading art critic and architectural authority, Ruskin had long emphasised the cultural significance of the French Gothic. The foundations of English architecture were to be found in medieval northern France and Belgium. As early as 1849 in *The Severn Lamps of Architecture*, Ruskin had argued for the superiority of the French style because it was so clearly grounded in the surrounding natural world. Above all though, the medieval architects of northern France, Belgium, and England had prioritised the drawing of light into their cathedrals and churches. Unlike Italian and Greek architects, this was of profound importance in such relatively gloomy regions: lofty knaves, choirs, and expansive windows were not just immensely beautiful, but optimised light in the darkness of northern Europe. For Ruskin, this was virtuous because it built in reference to local surroundings and nature.[7] And of all landscapes, he thought north France's supreme, having the 'purest air in the world'.[8] Since his first visit to lowland France in 1825, aged six, Picardy, Normandy, and valleys of the Loire, Marne, Meuse, and Somme formed

Ruskin's own 'perpetual Paradise'. He would continue to visit until 1888, including long periods of architectural study in 1848, 1868, and 1880.⁹

His 1868 two-month examination of the medieval Picardy port of Abbeville, which was about to be demolished and rebuilt, resulted in his Royal Institution lecture, 'The Flamboyant Architecture of the Valley of the Somme', delivered in 1869. Though finding Brussels quite repugnant, Ruskin cultivated an English appreciation for the Gothic of French and Flemish cities and towns. From the start, he had supported France during the 1870 Franco-Prussian War, but when the Germans laid siege to Paris, Ruskin rallied British audiences, arguing that this was not just a threat to French culture, but Britain's too. In 1871 he warned readers in *The Daily Telegraph* that the Prussians were targeting French architecture, and that Notre-Dame Cathedral and Sainte-Chapelle were both at risk. The loss of either precious work, of such perfect thirteenth-century Gothic art, would be as devastating to England as to France. Notre-Dame was the central edifice of a sacred ring of cathedrals consisting of Amiens, Reims, Chartres, Rouen, and Bourges, forming a 'cinque-foil' around Paris. The loss of any one of these would be a loss to all civilized Christendom. He eagerly promoted a fundraising campaign for the Bishop of Versailles and the Parisian clergy. By 1872 Ruskin feared that Paris had effectively become a new Venice: a city 'in ruin'.¹⁰

As much as Ruskin promoted Amiens Cathedral as a shared Anglo-French architectural heritage to British audiences, his most celebrated reader was undoubtedly a Frenchman. Few valued Ruskin's appreciation of the Gothic so much as Marcel Proust (1871-1922), making overt references to the English social reformer throughout his epic *À la recherche du temps perdu*, published in seven parts between 1913 and 1927.¹¹ Proust also translated Ruskin's *The Bible of Amiens*, recommending French readers visit the cathedral as a 'sort of Ruskinian pilgrimage'.[12] Lamenting how snobbish French audiences were towards their own works of Gothic art, Proust found Ruskin's rediscovery of the beauty of Amiens completely enchanting: Ruskin had understood the cathedral like no other. Proust explained that the term 'Bible' was literal, with the cathedral's porch 'not merely a stone book, a stone Bible ... it is "the Bible" in stone', depicting Christ in the centre, surrounded by saints and apostles.[13] The medieval wonder was 'not only a beauty to be felt', but a book to be understood, and Ruskin offered a reading like no other.

As much as Franco-British international relations were polarised during the late nineteenth century, Ruskin and Proust were overseeing a renewed appreciation of a shared architectural past. There was, for all the imperial rivalry, a profound and mutual respect of the two nations' rich histories, in which Amiens Cathedral took a central role. And Ruskin's celebration of French architecture was to precede a revival in Anglo-French relations during the early twentieth century that would go far beyond stone and spires. If Ruskin was sure that northern France and England were bound by a shared medieval past, then British and French politicians were becoming increasingly aware that they would have to unite to survive in the new industrial century. Almost enemies in a global conflict in 1898, just sixteen years later, France and Britain would enter a truly worldwide war as allies.

It would be a war that would undermine much of Ruskin's influence, as his brand of romantic socialism and emphasis of craft and non-industrialised economies had little place in an age of mechanised warfare. If you want to know what happened to Ruskin's teachings, then you could do worse than to look to the battlefields of the First World War, where chemicals, machines, and mass production proved so brutalising. In 1915, the *Westminster*

Gazette published an account in which Ruskin's works were literally buried in the mud of the trenches. A soldier, fatally wounded, was quietly reading one of Ruskin's most celebrated works, *The Crown of Wild Olive* (1866), 'enjoying it immensely'. The *Westminster Gazette's* reporter told of how this 'little book had been his companion all through and that when he died he wanted it to be buried with him. His end came the next day, and we buried the book with him.'[14] Ruskin's writings struggled to endure the dehumanising experience of the Western Front, as did the Anglo-French alliance. But together, Britain and France did endure it. This partnership came about over a decade of rapprochement between 1903 and 1914. By the end of it, the fates of the two countries were inseparably bound. In 1916, more than two decades after Ruskin had advised his readers to visit Amiens, British and French soldiers would fight and die together in the same Picardy fields of the Somme Valley from which the stone of Amiens Cathedral had been cut.

*

Queen Victoria had reigned for sixty glorious years. She had ascended the throne in 1837 as the youthful ruler of a United Kingdom with a considerable number of overseas colonies, but was now the infirm Empress of an Empire covering a quarter of the Earth. No one who witnessed her Diamond Jubilee Spithead naval review on 26 June 1897 could doubt Britain's might. Some 165 warships, including twenty-one first-class battleships and fifty-four cruisers, were testament to that. Crucially, Britain controlled Dover, Cape Town, Singapore, Gibraltar, and Alexandria; as Admiral Jacky Fisher put it, these 'five strategic keys lock up the globe'.[15] Along with railways and steamships, a colossal network of telegraphy cables delivered rapid communication to hold this all together. This was the world's greatest information network. With India connected to Britain in 1864, Canada in 1868, and links to Singapore, Japan, and China by 1871, this 'All-Red Line Around the World' was completed in 1902 with the Transpacific cable.[16] In 1900 a jealous French government noted enviously that 'England owes her influence in the world perhaps more to her cable communications than to her navy. She controls the news, and makes it serve her policy and commerce in a marvellous manner.'[17]

All was not, however, as well as it seemed. Since Fashoda, Britain's European rivals had grown increasingly hostile to the aggressively imperialistic power. Britain's clumsy and ruthless handling of the Second Boer War between 1899 and 1901 caused outrage across the Continent. It was not just that Britain's expansion in South Africa looked like little more than a greedy theft of the Boer's valuable gold fields, but the cruel use of concentration camps to control the Boer population shocked European and American audiences. Along with this collapse of international sympathy, Britain's naval strength was diminished. Britain had thirty-eight battleships in 1883, rising to sixty-two in 1897. This was not too bad, but it marked a relative decline, considering that France expanded its fleet from nineteen to thirty-six, Russia three to eighteen, and the United States from none to eleven during the same period.[18]

In particular, it was Germany's naval expansion that would eventually give British audiences the most anguish. In 1897, Admiral Alfred von Tirpitz had found approval with Kaiser Wilhelm II in his assertion that the German Empire required a huge battle fleet to gain diplomatic weight with Britain. Bernard von Bülow (1849–1929), German Chancellor between 1900 and 1909, launched a colossal battleship-building programme. In 1898 Tirpitz and the Kaiser had agreed on eleven new battleships within seven years, but by 1900 Bülow adopted Tirpitz's new proposals for forty-five battleships and armed cruisers. This move sent shock waves through the Admiralty in London. When Jacky Fisher ascended to the position of First Sea Lord in 1904, he vowed to overhaul the Royal Navy, enhancing its home waters capabilities and initiating a new class of super battleships, the first of which was launched in 1906, HMS *Dreadnought*. Bülow responded with a new naval act that year, and a 1908 bill expanding Germany's building programme from three to four ships per annum. Ultimately, it was Britain that triumphed in this naval race. Dreadnought building was an expensive business and, with the German national debt doubling between 1900 and 1908, Bülow was forced to resign. A final naval act in 1912 brought German naval aspirations to a halt.

Britain nevertheless struggled to keep up in the naval race. Still an imperial power, the nation's spending priorities were changing, moving towards more social concerns. The Boer War had revealed how malnourished and sickly much of Britain's working classes were. Between 1906 and 1914, the Liberal governments of Henry Campbell-Bannerman and Herbert Asquith were committed to reforming social welfare and moving the state away from its traditional *laissez-faire* ethos. Under the guidance of 'New Liberals' like Winston Churchill and David Lloyd George, the government introduced free school meals in 1906, followed by pensions for the over seventies in 1908. As Chancellor of the Exchequer, Lloyd George pushed through his radical 'People's Budget' between 1909 and 1910, ably assisted by Churchill as President of the Board of Trade. This dramatically increased social spending, paid for by taxes on the landed classes and super wealthy. Balancing such expenditure with the construction of battleships was a delicate task for the Liberal government. With spiralling welfare spending commitments, Asquith was forced to abandon Salisbury's two-power naval standard, replacing it with a new ratio of sixteen ships for every ten in the German fleet.[19] Nevertheless, by 1914, Britain boasted twenty-nine dreadnoughts to Germany's seventeen.

But in the early 1900s, this was all a long way off: Britain was very much alone. After initially considering Germany as a possible ally between 1900 and 1901, leading British statesmen, including Prime Minister Salisbury, regarded the Kaiser as an increasingly unreliable partner. It was improbable that Germany would help Britain's efforts to hold on to India in the event of a war with Russia. At the same time, the anti-British feeling among the German public following the Boer War made such an alliance unlikely.[20] As for Russia, it seemed equally hostile, having stirred up unrest in the areas cushioning India from the Tsarist empire, notably in Persia and Afghanistan.[21] In short, British policymakers desperately wanted an ally and they wanted one fast, and the most likely candidate was France.

The Third Republic might well have shared common anti-German sentiments in the early 1900s, but it was far from sympathetic to its Anglo-Saxon rival in the light of Fashoda and the Boer War. Under Delcassé, the Quai d'Orsay was perpetually suspicious of Germany. The two countries briefly courted the idea of an anti-British union in response to the Boer War in March 1900, but it proved impossible for Delcassé to move beyond his distrust of German militarisation.[22] Instead of Britain, the Russian alliance remained central to French foreign policy, with Delcassé promoting a string of loans to the Tsarist state on the Paris financial market. But Fashoda had shown how limited Russian support could be, having failed to declare its support for France during the confrontation.[23] At the same time as cultivating resistance to Germany through a Russian alliance, Delcassé was keen to exert French influence in the Mediterranean, especially over Morocco. Britain was crucial to both his management of the German question and his determination to expand along the north African coast.

Yet Britain remained unpopular with the French public, still bitter over Egypt, Fashoda, and the Boers. There remained a consensus that Britain was the single biggest threat to international peace. Nearing a German reconciliation, Delcassé told his journalist friend Jules Glarétie in March 1900 that the British Empire represented a threat to world civilization.[24] Fears echoed around the corridors of French government that British colonialists coveted total global domination. It would prove difficult to pull off a reversal in public relations and bring Britain onside in the face of German military and economic strength.

It took the wit and charm of Britain's new monarch to resolve this diplomatic isolation. Queen Victoria died in 1901, succeeded by her fun-loving sixty-year-old son, Edward VII (1841-1910). Popular and affable, the 'Uncle of Europe' was a real trendsetter, initiating a fashion for tweeds, homburg hats, black tie at dinner rather than the traditional white tie and tails, and pioneering a preference for the side, as opposed to the customary front, trouser press. With a huge appetite for food, he popularised the serving of horseradish and Yorkshire puddings with roast beef on Sundays. Crucially, however, he was unlike his mother in being ardently pro-French. No less significant was the influence of his wife, Queen Alexandra (1844–1925), who had married Edward in 1863. The daughter of King Christian IX of Denmark, she had not forgotten the Danish defeat of 1864. While Victoria had been pro-German, Alexandra and Edward opposed Prussia's aggression and Alexandra's anti-German feeling never abated. When the British government agreed to exchange Heligoland for Zanzibar in 1890, Alexandra wrote a memorandum to the cabinet, opposing the move. Edward shared this dislike of Germany, especially distrustful of his erratic nephew, Kaiser Wilhelm II (1859–1941).

Entente Renewed: The Drift to Global War

Since the start of his reign, Wilhelm had always had a troubled relationship with Britain. Both envious and admiring of its empire and navy, the Kaiser adored his grandmother, Victoria, but resented Edward. Rude and obnoxious, Wilhelm had few friends among his English relatives.

Edward's hostility to Germany and passion for all things French was no secret. As king, he made it his mission to restore the entente. This was music to French ears. Despite his reservations over Britain's reputation and threat to world peace, by 1903 Delcassé had come to accept that an entente was probably the only real solution to France's anxieties over Germany, even if this meant finally acknowledging British control over Egypt.[25] He wanted to secure British support, as did France's President, Émilie Loubert. The problem was that Britain was still profoundly unpopular with the French public, especially after the Boer War. But as Loubert predicted, 'a visit from the king would ... do an amount of good which is probably not realised in England ... In this capital, His Majesty, while Prince of Wales, had acquired an exceptional personal popularity.'[26] Edward's love of pleasure and easy-going humour might have raised eyebrows in England, but it had already won over many a Parisian. The Foreign Office advised against an official state visit, but both the king and Loubert ignored the suggestion.[27] Although talks in early 1902 between the Quai d'Orsay and the British Colonial Secretary, Joseph Chamberlain, preceded the king's intervention, it was very much his own initiative.[28]

On 1 May 1903, Loubert welcomed Edward to Paris and took him through the Bois de Boulogne to the Champs-Élysées. The whole city, it seemed, had turned out. After a stop at the British embassy, where a room had been prepared with a magnificent throne, the king and president attended the Théâtre Français that evening and spent the following day attending military parades.

At the Hôtel de Ville, Edward delivered a speech 'in praise of the beauty of Paris', before going to the races at Longchamp and a state dinner at the Élysée Palace. Aside from a few nationalistic outbursts in the more radical newspapers, the visit was a triumph.[29] Edward had always loved Paris, having known its most intimate charms and delights, including those less respectable, since his youth. Initially met with cries of 'vivent les Boers!', it was hard for Parisians to remain angry at the jolly king. He knew how to flatter, and how the French loved it. By his departure, the heckling had turned to cheers of 'vive le Roi!' and 'vive le bon Edouard!'[30]

In July, Edward personally orchestrated a return state visit, hosting Loubert and Delcassé in London. Here, Delcassé and the Conservative Foreign Secretary, Henry Petty-Fitzmaurice, 5th Marquess of Lansdowne (1845–1927), met and thrashed out an agreement that would culminate in 1904 in an all-out entente: the king's work was done. The *New York Times* recognised the affront this royal triumph presented to the Kaiser and the German people. To the American paper it seemed odd that the king of a democracy 'still decides war and peace without consulting Parliament', interpreting his efforts to reconcile Britain and France as a sort of personal revenge on his wife's behalf. 'Wait until I am King!' Edward had warned on learning of Germany's victory over France in 1870.[31]

The dining, charming, and flattering complete, now came the turn of the politicians. Under Delcassé's instruction, the French ambassador Pierre Paul Cambon (1843–1924) fashioned a hard-fought settlement with Lansdowne. Appointed to London in 1898, Cambon would serve as ambassador until 1920, embodying the new comradeship between the two nations. Signed on 8 April 1904 and ratified by Parliament in May, the *Entente Cordiale* consisted of three documents, covering spheres of influence in Siam, British and French influence over Egypt and Morocco, and an agreement over the Newfoundland fisheries.[32]

Entente Renewed: The Drift to Global War

Punch's portrayal of John Bull's courting of 'Madame La France', much to the annoyance of Kaiser Wilhelm. 'What a very uppish person!', Madame La France reflects, to which John Bull replies, 'Oh, I suppose it's what he calls being "correct".' (Author's collection)

Resolving this final question was an especially bizarre achievement, having been a sore point since the Treaty of Utrecht in 1713. Then, France had renounced its claims over the North American island of Newfoundland but retained fishing rights along its coast. In the 1820s, Newfoundland's permanent settlers found this presence a nuisance, especially as France owned the islands of St Pierre and Miquelon, just off the coast, which developed into a major fishing centre. This French rivalry slowed Newfoundland's economic growth, providing stiff competition for fish exports: by the 1880s the European markets were flooded with cheap catches from Newfoundland's waters. This was exacerbated by the French government's subsidising of St Pierre's fishing industry.[33]

In 1901, Cambon's proposal to swap France's Newfoundland fishing rights for The Gambia, a British colony, was flatly refused. But by 1903, their shared anxieties over Germany convinced Delcassé and Lansdowne to put aside their differences over Newfoundland's fish. Although the Foreign Office refused French demands for land in return for fishing rights, it did eventually agree to financially compensate French fishermen in the region in return for them consenting to Newfoundland's fishing regulations. Along with this, France also secured a favourable adjustment of borders with Nigeria and The Gambia and the acquisition of the Iles de Los off French-held Guinea. In return, it effectively gave up its fishing rights and, more importantly, recognised Britain's authority in Egypt.[34] In exchange for this, Britain acknowledged that Morocco was firmly a French area of influence. By any measure, the 1904 rebirth of the entente marked an astonishing turnaround in Anglo-French relations.

*

The renewed friendship between France and Britain that followed Edward's Parisian triumph sparked a flurry of cross-Channel exchanges and visits. When President Poincaré visited London in 1913, he was met with such a reception so as to remove any chance 'that England and France can ever again become enemies'.

'No one,' reported one British journalist, repeated 'the old anti-French cries of "Waterloo" or "Fashoda", no one seemed to remember.' Indeed, no visitor had ever been treated with 'greater splendour and dignity' than Poincaré, who enjoyed the hospitality of King George V and the City of London.[35] Nor were such meetings limited to political elites. As early as October 1904, the entente was extended into the world of medicine, with *The Hospital* reporting on a deputation of French doctors to London's hospitals and laboratories. Some 200 French physicians descended on the capital for a three-day tour, examining Britain's 'system of medical examination'. While English medical professionals regularly travelled to Paris, Vienna, and Berlin to adopt Continental practices, French doctors rarely travelled the other way. Britain had lessons both to follow and avoid. Its lack of state spending and government-supported healthcare were a national shame, but the caring culture of English nurses was to be envied. The French delegation thought Britain's *laissez-faire* system of voluntary provisions absurd, but seemed to admire the effects of liberalism on the patient. 'The care lavished upon the patient as an individual and not as a mere case is the direct outcome of the independence which is so marked a trait in our national character,' *The Hospital* concluded.[36] The entente's influence was fast filtering through to both British and French societies.

It was in terms of international diplomacy, however, that the alliance exerted its greatest influence, as Britain and France increasingly coordinated their foreign policies. Part of this was down to France's loss of confidence in its Russian allies, whose catastrophic defeat at the hands of the Japanese between 1904 and 1905 shocked European observers. Fortunately, Britain had been allied to Japan since January 1902 and it had been British pressure on the Ottoman Empire to prevent the Russian fleet from passing out of the Black Sea, as well as stopping Russian shipping from using the Suez Canal, that had contributed to Japan's naval supremacy in the Far East.[37] By 1907 Britain and Russia had allied, marking the completion of an Anglo-French-Russian entente.

The first real test of the entente came amid the growing tensions over Morocco. Kaiser Wilhelm was keen to secure influence over one of Morocco's Atlantic ports, travelling to Tangier to build relations with the Moroccan king in March 1905.[38] This move was anathema to French politicians, fresh from securing British recognition that Morocco was within France's sphere of influence. But the Kaiser hoped to mobilise international support against a French monopoly of control over the North African coast. In early 1905, Germany called for an international conference to resolve the matter, believing that Britain and the United States would oppose the encroachment of protectionist France into the country. German politicians hoped to use the Moroccan question to wreck the newly formed entente. As Chancellor Bülow put it, with Morocco under discussion he believed he could 'cause Delcassé's fall, break the continuity of aggressive French policy, knock the continental dagger out of the hands of Edward VII and the war group in England and, simultaneously, ensure peace, preserve German honour, and improve German prestige'.[39] Bülow could not be accused of modest ambitions.

Nevertheless, the German Chancellor found little support from President Theodore Roosevelt, who followed French policy over Africa and refused to trust the Kaiser. After all, how could one rely on 'a man who is so jumpy', the President asked rhetorically.[40] Initially, Britain and France also rejected German proposals for a conference. King Edward assured Delcassé that over Morocco, his 'government will give you every assistance in its power', while the Royal Navy mobilised for action during the summer of 1905.[41] British audiences, including *The Times*, were well aware that Germany's Moroccan intentions were largely to test the 1904

Entente Renewed: The Drift to Global War

entente and rupture Franco-British relations. Then in June, the weight of German pressure on France told. Eager not to antagonise its militaristic neighbours, the French cabinet ousted Delcassé from the Quai d'Orsay. In Britain, Conservative Prime Minister Arthur Balfour was taken aback by this jittery move. As he put it, Delcassé's resignation 'displayed a weakness on the part of France which indicated that she could not at present be counted on as an effective force in international politics'.[42] Despite this, Delcassé's successor, Maurice Rouvier, took the same hard line over Morocco. But with Britain, France, and Germany all sliding towards war, Rouvier and Lansdowne finally agreed to a conference to de-escalate tensions.

Bülow's success was short-lived. The ensuing Algeciras Conference was a complete diplomatic disaster for Germany, as the entente held firm. At the Spanish port of Algeciras, within ominous sight of the British-held Rock of Gibraltar, the negotiating began on 16 January 1906 and was all over by early April. Held in the town hall, the Ayuntamiento, it soon became very clear that it was now Germany, not Britain, that was isolated.[43] Fearing that Bülow planned to use an Atlantic port, most likely Casablanca, to expand into South America, Roosevelt threw American support behind Britain and France, as did Russia. The President even despatched part of the United States's North Atlantic fleet to Gibraltar as a visible display of American power.[44]

Throughout, Britain provided unwavering support of its new French partners, with the recently elected Liberal government continuing the entente that Lansdowne had fashioned. His successor as Foreign Secretary, Sir Edward Grey (1862–1933), would epitomise and manage Anglo-French cooperation for a decade. No other British Foreign Secretary matched Grey's continuous tenure of the office from 1905 until 1916. Expelled from Oxford in 1884, and earning more of a reputation for tennis than academic ability, he was the quintessential English gentleman. Continuing Lansdowne's pro-French stance, Grey dominated British foreign policy and ensured Asquith's government remained fully committed to the entente.[45]

From the start of the Algeciras Conference, Grey warned the German ambassador of Britain's pro-French position. On 3 March, a vote of ten to three passed resolving that the French and Spanish would share police powers in Moroccan ports, with a Swiss inspector general of police at Tangier. It also allowed France to establish a State Bank of Morocco, under French law, at Tangier, which would act as the nation's mint and treasury, with powers to issue paper money.[46] In effect, France had acquired Morocco as something nearing a protectorate in all but name. Having taken control of its police and finances, France was the real power in the region by international agreement. Germany had been humiliated in its attempt to test the entente. In the end, of the thirteen states represented, only Austria-Hungary and Morocco supported the German case. The conference confirmed Morocco's independence, just, but established that France was to have a privileged place in the country. This was some check on German imperial aspirations.

Throughout the late 1900s and early 1910s, this Anglo-French collaboration remained solid. When Germany supported the Austro-Hungarian annexation of Bosnia-Herzegovina between 1908 and 1909, despite Russian protest, France secured a new agreement over Morocco in exchange for neutrality in the Balkans. With Russia weak and Britain's army still developing, Prime Minister Georges Clemenceau (1841–1929) had little choice but to agree to remain out of any conflict at the Casablanca Agreement. Nevertheless, Germany ceded further influence to France over Morocco.[47]

For Britain's part, the Foreign Office worked with Germany to restrain Austro-Russian antagonism. Yet for all Grey's fancy

Entente Renewed: The Drift to Global War

footwork in using Germany to hold back Austrian aggression, he remained committed to the entente.[48] Things escalated in October 1912 when war broke out in the Balkans. Against the ever-disintegrating Ottoman Empire, a Balkan League of states, consisting of Bulgaria, Greece, Montenegro, Serbia, and Romania, took power in the region. A second war followed in 1913 among the victors over the spoils of the earlier conflict. Amid this instability, Russia and Austria both vied for influence and territory, hoping to draw in their allies. Russia looked to France to back its moves to check Austria-Hungary's Balkan ambitions, while the Austrians counted on Germany's support. Britain aligned with Germany as the apparently more moderate European power. France seemed determined to assist Russia.[49]

By 1913, Paris was demanding more than promissory notes from the British over naval support, calling for a formal military alliance. The Foreign Office, on the other hand, grew increasingly alarmed at France's inability to curtail Russia's territorial ambitions. In the spring of 1914, Anglo-French ties appeared to be loosening over the question of Russia and the Balkans. As much as Grey and his diplomats wanted French cooperation, they did not want to be shackled to increasingly unpredictable Russia looking to expand into the Balkan Peninsula.[50] It seemed that a détente with Germany was nearing, with Grey admitting that 'We are on good terms with Germany now and we desire to avoid a revival of friction with her.'[51] Nevertheless, the Franco-British entente endured, despite their varying commitments to Russia in the Balkans. Away from the international bargaining, the governments and armed forces of Britain and France were in fact moving ever closer together.

The real question after 1904 for British and French politicians was how, and even if, the two countries would work together should it come to war with Germany. It was a common, if flippant, nineteenth-century observation that there were five fundamentally stable perfect institutions on which European civilization rested: the Houses of Parliament in London, the Curiâ in Rome, the Opera in Paris, the Russian Ballet in St Petersburg, and the Great General Staff in Berlin.⁵² So the challenge of taking on the German war machine was immense. Having so long been rivals, British and French policymakers would need to act fast to establish a robust relationship.

Under Campbell-Bannerman between 1905 and 1908 and Asquith during the following six years, the Liberal government was firmly committed to the alliance. The Foreign Secretary, Grey, declared in February 1906 that his leading policy was 'to maintain the entente with France'.⁵³ Seven months later he made it clear that he would resign should Britain not support France in the event of German hostility. Grey saw that the entente would only endure if it was made clear that Britain would provide military and naval support when called on. Yet Asquith's cabinet opposed any participation in a Continental war, preferring to keep military intervention as a choice rather than an obligation, should Germany invade France. In early 1906 Britain agreed to form the British Expeditionary Force (BEF), in response to the Moroccan Crisis, with the intention of this small army being deployed to France in the event of a German invasion. The Liberal Secretary of State for War, Richard Haldane, subsequently oversaw British army reforms and planned the creation of the BEF, but it was unclear what the function of this force would be.⁵⁴

Admiral Fisher certainly had his own views on the matter. The First Sea Lord proposed in 1908 that the BEF not engage on the Continent except for sudden maritime assaults. With naval support, he envisioned the BEF tasked with garrisoning Antwerp and recapturing Heligoland in the first instance, assuming Germany had violated Belgian neutrality. With these in hand, he believed he could land the British army on the Pomeranian coast, 90 miles from Berlin, where it would dig in and distract a million German soldiers from the French frontier thanks to the overwhelming supremacy of the Royal Navy.[55]

Others saw the flaws in this: the German army could easily tie down the BEF and still invade France. Some in the army favoured fighting alongside the French, but it was soon clear the priority should be Belgium. In the Cabinet and General Staff there were fears that as the Belgians relied too much on Antwerp as a defensive fort, leaving the line between Liège and Namur poorly defended, this was where the Germans would look to outflank the French. Should the Germans march on the Somme, the BEF might be best deployed to help hold the Belgian flank along the River Meuse. Churchill in particular was a supporter of this plan, conceiving of an Anglo-Belgian army holding the Liège-Namur line, pinning down German units away from their central assault on Paris. Of course, this assumed Belgian neutrality had been violated. By 1914, the nominal plan in the event of war was for the BEF to land in France within two weeks of the commencement of hostilities and work alongside the French and Belgian armies.[56] One thing that was settled on was naval cooperation, with the 1912 Anglo-French Mediterranean agreement dividing up responsibility in the Mediterranean to the French navy, and the Atlantic and North Sea to the Royal Navy.

It was not just the fashioning of a shared strategy between the governments in London and Paris that mattered. Equally important was the cultivation of relations between the French and British armies. Initially, this involved talks between their respective high commands, the newly established British General Staff and France's experienced État-Major, throughout the winter of 1905–06, amid the Morocco Crisis. The British General Staff even conducted a war game in which the British army responded to a German invasion of France and Belgium.[57] But it was soon clear to all that the British army lacked the organisation and knowledge required to conduct Continental warfare. The French General Staff recognised that it had to offer instruction to the enthusiastic, but embryonic, BEF. For their part, Britain's military commanders were eager to learn all they could from their new French allies. Together, the two armies would make preparations for a shared Western Front, away from the high politics of London and Paris.

The leading architects of this cooperation were Brigadier-General Sir Henry Wilson, director of military operations at the war office from 1910, and General Ferdinand Foch (1851–1929). Before 1910, Wilson and Foch were heads of their country's respective staff colleges and fostered a culture of exchange between British and French officers.[58] In late 1909 Wilson visited France's École Supérieure de Guerre, where Foch gave him a personal tour. Wilson was impressed and invited himself back the next day and returned for a third visit in January 1910, eager to gain instruction in how to reform the British officer training programme at Camberley according to the more practical style of France's learned military academy.[59]

As commandant of the British Staff College, Wilson reoriented Camberley's educational framework towards a Continental war versus Germany, rather than the customary focus on small colonial warfare. Maps of the frontier between Belgium, France, and Germany went up in classrooms and French-style inspections and manoeuvres became commonplace. Wilson was so enthusiastic over this collaboration that he spent his holidays cycling the frontier regions of Belgium and France with French staff officers; but he would never the see the fruit of this partnership, succumbing to a heart attack in August 1914.[60]

Although the Foch-Wilson friendship was crucial to shaping Anglo-French military integration, these close relations went beyond the dynamic duo. The star of the British army and future

Entente Renewed: The Drift to Global War

BEF commander Sir John French (1852–1925) was also very French, or at least, pro-French. A notorious womaniser, he had served under Wolseley in Egypt and the Sudan before gaining more military experience in the Boer War. In 1909, one French general observed that Sir John showed 'a strong and real sympathy for France, and has confidence in her army ... He has only one wish, reiterated at every opportunity ... that is, to see the British army fighting at our side in the event of a war with Germany.'[61] In September 1906, Sir John had attended the manoeuvres of the II Corps d'Armée. The favour was returned in 1907, when French generals were invited to Aldershot to see the BEF emulate the French practice. The British government spared no expense on this return visit, sending a deputation of staff officers to welcome the French party at Charing Cross station, who were then treated to dinner at Windsor Castle and later met Edward VII, the Prince of Wales, Asquith, Haldane, and Grey.[62]

Through such interaction, the two armies built a firm affinity and fashioned a shared sense of purpose and strategy for managing a German invasion. In the press, too, these military connections were fostered. *The Times*'s military correspondent, Charles à Court Repington, worked to enhance public sympathy for the French army.[63] Under his guidance, *The Times* became a champion of the entente, with the Franco-British alliance the foundation of the influential newspaper's foreign policy. When war broke out in 1914, the newspaper was crucial to rallying public support to send the BEF to the aid of France and 'brave little Belgium'.[64]

*

For all their differences over Russia, the Balkans, and Germany, by 1914 the governments and general staffs of Britain and France were ready to collaborate. This marked an astonishing turnaround since 1903. King Edward VII's Parisian triumph had heralded a new era of Anglo-French cooperation, reminiscent of the heady days of Palmerston and Napoléon III. Yet the nature of the 1904 *entente cordiale* was in fact very different to the alliances of the 1850s. This was not a moment of Franco-British global dominance: it was not the sharing of grand imperial ambitions and pursuit of economic partnership. Rather than a new Anglo-French ordering of world affairs, the partnership of 1904 to 1914 was one of anxiety. It was built on a mutual fear of German economic and military expansion. Even together, Britain and France could not restore the global hegemony they had enjoyed in the mid-nineteenth century. After two decades of competition and rivalry, the two Old World powers were shackled together for survival.

Epilogue

AN ANGLO-FRENCH WORLD ORDER?

Just before 2 a.m. on 5 August 1914 a little boat, the *Alert*, sailed out of Dover. An hour later, she lowered a hook and began dredging the seabed in the morning darkness. Before too long, the *Alert*'s crew had caught hold of something: a telegraph cable connecting Germany to the United States and the world beyond. After severing this vital communications link, the *Alert* returned home to Dover, leaving the German Empire detached from world affairs. Though the crew did not know it, this curious little act had in fact marked Britain's entry into the First World War. Within minutes of the expiry of Britain's ultimatum to Germany at midnight, Winston Churchill, as First Lord of the Admiralty, had telegraphed the order to Dover for the line to be cut. Britain's first move in what would rapidly escalate into a global war had been to isolate Germany and seize control of the world's information networks.

Things had really got out of hand that summer. After Archduke Franz Ferdinand, heir to the Austrian throne, had been assassinated in Sarajevo on 28 June by a Bosnian Serb nationalist, Austria-Hungary had demanded huge concessions from neighbouring Serbia in compensation. Russia declared its support for Serbia. Germany threw its weight behind Austria, advising a quick move on Serbia to prevent Russian intervention. But the ailing Austro-Hungarian Empire dithered. By 30 July, Russia had mobilised its armies, followed by Germany on 1 August, who declared war on Russia. France remained committed to its Russian ally, so Germany looked to seize the advantage. Anticipating that the French could mobilise faster than the Russians, German troops captured Luxembourg on 2 August, and declared war on France the next day. On the 4th, German armies marched into Belgium, outflanking French forces on the Franco-German border, looking to advance on Paris. The scenario so long feared by European statesmen and military commanders had unfolded with explosive rapidity.

And Britain? Throughout July, the Liberal government had been indecisive, provoking anxieties in Paris over Britain's commitment to the entente. As late as 1 August, Asquith's Cabinet had voted against despatching the BEF, preferring to remain neutral should war break out. In the end, it was Grey, the Foreign Secretary, who compelled his fellow ministers to honour their commitments to France and Belgium. On 2 August Grey promised that the Royal Navy would protect France's Atlantic coast if attacked, while informing the German ambassador that should Germany's fleet steam into the North Sea or its armies enter Belgium, Britain would act. Berlin ignored the warning and Grey backed the Cabinet in delivering an ultimatum. With the support of Asquith, Churchill, Haldane, and Lloyd George, Grey's interventionist minority was influential, threatening to split the Liberal Party and bring down the government should it abandon Belgium and France.[1] The Cabinet faced little choice: Britain issued an ultimatum on the 4th in response to Germany's violation of Belgian neutrality, which was never answered. By midnight, Britain and France were both at war with the German Empire.

An Anglo-French World Order?

Over the next four years, the Franco-British collation struggled towards victory.² Though close, relations between the two military commands were always strained. To France's five armies of eighty-two divisions, the BEF in 1914 was just a token, with four. General Joseph Joffre (1852–1931), Commander-in-Chief of the French forces on the Western Front and a veteran of the defence of Paris in 1870, was unimpressed. With the French commander-in-chief ignoring warnings of the German advance through Belgium, the Belgian armies were forced to take refuge in Antwerp, where they were isolated for a month, and the BEF was left exposed, fleeing its position at Mons. These first chaotic exchanges constituted a disaster for the entente that would burden the partnership throughout the war.³ As the conflict descended into the deadlock of trench warfare, the British focus was firmly on Belgium at Ypres, with Churchill favouring an offensive up the Belgian coast towards the port of Zeebrugge, utilising naval support. But Joffre was determined to recapture France's industrial regions, lost in 1914. When the Germans launched a ruthless assault on Verdun in early 1916, the BEF's attention was dragged away from Ypres towards the Somme Valley. The ensuing shambolic offensive of 1 July, in which Kitchener's volunteer army suffered some 60,000 casualties in a day, was very much an attempt to relieve pressure on the buckling French defences at Verdun.⁴

At the highest level, Joffre and Sir John French did not get on, with the British commander writing to his mistress, Winifred Bennett, in April 1915 that the French 'are a funny people ... not very reliable "allies" and one always has to be watching them ... Truly I don't want to be allied with them more than once in a lifetime. You can't trust them.'⁵ This was a long way from the happy pre-war days in which Sir John had appeared such a Francophile. The position between the French high command and the BEF was never completely clear. Predictably, Joffre favoured assuming complete control over the British army, but London politicians were eager to keep the BEF independent. Kitchener's orders to Sir John in August 1914 vaguely specified that although 'every effort must be made to coincide most sympathetically with the plans and wishes of our Ally ... I wish you to distinctly understand that your command is an entirely independent one, and you will in no case come under the orders of any Allied General.'[6]

By the time Sir Douglas Haig (1861–1928) replaced him as commander of the BEF in 1915, Sir John was universally hated at French command. Haig, by contrast, was a marked improvement, managing testing but business-like relations with the succession of French commanders-in-chief.[7] Unlike Sir John, Haig had fluent French. But the two staffs struggled to cooperate. While British generals regarded their counterparts as autocratic and secretive, they were themselves considered unreliable and awkward. Few British officers spoke clear French and French officers generally refused to speak English.[8] Lord Esher, Kitchener's special envoy in Paris, noted dryly in March 1915 that it was

> ... rather absurd ... but you cannot bring an Englishman and a Frenchman, if they are pure bred of their race, together. The Anglo-Saxon ... has so little in common with the Gaul in temperament, education, habits or feeling. It shows how little our allies are understood. They yield to reason, but they cannot grasp the meaning of our cold reserve.[9]

If Britain's politicians and generals sometimes underestimated France's military efforts, then the French were equally guilty of under-appreciating Britain's maritime contribution. France's astonishing wartime munitions production figures made a stark contrast to Britain's early deficiencies, especially in shell manufacturing. But France's remarkable industry was dependent on coal and steel imported on British ships, often from British sources.¹⁰ The two allies were unaware of just how mutually dependent they had become. By 1917, Britain took on the brunt of the fighting on the Western Front, at Ypres and Passchendaele, amid fears that France might capitulate altogether. The following winter, British troops occupied a growing proportion of the line as France's armies wilted; both desperately awaited the arrival of the Americans, who had entered the war in 1917.

Cooperation on the battlefield was important, but Anglo-French finance was crucial to the shared war effort. In 1914, Britain and France were the greatest creditors on Earth, with France having £1.8 billion invested globally, compared to Britain's £4 billion. The City of London was the world's leading financial hub and central exchange, and the British pound the global currency, backed by the gold standard. Likewise, Paris's Bourse and the Bank of France were pillars of the international financial system. Together, the Banks of England and France held some £180 million of gold, and the Paris Bourse and London Stock Exchange were the premier money markets for raising loans.¹¹ All this would be thrown into the fight against Germany.

At the outbreak of war, British and French financial policies differed greatly. Determined to survive at all costs, France's leaders were content to sacrifice their international standing to finance a colossal wartime budget. Minister of Finance Alexandre Ribot oversaw an immediate payment of 500 million francs for mobilisation, followed by 2.9 billion more to kick-start France's wartime economy.¹² His financial policy was to spare no expense, to spend without question, and raise the cash in any way possible. Britain was, in contrast, keen to preserve its financial eminence. In 1902, First Lord of the Admiralty Lord Selborne had largely predicted this when he asserted that the Royal Navy and London finance were 'the two main pillars on which the strength of this country rests, and each is essential to the other'.[13] While Russia abandoned its gold standard in July 1914, and Germany and France did the same in August, Britain clung on to this prestigious commitment until 1916. Lloyd George's first wartime budget, in November 1914, included a timid loan of £350 million floated at 3.5 per cent. By February 1915, however, Russia's credit had dissipated and when the Tsar came cap in hand for a £100 million loan to keep his empire in the war, Lloyd George and Ribot could only manage a £50 million flotation on the London and Paris markets. Rapidly, even these centres of capital were becoming swamped with allied war bonds. France agreed to support Russia's debts, but by May 1915 was unable to meet these obligations. When Ribot proposed a huge £800 million allied war loan be raised in London, Lloyd George was shocked, rejecting the measure in fear of completely exhausting all available capital.[14]

Instead, Britain and France had to rely increasingly on America's markets, liquidating securities, selling off pounds and francs, and shipping out gold reserves. Together, they sacrificed their dominance of global finance on the bloody altar of trench warfare. In the autumn of 1915, a joint Anglo-French delegation to New York sought to raise a $1 billion loan, but returned with just $500 million at 5 per cent. The two imperial powers had to use much of this to subsidise their allies, including Belgium, Serbia, and Italy. Russia alone took a fifth. The bedrock of the allied war effort from 1914 until 1916 was Anglo-French finance. As British economist John Maynard Keynes (1883–1946) concluded in March 1916, 'We have one ally, France. The rest, mercenaries.'[15]

But then French credit imploded. In April, France requested a joint offensive and a loan of £160 million from the British government, which responded with £60 million and an assault on the Somme. From then until 1917, Britain bankrolled its French partner, paying a monthly £4 million subsidy, increasing to £25 million a month

An Anglo-French World Order?

by August.[16] Between 1916 and 1917, Britain loaned France £171 million in total, amid Ribot's dire warnings that without such aid France would have to throw in the towel.[17] France's expenditure was pulling the government apart, with its estimated expenditure for 1916 of 5.6 billion francs escalating to over 6.77 billion.

With Britain and France completely exhausted, their once eminent markets flooded with allied loans, they turned to the United States. In November 1916, British credit had collapsed, with the bank of J. P. Morgan & Co. acting to secure the American loans that would finance the entente until victory in 1918. After 1916, British and French financial policy was no longer dictated in London and Paris, but by New York. This marked a staggering shift in global power that would last well beyond the war.[18]

In many respects, the First World War represented the historic 'high noon' of the entente.[19] At the Paris Peace Conference, Britain and France pursued differing ideas of what to do with Germany. During the 1920s, with Germany neutralised, British and French politicians drifted apart, as both struggled to control their post-war empires without their pre-war financial strength. Britain's ambassador in Paris, Lord Hardinge, expressed the animosity succinctly in 1921, declaring that 'No sane Englishman could possibly be tempted by the idea of being dragged at the wheels of Chauvinism and pseudo-Imperialism of France ... [w]ith Latin races it is essential to stand up to them.'[20] Part of the problem was that British and French audiences had very different memories of the war and each other's performance in it. French commentators tended to remember the slow, half-hearted British contribution before 1916. British contemporaries, in contrast, tended to forget how France had shouldered the brunt of the fighting during the first two years of the war.[21]

Nevertheless, British and French imperial aspirations survived throughout the 1930s and past the Second World War, into the 1950s. The imperial entente culminated in the hugely embarrassing Suez Crisis of 1956, where the failure of the two ex-global powers to cling on to this vital trade link served up a dose of cold reality in an increasingly cold war. In the post-1945 world of Russo-American dominance, the Foreign Office and Quai d'Orsay had initially seen cooperation as a means to rectify the collapse in European power witnessed after the Second World War. The short-lived Eurafrique initiative of pooling Franco-British African resources to recover economic independence from the United States was shelved in 1950 but had conjured up the ghosts of the ententes of the 1850s and 1900s.[22]

After Suez, British and French national interests diverged further still. With Britain looking towards its post-imperial network of Commonwealth nations and ever-closer Anglo-American partnership (some might say subservience), France looked to Europe and the growing European Economic Community (EEC). By the 1960s, this was a community that France was very eager to exclude Britain from. President Charles de Gaulle was adamant that the British economy was incompatible with France's inside the EEC. While France focused on European markets and anxiously sought agricultural protection, the United Kingdom's reliance on cheap food imports, overseas trade, and closeness to the United States made it an unusual European partner. When Prime Minister Harold Macmillan applied for EEC membership, de Gaulle vetoed the application with a resounding 'non'. In private, a distraught Macmillan reflected that for all the uncertainties in the world, one thing was ever true: 'The French always betray you in the end.'[23] Harold Wilson's bid to enter the 'Free Market' met a similar fate in 1967, and it was not until after de Gaulle's departure from power in 1969 that Britain could finally join the EEC in 1973.

An Anglo-French World Order?

As Britain and France's global influence has declined, so too has the importance of the entente cordiale.[24]

*

If you want to identify the moment at which a country was at the absolute apex of global dominance, you should look to Britain in the 1850s. And yet the lessons from this moment are usually misinterpreted. Despite its unprecedented wealth and influence, mid-nineteenth-century Britain never acted as a lone power, independent of collaboration with Continental Europe. It was France with whom Britain shared in its international aspirations. Being the premier global power did not mean operating in splendid isolation. Indeed, without French cooperation, Victorian Britain found it virtually impossible to exert political influence on the Continent. This was brought home to politicians during the early 1860s. This is not only an important moment for those interested with Victorian Britain. It is something equally relevant to the American dominance of the twentieth century. And while the next century might well belong to China, the ruins of the Summer Palace provide a powerful, if distasteful, warning on the dangers of isolation in the face of international collaboration.

Britain's relationship with France during the 1850s and the subsequent decline both in entente and global hegemony after 1863 demonstrate that those commentators who look to the nineteenth century as a time when Britain did not have to cooperate with Europe are mistaken. When looking for what Britain's place in the world is today, it is very easy to think that if only the nation had a little more power, it would not have to collaborate with its neighbours or work towards solidarity. To a certain extent the 1850s feel familiar. Although an imperial power, Britain's place in the world was in many ways uncertain.

Entente Imperial

For all the internationalism, there was something parochial about England. Politicians fuelled panic that, at any moment, the French might invade. Often there was little basis to the hysteria that the Channel would soon be covered in an armada of foreign battleships, but such scaremongering provided governments with a valuable distraction from more urgent domestic concerns. Lord Palmerston, for example, in 1859 resumed his role as Prime Minister after the existing Conservative administration appeared to have underfunded naval expansion; military spending was a popular way of staying in government. When not worrying about a French invasion, questions of sovereignty were never far from public thought. Increasing trade with France meant some degree of political integration. In particular, free trade involved sharing measurement standards, but introducing the metre was far from popular. Parliament's attempts to force society into converting to the metric system fuelled fears that Britain was not only accepting a foreign system, but that the state was becoming more autocratic. It seemed that trade integration with France was jeopardising British liberalism through excessive regulation and undemocratic governance. When, in 1858, Palmerston responded to Napoléon III's calls for Britain to give France legal powers over French refugees living in Britain, it seemed that British independence was under direct threat. For all Britain's industrial wealth and imperial possessions, there was a very real sense that France, either through regulating measurements, legal powers, or possible military invasion, was compromising Britain's independence.

Integration was politically controversial, even for a great imperial and industrial powerhouse. It seems that, despite an empire and global dominance, the British people in the 1850s were as concerned over questions of sovereignty and independence as they seem to be in the 2010s. Yet the mid-Victorian generation of statesmen that included Palmerston were a shrewd bunch. While they happily mobilised anti-French sentiment among the voting middle classes, they carefully cultivated relations with Napoléon III. Here was an emperor and a nation with whom they could do business. Through this Anglo-French alliance the two nations exerted global influence. It was an *entente cordiale* that sustained a unique moment of European dominance throughout the world. Both in its imperial past and its twenty-first-century future, cooperation with European partners was, and is, crucial to Britain's place in the world.

BIBLIOGRAPHY

Adams, Steven, *The Barbizon School & the Origins of Impressionism* (Phaidon Press: New York, 1994).

Airy, George Biddell, *Mathematical Tracts on Physical Astronomy, the figure of the earth, precession and nutation, and the calculus of variations* (Cambridge University Press: Cambridge, 1826).

Albritton, Vicky and Jonsson, Fredrik Albritton, *Green Victorians: the simple life in John Ruskin's Lake District* (University of Chicago Press: Chicago, 2016).

Alder, Ken, 'A Revolution in Measure: the political economy of the Metric System in France', in M. Norton Wise (ed.), *The Values of Precision* (Princeton University Press: Princeton, 1995), pp. 39-71.

Allgood, G., *China War, 1860: letters and journal* (Longman's, Green, and Co.: London, 1901).

Anglo-French Convention. *A bill for approving and carrying into effect a convention between His Majesty and the President of the French Republic* (House of Commons Papers: No. 205, 1904).

(Anon.), *The Great Industrial Exhibition, in 1851. The disastrous consequences which are likely to arise to the manufacturing trade of this country, from the carrying out of the proposed Great Exhibition of All Nations, in 1851. Address to all ranks of society, more particularly the manufacturers and working classes of Great Britain and Ireland* (London, 1851).

Bibliography

(Anon.), *On the conduct of the war in the East. The Crimean Expedition. Memoir addressed to the government of H. M. the Emperor Napoléon III, by a General Officer* (W. Jeffs: London, 1855).

(Anon.), 'France and England', *Littell's Living Age* (1844-96); 17 Apr., 1858; 725; American Periodicals, pg. 224.

(Anon.), 'An Imperial Pitchfork', *The Spectator*, 28 Aug. 1858 (London, England), pp. 910-11.

(Anon.), *A foreigner's evidence on the China question* (Smith, Elder & Co.: London, 1859).

(Anon.), 'Egypt', *The Times*, 21 Jun. 1859 (London, England), Issue 23338, p. 11.

(Anon.), *Some remarks on our affairs in China* (James Ridgway: London, 1860).

(Anon.), 'The Entente Cordiale', *Punch*, Vol. 38 (31 Mar. 1860), p. 127.

(Anon.), 'Uniform musical pitch. Minutes of a meeting of musicians, amateurs, and others interested in music, held at the house of the society of arts, when the report of the committee appointed by the council of the society was received and adopted', *The Journal of the Society of Arts* 8, no. 417 (1860), pp. 1-8.

(Anon.), 'The Treaty of Commerce was signed at Paris...', *The Times*, 24 Jan. 1860 (London, England) Issue 23524, p. 8.

(Anon.), 'While M. Lesseps was expatiating last week ...', *The Times*, 24 May 1860 (London, England), Issue 23628, p. 8.

(Anon.), 'The Third China War', *New York Times*, 27 Jul. 1860 (New York, United States), p. 4.

(Anon.), 'Tuning-forks and musical pitch', *Chamber's Journal of Popular Literature Science and Arts*, Vol. 34, No. 346, Jul.-Dec. 1860 (London, England), 18 Aug. 1860, pp. 98-101.

(Anon.), 'The Third China War', *New York Times*, 17 Nov. 1860 (New York, United States), p. 4.

(Anon.), 'The China War', *The Examiner*, 1 Dec. 1860 (London, England), No. 2757; p. 753.

(Anon.), 'Fox-hunting in France', *Punch*, Vol. 42 (8 Nov. 1862), p. 188.

(Anon.), *Debate in the House of Commons on the proposed introduction of the Metric System of Weights and Measures, 1st July, 1863, corrected by the respective members who took* *part in the discussion* (Bell and Daldy: London, 1863).

(Anon.), *Debates in both houses of Parliament on the Metric Weights & Measures Bill. Session 1864* (Bell and Daldy: London, 1864).

(Anon.), 'The Schleswig-Holstein War', *The Round Table: a Saturday Review of politics, finance, literature, society, and art* (1863-1869); 27 Feb. 1864; 1; p. 161.

(Anon.), 'The Siege of Paris', *Pall Mall Gazette* (London, England), 14 Nov. 1870; Issue 1795.

(Anon.), 'France and Egypt', *Morning Post* (London, England), 11 Jan. 1883; Issue 34492; p. 5.

(Anon.), 'The Anglo-French Agreement', *Morning Post* (London, England), 28 June 1884; Issue 34950; p. 5.

(Anon.), 'France and Egypt', *The Daily News* (London, England), 30 Sep. 1886; Issue 12628.

(Anon.), 'Ferdinand de Lesseps', *Nature*, 13 Dec. 1894, No. 1311, Vol. 51 (London, England) pp. 155–6.

(Anon.), 'French at Fashoda', *Lloyd's Illustrated Newspaper* (London, England), 18 Sep. 1898; Issue 2913.

(Anon.), 'Marchand leaves Fashoda', *Western Mail* (Cardiff, Wales), 29 Oct. 1898; Issue 983.

(Anon.), 'The Anglo-French Agreement', *York Herald* (York, England), 28 Mar. 1899; Issue 14195; p. 5.

(Anon.), 'Anglo-French Niger-Nile Convention', *New York Times* (New York, United States), 13 May 1899; p. 7.

(Anon.), 'King Edward in Rome and Paris', *The Independent* (London, England), 17 May 1903; 55, 2840, p. 1059.

(Anon.), 'Anglo-French Entente Worries Germany: agreement over Morocco rouses the Pan-German Party', *New York Times* (New York, United States), 17 Apr. 1904; p. 4.

(Anon.), 'L'Entente Cordiale', *The Hospital* (London, England), 8 Oct. 1904, p. 20.

(Anon.), '*The Anglo-French Convention and its sequel*, by Sir Harry Johnston', *The Review of Reviews*, June 1904; 29, 174; p. 583.

(Anon.), 'Anglo-French Relations', *Outlook* (London, England), 5 July 1913; 104: 10; p. 493.

Aronson, Theo, *Queen Victoria and the Bonapartes* (Cassell: London, 1972).

Ashburner, F., 'Escoffier, Georges Auguste (1846–1935), master chef and writer on cookery.' *Oxford Dictionary of National Biography*. 23 Sep. 2004; Accessed 2 Apr. 2020. https://www.oxforddnb.

com/view/10.1093/ref:odnb/9780198614128.001.0001/odnb-9780198614128-e-50441.

Barnwell, P. S., Geoffrey Tyack, and William Whyte (eds.), *George Gilbert Scott, 1811-1878: an architect and his influence* (Donington: Shaun Tyas, 2014).

Barry, Alfred, *The Lessons of the war, and the duties of the peace. A sermon preached at the parish church, Leeds, on the evening of Sunday, May 4th, 1856, being the day appointed for public thanksgiving on the restoration of peace* (Thomas Harrison: Leeds, 1856).

Bates, Darrell, *The Fashoda Incident of 1898: encounter on the Nile* (Oxford University Press: Oxford, 1984).

Baylen, Joseph O. and Conway, Alan (eds.), *Soldier-Surgeon: the Crimean War letters of Dr Douglas A. Reid, 1855–1856* (University of Tennessee Press: Knoxville, 1968).

Bazancourt, Baron de, *The Crimean Expedition, to the capture of Sebastopol. Chronicles of the war in the East, from its commencement to the signing of the Treaty of Paris*, Vols. I and II (Sampson Low, Son, & Co.: London).

Bektas, Yakup, 'The Crimean War as a technological enterprise', *Notes and Records*, 71 (2017), pp. 233-62.

Bickers, Robert, *The Scramble for China: foreign devils in the Qing Empire, 1832–1914* (Penguin: London, 2012).

Birch, Lionel, *Stanhope A. Forbes A.R.A., and Elizabeth Stanhope Forbes, A.R.W.S.* (Cassell: London, 1906).

Blake, R. L. V. Ffrench, *The Crimean War* (Sphere Books Limited: London, 1971).

Boyce, Robert, 'Behind the façade of the Entente Cordiale after the Great War', in Antoine Capet (ed.), *Britain, France and the Entente Cordiale since 1904* (Palgrave: London, 2006), pp. 41-63.

Bradley, Margaret and Perrin, Fernand, 'Charles Dupin's study visits to the British Isles, 1816-1824', *Technology and Culture*, Vol. 32, No. 1 (Jan. 1991), pp. 47-68.

Bresler, Fenton, *Napoléon III: a life* (Harper Collins Publishers: London, 1999).

Brown, David, 'Palmerston and Anglo-French Relations, 1846-1865', *Diplomacy and Statecraft*, 17:4 (2006), pp. 675-92.

Brown, George, *Memoranda and observations on the Crimean War, 1854-6, and notes on Mr. Kinglake's second volume* (James

Watson: London, 1879).

Brown, Roger Glenn, *Fashoda Reconsidered: the impact of domestic politics on French policy in Africa, 1893-1898* (John Hopkins University Press: Baltimore, 1970).

Burn, W. L., *The Age of Equipoise: a study of the mid-Victorian generation* (Taylor & Francis Group: London, 2017).

Butler, Josephine Elizabeth Grey, *Recollections of George Butler* (J. W. Arrowsmith: London, 1892).

Cannadine, David, *Victorious Century: the United Kingdom* (Allen Lane: London, 2017).

Conrad, Joseph, *The Secret Agent: a simple tale* (Penguin: London, 2012).

Cooper, Barbara M., '"Our Anglo-Saxon Colleagues": French administration of Niger and the Constraining embrace of Northern Nigeria', in James R. Fichter (ed.), *British and French Colonialism in Africa, Asia and the Middle East: connected empires across the eighteenth to the twentieth centuries* (Palgrave Macmillan: Basingstoke, 2019), pp. 35-64.

Cox, Edward Franklin, 'The Metric System: a quarter-century of acceptance (1851-1876)', *Osiris*, Vol. 13 (1958), pp. 358-79.

Cantor, Geoffrey, *Religion and the Great Exhibition of 1851* (Oxford University Press: Oxford, 2011).

Cantor, Geoffrey (ed.), *The Great Exhibition: a documentary history*, Vol. 4 of 4 (Pickering & Chatto: London, 2013).

Capet, Antoine (ed.), *Britain, France and the Entente Cordiale since 1904* (Palgrave: London, 2006).

Cardwell, Donald S. L., *From Watt to Clausius: the rise of thermodynamics in the early industrial age* (Heinemann: London, 1971).

Carnot, Sadi, *Reflexions on the motive power of fire: a critical edition with the surviving scientific manuscripts* (Trans.) Robert Fox (Manchester University Press: Manchester, 1986).

Chafer, Tony and Cummin, Gordon, 'Beyond Fashoda: Anglo-French security cooperation in Africa since Saint-Malo', *International Affairs (Royal Institute of International Affairs, 1944-)*, Vol. 86, No. 5 (Sep. 2010), pp. 1129-47.

Chamberlain, M. (27 May 2010). 'Gordon, George Hamilton-, fourth earl of Aberdeen (1784–1860), prime minister and scholar.' *Oxford Dictionary of National Biography*. Ed. Retrieved 29 Mar. 2019, from http://www.oxforddnb.com.ezp.lib.cam.

Bibliography

ac.uk/view/10.1093/ref:odnb/9780198614128.001.0001/odnb-9780198614128-e-11044.

Chassaigne, P. and Dockrill, M. (eds.), *Anglo-French relations, 1898-1998: from Fashoda to Jospin* (Palgrave Macmillan: Basingstoke, 2002).

Conlin, Jonathan, *Tales of Two Cities: Paris, London and the birth of the modern city* (Atlantic Books: London, 2013).

Correspondence respecting the Anglo-French financial control (Houses of Parliament Paper: Egypt, No. 20, 1882) (Harrison and Sons: London, 1882).

Croly, George, 'The Preacher No. III. England's Greatness. A Sermon, delivered on Sunday morning, May 4, 1856', *The Penny Pulpit*, No. 2,592, 5 June 1856 (London, England), pp. 388-92.

Crosland, Maurice, *Gay-Lussac: scientist and bourgeois* (Cambridge University Press: Cambridge, 1978).

David, Saul, *Victoria's Wars: the rise of empire* (Penguin Books: London, 2006).

De Lesseps, Ferdinand, *The Isthmus of Suez Question* (Longman, Brown, Green, and Longman's: London, 1855).

De Lesseps, Ferdinand, *Inquiry into the opinions of the commercial classes of Great Britain on the Suez ship canal* (John Weale: London, 1857).

De Lesseps, Ferdinand, *The History of the Suez Canal: a personal narrative* (William Blackwood and Sons: Edinburgh, 1876).

Denmark and Germany. No. 2. Correspondence respecting the affair of the Duchies of Holstein, Laurenburg, and Schleswig (Harrison and Sons: London, 1864).

Dickens, Charles, *A Tale of Two Cities* (Macmillan: London, 2003).

Dunham, Arthur Louis, *The Anglo-French Treaty of Commerce of 1860 and the progress of the industrial revolution in France* (University of Michigan Press: Ann Arbor, 1930).

Duplais, Pierre, *A treatise on the manufacture and distillation of alcoholic liquors* (Henry Carey Baird: Philadelphia, 1871).

Eagles, Stuart, 'Political legacies', in Francis O'Gorman (ed.), *The Cambridge Companion to John Ruskin* (Cambridge University Press: Cambridge, 2015), pp. 249-62.

Echard, William E., *Napoléon III and the Concert of Europe* (Louisiana State University Press: Baton Rouge, 1983).

'Economist', 'The Treaty with France', *The Times*, 6 Feb. 1860

(London, England) Issue 23535, p. 7.

Edsall, Nicholas C., *Richard Cobden: Independent Radical* (Harvard University Press: Massachusetts, 1986).

Farnie, D. A., *East and West of Suez: the Suez Canal in History, 1854-1956* (Oxford University Press: Oxford, 1969).

Fichter, James R. (ed.), *British and French Colonialism in Africa, Asia and the Middle East: connected empires across the eighteenth to the twentieth centuries* (Palgrave Macmillan: Basingstoke, 2019).

Fichter, James R., 'Britain and France, connected empires', in James R. Fichter (ed.), *British and French Colonialism in Africa, Asia and the Middle East: connected empires across the eighteenth to the twentieth centuries* (Palgrave Macmillan: Basingstoke, 2019), pp. 1-15.

Fichter, James R., 'Imperial Interdependence on Indochina's Maritime Periphery: France and coal in Ceylon, Singapore, and Hong Kong, 1859-1895', in James R. Fichter (ed.), *British and French Colonialism in Africa, Asia and the Middle East: connected empires across the eighteenth to the twentieth centuries* (Palgrave Macmillan: Basingstoke, 2019), pp. 151-79.

Fox, Caroline, *Stanhope Forbes and the Newlyn School* (David & Charles: Newton Abbot, 1993).

Fox, Robert, 'Introduction', in Sadi Carnot, *Reflexions on the motive power of fire: a critical edition with the surviving scientific manuscripts* (Trans.) Robert Fox (Manchester University Press: Manchester, 1986), pp. 1-44.

Gamble, Cynthia, 'France and Belgium', in Francis O'Gorman (ed.), *The Cambridge Companion to John Ruskin* (Cambridge University Press: Cambridge, 2015), pp. 66-80.

Geppert, Dominik, William Mulligan, and Andreas Rose (eds.), *The Wars Before the Great War: conflict and international politics before the outbreak of the First world war* (Cambridge University Press: Cambridge, 2015).

Gifford, Prosser and Louis, William Roger (eds.), *France and Britain in Africa: imperial rivalry and colonial rule* (Yale University Press: New Haven, 1972).

Gillin, Edward, 'Prophets of Progress: authority in the scientific projections and religious realizations of the "Great Eastern" steamship', *Technology and Culture*, Vol. 56, No. 4 (October 2015), pp. 928-56.

Glencross, Matthew, *The State Visits of Edward VII: reinventing royal diplomacy for the twentieth century* (Palgrave Macmillan: Basingstoke, 2015).

Goldie, Sue M. (ed.), *'I have done my duty': Florence Nightingale in the Crimean War, 1854-56* (Manchester University Press: Manchester, 1987).

Gooch, Brison D., *The New Bonapartist Generals in the Crimean War: distrust and decision-making in the Anglo-French alliance* (Martinus Nijhoff: The Hague, 1959).

Goode, James Hubbard, 'The Fashoda Crisis: a survey of Anglo-French Imperial Policy on the Upper Nile Question, 1882-1899' (PhD thesis: North Texas State University, 1971).

Greenhalgh, Elizabeth, *Victory Through Coalition: Britain and France during the First World War* (Cambridge University Press: Cambridge, 2005).

Gribenski, Fanny and Gillin, Edward, 'The politics of musical standardization in nineteenth-century France and Britain', *Past and Present*, Vol. 251, Issue 1, (May 2021), pp. 153-87.

Grattan-Guinness, I., 'Mathematics and mathematical physics from Cambridge, 1815-40: a survey of the achievements and of the French influences', in P. M. Harman (ed.), *Wranglers and Physicists: studies on Cambridge mathematical physics in the nineteenth century* (Manchester University Press: Manchester 1985), pp. 84-111.

Guymer, Laurence, 'The wedding planners: Lord Aberdeen, Henry Bulwer, and the Spanish marriages, 1841-1846', *Diplomacy & Statecraft*, 21:4 (2010), pp. 549-73.

Guymer, Laurence, 'Pressing the French and defending the Palmerstonian line: Lord William Harvey and *The Times*', *Historical Research*, Vol. 87, No. 235 (Feb. 2014), pp. 116-133.

Hamilton, C. I., *Anglo-French Naval Rivalry, 1840-1870* (Clarendon Press: Oxford, 1993).

Harding, Robert Graham, 'The Establishment of Champagne in Britain, 1860-1914' (DPhil., thesis: University of Oxford, 2018).

Harman, P. M. (ed.), *Wranglers and Physicists: studies on Cambridge mathematical physics in the nineteenth century* (Manchester University Press: Manchester, 1985).

Hayne, M. B., *The French Foreign Office and the Origins of the First World War, 1898-1914* (Oxford University Press: Oxford, 1993).

Heitzman, Matthew, '"A Long and Constant Fusion of the Two

Great Nations": Dickens, the Crossing, and *A Tale of Two Cities*', *Dickens Studies Annual*, Vol. 45 (2014), pp. 275-92.

Herkomer, Sir Hubert von, and Frederick Goodall, 'Kitchener, Horatio Herbert, Earl Kitchener of Khartoum (1850–1916).' *Oxford Dictionary of National Biography*. 23 Sep. 2004; Accessed 2 Apr. 2020. https://www.oxforddnb.com/view/10.1093/ref:odnb/9780198614128.001.0001/odnb-9780198614128-e-1001401.

Hewitt, Martin (ed.), *An Age of Equipoise? Re-assessing mid-Victorian Britain* (Routledge: London, 2000).

Hewitt, Martin, 'Prologue: reassessing *The Age of Equipoise*', in Martin Hewitt (ed.), *An Age of Equipoise? Re-assessing mid-Victorian Britain* (Routledge: London, 2000), pp. 1-38.

Hewitt, Martin (ed.), *The Victorian World* (Routledge: London, 2012).

Hicks, Geoffrey, 'An overlooked entente: Lord Malmesbury, Anglo-French relations and the Conservatives' recognition of the Second Empire, 1852', *History*, Vol. 92, No, 2 (309) (2007), pp. 187-206, 188-93.

Hicks, Geoffrey, 'The Struggle for Stability: the fourteenth earl and Europe, 1852-1868', in Geoffrey

Hicks, Geoffrey (ed.), *Conservatism and British Foreign Policy, 1820-1920: the Derbys and their world* (2011).

Hicks, Geoffrey, 'Disraeli, Derby and the Suez Canal, 1875: some myths reassessed', *History*, Vol. 97, No. 2 (326) (April 2012), pp. 182-203.

Hiller, James K., 'The 1904 Anglo-French Newfoundland Fisheries Convention: another look', *Acadiensis*, Vol. 25:1 (Autumn 1995), pp. 82-98.

Hind, Charles Lewis, *Stanhope A. Forbes, Royal Academician* (Virtue & Company: London, 1911).

Hopkins, Anthony G., 'The Victorians and Africa: a reconsideration of the occupation of Egypt, 1882', *Journal of African History*, 27.2 (1986), pp. 363–391.

Horn, Martin, 'External finance in Anglo-French relations in the First World War, 1914-1917', *The International History Review*, Vol. 17, No. 1 (Feb. 1995), pp. 51-77.

Howard, Michael, *Franco-Prussian War: German Invasion of France, 1870-1871* (Routledge: London, 1991).

Howe, Anthony and Morgan, Simon (eds.), *The Letters of Richard Cobden*, Vol. 3 of 4 (Oxford University Press: Oxford, 2012).

Howe, Anthony and Morgan, Simon (eds.), *The Letters of Richard Cobden*, Vol. 4 of 4 (Oxford University Press: Oxford, 2015).

Howse, Derek, *Greenwich Time and the Longitude* (Philip Wilson: London, 1997).

Hugo, Victor, 'The Chinese Expedition: Victor Hugo on the sack of the Summer Palace – letter from Hugo to Captain Butler', 25 Nov. 1861.

Iliasu, A. A., 'The Cobden-Chevalier Commercial Treaty of 1860', *The Historical Journal*, XIV, 1 (1971), pp. 67-98.

Jantzen, Hans, *High Gothic: a comparative analysis of the Great Gothic Cathedrals of Chartres, Rheims, and Amiens* (Constable and Co: Letchworth, 1962).

Jennings, Eric T., 'Britain and free France in Africa, 1940-1943', in James R. Fichter (ed.), *British and French Colonialism in Africa, Asia and the Middle East: connected empires across the eighteenth to the twentieth centuries* (Palgrave Macmillan: Basingstoke, 2019), pp. 277-96.

'J. P.', 'The result of the Washington Conference', *Graphic* (London, England), 1 Aug. 1885; Issue 818.

Kennedy, Paul, 'The Costs and Benefits of British Imperialism, 1846-1914', *Past & Present*, Vol. 125 (Nov. 1989), pp. 186-192.

Kennedy, Paul, *The Rise and Fall of British Naval Mastery*, 3rd edition (FontanaPress: London, 1991).

Kent, David, 'Containing disorder in the "Age of Equipoise": troops, trains and the telegraph', *Social History*, 38:3 (August 2013), pp. 308-27.

Kent, John, *The Internationalization of Colonialism: Britain, France, and Black Africa, 1939-1956* (Clarendon Press: Oxford, 1992).

Kern, Stephen, *The Culture of Time and Space, 1880-1918* (Harvard University Press: Harvard, 2003).

Kiernan, Michael T., *The Engineers of Cornwall at the Mines of Pontgibaud in France* (Redruth Cornish Global Migration Programme: Redruth, undated).

Kießling, Fredrich, 'Anglo-French relations and the wars before the war', in Dominik Geppert, William Mulligan, and Andreas Rose (eds.), *The Wars Before the Great War: conflict and international politics before the outbreak of the First World War* (Cambridge University Press: Cambridge, 2015), pp. 283-97.

Lampe, Markus, 'Explaining nineteenth-century bilateralism: economic and political determinants of the Cobden-Chevalier network', *Economic History Review* 64:2 (2011), pp. 644-668.

Leggett, Don, *Shaping the Royal Navy: technology, authority and naval architecture, c. 1830-1906* (Manchester University Press: Manchester, 2015).

Lehman, Jörg, 'Civilization versus Barbarism: the Franco-Prussian War in French History Textbooks, 1875-1895', *Journal of Educational Media, Memory & Society*, Vol. 7, No. 1 (Spring, 2015), pp. 51-65.

Lewis, David Levering, *Race to Fashoda* (Henry & Company: New York, 2001).

Lightman, Bernard (ed.), *Victorian Science in Context* (University of Chicago Press: Chicago, 1997).

Low, Charles Rathbone, *General Lord Wolseley (of Cairo), G.C.B., G.C.M.G., D.C. L., LL.D. A memoir* (Richard Bentley and Son: London, 1883).

Mace, Harry J., 'The Eurafrique Initiative: Ernest Bevin and Anglo-French relations in the Foreign Office, 1945-1950', *Diplomacy & Statecraft*, Vol. 28, Issue 4 (2017), pp. 601-18.

Macksey, Richard, 'Introduction', in Marcel Proust, *On Reading Ruskin: prefaces to La Bible d'Amiens and Sésame et Les Lys with selections from the notes to the translated texts* (trans.) Jean Autret, William Burford, and Phillip J. Wolfe (Yale University Press: New Haven, 1987), pp. xiii-liii.

Maneglier, Hervé, *Paris Impérial – La vie quotidienne sous le Second Empire* (Armand Colin: Paris, 2009).

Mann, Michael, *China, 1860* (Michael Russell: Salisbury, 1989).

Marsden, Ben and Smith, Crosbie, *Engineering Empires: a cultural history of technology in nineteenth-century Britain* (Palgrave Macmillan: Basingstoke, 2005).

Marx, Karl, 'Persia-China', *New York Daily Tribune*, 5 Jun. 1857, in Dona Torr (ed.), *Marx on China, 1853-1860: articles from the New York Daily Tribune* (Lawrence & Wishart: 1968), pp. 45-51.

Marx, Karl, 'Free trade and monopoly', *New York Daily Tribune*, 25 Sep. 1858, in Dona Torr (ed.), *Marx on China, 1853-1860: articles from the New York Daily Tribune* (Lawrence & Wishart: 1968), pp. 56-9.

Marx, Karl, 'Another civilization war', *New York Daily Tribune*, 10 Oct. 1859, in Dona Torr (ed.), *Marx on China, 1853-1860: articles from the New York Daily Tribune* (Lawrence & Wishart: 1968), pp. 78-82.

Massie, Alastair, *The National Army Museum Book of the Crimean War: the untold stories* (Sidgwick & Jackson: London, 2004).

Massie, Robert K., *Dreadnought: Britain, Germany, and the Coming of the Great War* (Jonathan Cape: London, 1992).

McConkey, Kenneth, 'Forbes, Stanhope Alexander (1857–1947), genre painter.' *Oxford Dictionary of National Biography.* 23 Sep. 2004; Accessed 2 Apr. 2020. https://www.oxforddnb.com/view/10.1093/ref:odnb/9780198614128.001.0001/odnb-9780198614128-e-33194.

McDonald, Lynn, 'Florence Nightingale, statistics and the Crimean War', *Journal of the Royal Statistical Society*, Series A, 177, Part 3 (2014), pp. 569-86.

Merriman, H. G., *God's power and a nation's presumption. A sermon, preached in the parish church of Badger Salop, on the first day, Wednesday, 21st of March, 1855* (John Henry Parker: London, 1855).

Mill, John Stuart, *On Liberty and The Subjection of Women* (Penguin Books: London, 2006).

Miller, Gregory D., *The Shadow of the Past: reputation and military alliances before the First World War* (Cornell University: Ithaca, 2012).

Moncan, Patrice de, *Le Paris d'Haussmann* (Les Éditions du Mécène, 2002).

Morgan, Kenneth O., 'Lloyd George and Clemenceau: Prima Donnas in Partnership', in, Antoine Capet (ed.), *Britain, France and the Entente Cordiale since 1904* (Palgrave: London, 2006), pp. 28-40.

Mosse, W. E., 'Queen Victoria and Her Ministers in the Schleswig-Holstein Crisis 1863-1864', *English Historical Review*, Vol. 78, No. 304 (Apr. 1963), pp. 263-83.

Mossman, Samuel, *General Gordon's private diary of his exploits in China; amplified* (Sampson Low, Marston, Searle, & Rivington: London, 1885).

Mowat, R. C., 'From Liberalism to Imperialism: the case of Egypt 1875-1887', *The Historical Journal*, XVI, 1 (1973), pp. 109-24.

Mutibwa, Phares M., 'Britain's "Abandonment" of Madagascar: the Anglo-French Convention of August 1890', *Transafrican Journal of History*, Vol. 3, No. 1/2 (1973), pp. 96-111.

Newsinger, John, 'Liberal Imperialism and the Occupation of Egypt in 1882', *Race & Class*, 49.3 (2008), pp. 54–75.

Nye, John V. C., *War, Wine, and Taxes: the political economy of*

Anglo-French trade, 1689-1900 (Princeton University Press: Princeton, 2007).

O'Brien, Patrick K., 'The Costs and Benefits of British Imperialism, 1846-1914', *Past & Present*, Vol. 120 (Aug. 1988), pp. 163-200.

O'Gorman, Francis (ed.), *The Cambridge Companion to John Ruskin* (Cambridge University Press: Cambridge, 2015).

Otte, T. G., 'From "War-in-Sight" to Nearly War: Anglo-French relations in the age of high imperialism, 1875-1898', *Diplomacy & Statecraft*, Vol. 17, Issue 4 (2006), pp. 693-714.

Otte, T. G., *The Foreign Office Mind: the making of British foreign policy, 1865-1914* (Cambridge University Press: Cambridge, 2011).

Otte, T. G., 'Entente diplomacy v détente, 1911-1914', in Dominik Geppert, William Mulligan, and Andreas Rose (eds.), *The Wars Before the Great War: conflict and international politics before the outbreak of the First World War* (Cambridge University Press: Cambridge, 2015), pp. 264-82.

Palmer, Allen W., 'Negotiation and Resistance in Global Networks: 1884 International Meridian Conference', *Mass Communication and Society*, Vol. 5, Iss. 1 (2002), pp. 7-24.

Parry, J. P., 'The Impact of Napoleon III on British Politics, 1851-1880', *Transactions of the Royal Historical Society* (2000), pp. 147-75.

Perry, John, 'A shared sea: the axes of French and British Imperialism in the Mediterranean, 1798-1914', in James R. Fichter (ed.), *British and French Colonialism in Africa, Asia and the Middle East: connected empires across the eighteenth to the twentieth centuries* (Palgrave Macmillan: Basingstoke, 2019), pp. 113-130.

Philpott, William, 'Britain and France go to war: Anglo-French relations on the Western Front, 1914-1918', *War in History*, 2:1 (1995), pp. 43-64.

Philpott, William J., 'The making of the military entente, 1904-14', *English Historical Review*, Vol. CXXVIII, No. 534 (Oct. 2013), pp. 1155-85.

Pinkney, David H., *Napoléon III and the rebuilding of Paris* (Princeton University Press: Princeton, 1958).

Port, M. H., 'George Gilbert Scott: state architect?', in P. S. Barnwell, Geoffrey Tyack, and William Whyte (eds.), *George Gilbert Scott, 1811-1878: an architect and his influence* (Donington: Shaun Tyas, 2014), pp. 172-92.

Bibliography

Porter, Bernard, *The Battle of the Styles: society, culture and the design of the New Foreign Office, 1855-1861* (Bloomsbury: London, 2011).

Powell, Harry, *Recollections of a young soldier during the Crimean War* (Upstone and Doe: Oxford, 1876).

Price, Roger, *The French Second Empire: an anatomy of political power* (Cambridge University Press: Cambridge, 2001).

Proust, Marcel, *On Reading Ruskin: prefaces to La Bible d'Amiens and Sésame et Les Lys with selections from the notes to the translated texts* (trans.) Jean Autret, William Burford, and Phillip J. Wolfe (Yale University Press: New Haven, 1987).

Proust, Marcel, 'Preface to John Ruskin's *Bible of Amiens*', in Marcel Proust, *On Reading Ruskin: prefaces to La Bible d'Amiens and Sésame et Les Lys with selections from the notes to the translated texts* (trans.) Jean Autret, William Burford, and Phillip J. Wolfe (Yale University Press: New Haven, 1987), pp. 5-71.

Queen Victoria's Journals Online, Vols. 31, 39, and 40.

Raymond, Dora Neill, *British Policy and Opinion during the Franco-Prussian War* (Columbia University: New York, 1921).

Report from the Select Committee on weights and measures; together with the proceedings of the committee, minutes of evidence, appendix, and index, House of Commons Paper 411 (1862).

Rich, Rachel, *Bourgeois Consumption: food, space and identity in London and Paris, 1850-1914* (Manchester University Press: Manchester, 2011).

Riker, T. W., 'A Survey of British Policy in the Fashoda Crisis', *Political Science Quarterly*, Vol. 44, No. 1 (Mar. 1929), pp. 54-78.

Robbins, Keith, 'Grey, Edward, Viscount Grey of Fallodon (1862–1933), politician, countryman, and author.' *Oxford Dictionary of National Biography*. 23 Sep. 2004; Accessed 2 Apr. 2020. https://www.oxforddnb.com/view/10.1093/ref:odnb/9780198614128.001.0001/odnb-9780198614128-e-33570.

Robinson, Frederick, *Diary of the Crimean War* (Richard Bentley: London, 1856).

Ruskin, John, *On the Nature of Gothic Architecture: and herein of the true functions of the workman in art* (Smith, Elder, & Co.: London, 1854).

Ruskin, John, *Our fathers have told us. Part 1: The Bible of Amiens* (George Allen: Sunnyside, Orpington, 1881).

Russell, W. H., *Complete History of the Russian War, from its commencement to its close: giving a graphic picture of the great drama of war* (John G. Wells: New York, 1856).

Sandiford, Keith A. P., 'The British Cabinet and the Schleswig-Holstein Crisis, 1863-1864', *History*, Vol. 58, No. 194 (1973), pp. 360-83.

Schaffer, Simon, 'Metrology, Metrication, and Victorian Values', in Bernard Lightman (ed.), *Victorian Science in Context* (University of Chicago Press: Chicago, 1997), pp. 438-74.

Semmel, Bernard, 'Parliament and the Metric System', *Isis*, Vol. 54, No. 1 (Mar. 1963), pp. 125-33.

Sharp, Alan and Stone, Glyn (eds.), *Anglo-French relations in the twentieth century: rivalry and cooperation* (Routledge: Abingdon, 1999).

Sinclair, John, *The war in 1855. A sermon, preached on Wednesday, March 21, 1855, in the parish church of St. Mary Abbotts, Kensington* (Rivingtons: London, 1855).

Small, Ian and Crossley, Ceri (eds.), *Studies in Anglo-French cultural relations* (Palgrave Macmillan: Basingstoke, 1988).

Smith, Crosbie, *Coal, Steam and Ships: engineering, enterprise and empire on the nineteenth-century seas* (Cambridge University Press: Cambridge, 2018).

Smith, Hillas, *The Unknown Frenchman: the story of Marchand and Fashoda* (Book Guild Publishing: Lewes, 2001).

Spencer-Churchill, Winston, 'The Fashoda Incident', *The North American Review*, Vol. 167, No. 505 (Dec. 1898), pp. 736-43.

Stamp, Gavin, *Gothic for the Steam Age: an illustrated biography of George Gilbert Scott* (Aurum Press: London, 2015).

Standage, Tom, *The Victorian Internet: The Remarkable Story of the Telegraph and the Nineteenth Century's On-Line Pioneers* (Walker & Company: London, 1998).

Steele, D. (2009, May 21). 'Temple, Henry John, third Viscount Palmerston (1784–1865), prime minister.' *Oxford Dictionary of National Biography* Ed. Retrieved 29 Mar. 2019, from http://www.oxforddnb.com.ezp.lib.cam.ac.uk/view/10.1093/ref:odnb/9780198614128.001.0001/odnb-9780198614128-e-27112.

Stourton, James, *British Embassies: their diplomatic and architectural history* (Quarto Publishing: London, 2017).

Bibliography

Studio, René, 'Ritz, César Jean (1850–1918).' *Oxford Dictionary of National Biography*. 23 Sep. 2004; Accessed 2 Apr. 2020. https://www.oxforddnb.com/view/10.1093/ref:odnb/9780198614128.001.0001/odnb-9780198614128-e-1005507.

Taylor, M. (2009, May 21). Cobden, Richard (1804-1865), manufacturer and politician. Oxford Dictionary of National Biography. Ed. Retrieved 29 Mar. 2019, from http://www.oxforddnb.com.ezp.lib.cam.ac.uk/view/10.1093/ref:odnb/9780198614128.001.0001/odnb-9780198614128-e-5741.

Taylor, Philip, https://www.rmg.co.uk/discover/explore/astronomers-and-anarchist-bomber

Tena-Junginto, Antonio, Markus Lampe, and Felipe Tâmega Fernandes, 'How much trade liberalization was there in the world before and after Cobden-Chevalier', *Journal of Economic History*, Vol. 72, No. 3 (Sep. 2012), pp. 708-40.

Thomas, Martin, and Richard Toye, 'Arguing about intervention: a comparison of British and French rhetoric surrounding the 1882 and 1956 invasions of Egypt', *Historical Journal*, 58.4 (2015), pp. 1081–1113.

'T. M. J.', 'The Schleswig-Holstein difficulty: is a general European war probable?', *The Merchants' Magazine and Commercial Review* (1839-1870); 1 Feb. 1864; 50, 2, p. 119.

Todd, David, 'A French Imperial Meridian, 1814-1870', *Past and Present*, No. 210 (Feb. 2011), pp. 155-86.

Todd, David, *Free Trade and its Enemies in France, 1814-1851* (Cambridge University Press: Cambridge, 2015).

Tombs, Robert and Chabel, Emilie (eds.), *Britain and France in Two World Wars: truth, myth and memory* (Bloomsbury: London, 2013).

Torr, Dona (ed.), *Marx on China, 1853-1860: articles from the New York Daily Tribune* (Lawrence & Wishart: 1968).

Varouxakis, Georgios, *Victorian political thought on France and the French* (Palgrave: Basingstoke, 2002), pp. 80-1.

Verney, Frederick, 'Note on the Anglo-French Convention in Siam', *The Nineteenth Century: a monthly review* (Mar., 1877-Dec. 1900); Feb. 1896; 39, 228; pp. 332-4.

Walkowitz, Judith, *Prostitution and Victorian Society: women, class, and the state* (Cambridge University Press: Cambridge, 1980).

Walton, Whitney, *France at the Crystal Palace: Bourgeois taste and artisan manufacture in the nineteenth century* (University of California Press: Berkeley, 1992).

Wawro, Geoffrey, *The Franco-Prussian War: the German conquest of France in 1870-1871* (Cambridge University Press: Cambridge, 2003).

Weeks, Willet, *The Man Who Made Paris: the illustrated biography of Georges-Eugene Haussmann* (London House: London, 2000).

Weights and Measures. A bill for decimalizing our existing system of weights and measures, and for establishing an accordance between them and those of foreign countries, House of Commons Papers 120 (1863).

Wells, H. G., *Classics Collection 1: The Time Machine, The Island of Doctor Moreau, The War of the Worlds, The First Men in the Moon, The Invisible Man* (Gollancz: London, 2010).

Whewell, William, *Inaugural Lecture, November 26, 1851, the general bearing of the Great Exhibition on the progress of art and science* (David Bogue: London, 1852).

White, John Albert, *Transition to Global Rivalry: alliance diplomacy and the Quadruple Entente, 1895-1907* (Cambridge University Press: Cambridge, 1995).

Wilson, David B., 'The educational matrix: physics education at early-Victorian Cambridge, Edinburgh and Glasgow Universities', in P. M. Harman (ed.), *Wranglers and Physicists: studies on Cambridge mathematical physics in the nineteenth century* (Manchester University Press: Manchester, 1985), pp. 12-48.

Wilson, Keith M., *The Policy of the Entente: essays on the determinants of British Foreign Policy, 1904-1914* (Cambridge University Press: Cambridge, 1985).

Wise, M. Norton (ed.), *The Values of Precision* (Princeton University Press: Princeton, 1995).

Wolseley, G. J., *Narrative of the war with China in 1860* (Longman, Green, Longman, and Roberts: London, 1862).

Woodham-Smith, Cecil, *The Reason Why* (Penguin Books: London, 1958).

ENDNOTES

Introduction: Europe Ascendant
1. W. L. Burn, *The Age of Equipoise: a study of the mid-Victorian generation* (Taylor & Francis Group: London, 2017). First published in 1964.
2. Martin Hewitt, 'Prologue: reassessing *The Age of Equipoise*', in Martin Hewitt (ed.), *An Age of Equipoise? Re-assessing mid-Victorian Britain*, (Routledge: London, 2000), pp. 1-38, 5-6; for studies of Britain at this time, also see Martin Hewitt (ed.), *The Victorian World*, (Routledge: London, 2012).
3. David Kent, 'Containing disorder in the "Age of Equipoise": troops, trains and the telegraph', *Social History*, 38:3, (August, 2013), pp. 308-27, 310 and 313-5.
4. Paul Kennedy, *The Rise and Fall of British Naval Mastery*, 3rd edition (FontanaPress: London, 1991), p. 175.
5. Ibid., p. 176.
6. Ibid., pp. 183-5.
7. Ibid., pp. 180-2.
8. Most prominently demonstrated in, Tom Standage, *The Victorian Internet: The Remarkable Story of the Telegraph and the Nineteenth Century's On-Line Pioneers*, (Walker & Company: London, 1998).

9. D. Steele, (2009, May 21). Temple, Henry John, third Viscount Palmerston (1784–1865), prime minister. *Oxford Dictionary of National Biography*. Ed. Retrieved 29 Mar. 2019, from http://www.oxforddnb.com.ezp.lib.cam.ac.uk/view/10.1093/ref:odnb/9780198614128.001.0001/odnb-9780198614128-e-27112.
10. David Cannadine, *Victorious Century: the United Kingdom*, (Allen Lane: London, 2017), pp. 245-52.
11. D. Steele, (2009, May 21). Temple, Henry John, third Viscount Palmerston (1784–1865), prime minister. *Oxford Dictionary of National Biography*. Ed. Retrieved 29 Mar. 2019, from http://www.oxforddnb.com.ezp.lib.cam.ac.uk/view/10.1093/ref:odnb/9780198614128.001.0001/odnb-9780198614128-e-27112.
12. Quoted in, Kennedy, *The Rise and Fall of British Naval Mastery*, p. 198.
13. Scott quoted in M. H. Port, 'George Gilbert Scott: state architect?', in P. S. Barnwell, Geoffrey Tyack, and William Whyte (eds.), *George Gilbert Scott, 1811-1878: an architect and his influence*, (Donington: Shaun Tyas, 2014), pp. 172-92, 177.
14. Gavin Stamp, *Gothic for the Steam Age: an illustrated biography of George Gilbert Scott*, (Aurum Press: London, 2015), pp. 64 and 67; also see Bernard Porter, *The Battle of the Styles: society, culture and the design of the New Foreign Office, 1855-1861*, (Bloomsbury: London, 2011).
15. D. Steele, (2009, May 21). Temple, Henry John, third Viscount Palmerston (1784–1865), prime minister. *Oxford Dictionary of National Biography*. Ed. Retrieved 29 Mar. 2019, from http://www.oxforddnb.com.ezp.lib.cam.ac.uk/view/10.1093/ref:odnb/9780198614128.001.0001/odnb-9780198614128-e-27112; on British and French interests in the Mediterranean see, John Perry, 'A shared sea: the axes of French and British Imperialism in the Mediterranean, 1798-1914', in James R. Fichter (ed.), *British and French Colonialism in Africa, Asia and the Middle East: connected empires across the eighteenth to the twentieth centuries* (Palgrave Macmillan: Basingstoke, 2019), pp. 113-30.
16. Quoted in J. P. Parry, 'The Impact of Napoleon III on British Politics, 1851-1880', *Transactions of the Royal Historical Society* (2000), pp. 147-75, 149.

17. On the renovation of Paris see, Patrice de Moncan, *Le Paris d'Haussmann* (Les Éditions du Mécène, 2002); Hervé Maneglier, *Paris Impérial – La vie quotidienne sous le Second Empire* (Armand Colin: Paris, 2009); David H. Pinkney, *Napoléon III and the rebuilding of Paris* (Princeton University Press: Princeton, 1958); Willet Weeks, *The Man Who Made Paris: the illustrated biography of Georges-Eugene Haussmann* (London House: London, 2000).
18. James Stourton, *British Embassies: their diplomatic and architectural history* (Quarto Publishing: London, 2017), pp. 24 and 27-8.
19. For a comparison see, Jonathan Conlin, *Tales of Two Cities: Paris, London and the birth of the modern city* (Atlantic Books: London, 2013).
20. David Todd, 'A French Imperial Meridian, 1814-1870', *Past and Present*, No. 210 (Feb., 2011), pp. 155-86, 155-63.
21. See James R. Fichter, 'Britain and France, connected empires', in James R. Fichter (ed.), *British and French Colonialism in Africa, Asia and the Middle East: connected empires across the eighteenth to the twentieth centuries* (Palgrave Macmillan: Basingstoke, 2019), pp. 1-15.
22. On Dickens and Anglo-French relations after the Orsini affair, see Matthew Heitzman, '"A Long and Constant Fusion of the Two Great Nations": Dickens, the Crossing, and "A Tale of Two Cities"', *Dickens Studies Annual*, Vol. 45 (2014), pp. 275-292.
23. Charles Dickens, *A Tale of Two Cities* (Macmillan: London, 2003), p. 149.
24. Ibid., pp. 174 and 177.
25. Ibid., p. 321.
26. Ibid., pp. 375-6.

1 A World to Display: Britain and France at the Great Exhibition
1. Robert Fox, 'Introduction', in Sadi Carnot, *Reflexions on the motive power of fire: a critical edition with the surviving scientific manuscripts* (Trans.) Robert Fox (Manchester University Press: Manchester, 1986), pp. 1-44, 4.
2. Donald S. L. Cardwell, *From Watt to Clausius: the rise of thermodynamics in the early industrial age* (Heinemann: London, 1971), pp. 156-7; also see, Margaret Bradley and Fernand Perrin, 'Charles Dupin's study visits to the British

Isles, 1816-1824', *Technology and Culture*, Vol. 32, No. 1 (Jan. 1991), pp. 47-68; thanks to Simon Schaffer for directing me towards inspector Dupin in this context.
3. Cardwell, *From Watt to Clausius*, pp. 157-9.
4. Fox, 'Introduction', in Carnot, *Reflexions on the motive power of fire*, pp. 1-44.
5. Ben Marsden and Crosbie Smith, *Engineering Empires: a cultural history of technology in nineteenth-century Britain* (Palgrave Macmillan: Basingstoke, 2005), p. 82.
6. Fox, 'Introduction', in Carnot, *Reflexions on the motive power of fire*, pp. 5 and 8.
7. Cardwell, *From Watt to Clausius*, p. 192.
8. I. Grattan-Guinness, 'Mathematics and mathematical physics from Cambridge, 1815-40: a survey of the achievements and of the French influences', in P. M. Harman (ed.), *Wranglers and Physicists: studies on Cambridge mathematical physics in the nineteenth century* (Manchester University Press: Manchester, 1985), pp. 84-111, 84.
9. Laurence Guymer, 'The wedding planners: Lord Aberdeen, Henry Bulwer, and the Spanish marriages, 1841-1846', *Diplomacy & Statecraft*, 21:4 (2010), pp. 549-73.
10. Laurence Guymer, 'Pressing the French and defending the Palmerstonian line: Lord William Harvey and *The Times*', *Historical Research*, Vol. 87, No. 235 (Feb. 2014), pp. 116-133.
11. David Brown, 'Palmerston and Anglo-French Relations, 1846-1865' *Diplomacy and Statecraft*, 17:4, (2006), pp. 675-92, 679-80.
12. Ibid., p. 680.
13. Palmerston quoted in, Brown, 'Palmerston and Anglo-French Relations, 1846-1865', p. 686.
14. Geoffrey Hicks, 'An overlooked entente: Lord Malmesbury, Anglo-French relations and the Conservatives' recognition of the Second Empire, 1852', *History*, Vol. 92, No, 2 (306) (2007), pp. 187-206, 188-93.
15. Ibid., pp. 197-200.
16. Ibid., p. 203.
17. Cannadine, *Victorious Century*, p. 290.
18. Parry, 'The Impact of Napoleon III on British Politics, 1851-1880', pp. 148-52; for British thought on the autocratic

nature of French politics, see Georgios Varouxakis, *Victorian political thought on France and the French* (Palgrave: Basingstoke, 2002), pp. 80-1.
19. Parry, 'The Impact of Napoleon III on British Politics, 1851-1880', pp. 154-5.
20. Whitney Walton, *France at the Crystal Palace: Bourgeois taste and artisan manufacture in the nineteenth century* (University of California Press: Berkeley, 1992), p. 1; Geoffrey Cantor, *Religion and the Great Exhibition of 1851* (Oxford University Press: Oxford, 2011), p. 1.
21. 1 May, 1851, *Queen Victoria's Journals Online*, Vol. 31, pp. 211-6.
22. John Lemoinne, 'Letters of M. John Lemoinne', in Geoffrey Cantor (ed.), *The Great Exhibition: a documentary history*, Vol. 4 of 4 (Pickering & Chatto: London, 2013), pp. 3-14, 5.
23. Ibid., p. 5.
24. Ibid., p. 10.
25. Ibid., p. 12.
26. Ibid., p. 6.
27. William Whewell, *Inaugural Lecture, November 26, 1851, the general bearing of the Great Exhibition on the progress of art and science* (David Bogue: London, 1852), p. 6.
28. Ibid., pp. 7-8.
29. Ibid., p. 9.
30. Cantor, *Religion and the Great Exhibition of 1851*, p. 11. Though of the 7¼ million, some individuals attended church twice on the same day which inflated the figure somewhat.
31. Ibid., p. 3.
32. Ibid., pp. 6, 19, and 32.
33. *The Times* quoted in Cantor, *Religion and the Great Exhibition of 1851*, p. 30.
34. (Anon.), *The Great Industrial Exhibition, in 1851. The disastrous consequences which are likely to arise to the manufacturing trade of this country, from the carrying out of the proposed Great Exhibition of All Nations, in 1851. Address to all ranks of society, more particularly the manufacturers and working classes of Great Britain and Ireland* (London, 1851), p. 4.
35. Ibid., p. 9.
36. Quoted in Walton, *France at the Crystal Palace*, p. 199.
37. Lemoinne, 'Letters of M. John Lemoinne' in Cantor (ed.), *The Great Exhibition: a documentary history*, p. 12.

38. Quoted in Walton, *France at the Crystal Palace*, p. 207.
39. Walton, *France at the Crystal Palace*, p. 7.
40. Ibid., pp. 51-60.
41. Ibid., p. 176.
42. Quoted in ibid., p. 184.
43. John Ruskin, *On the Nature of Gothic Architecture: and herein of the true functions of the workman in art* (Smith, Elder, & Co.: London, 1854), p. 8.
44. Ibid., p. 8.
45. Ibid., p. 8.
46. Ibid., p. 6.
47. Ibid., pp. 6-7.
48. Stuart Eagles, 'Political legacies' in Francis O'Gorman (ed.), *The Cambridge Companion to John Ruskin* (Cambridge University Press: Cambridge, 2015), pp. 249-62.
49. Ben Marsden and Crosbie Smith, *Engineering Empires: a cultural history of technology in nineteenth-century Britain* (Palgrave Macmillan: Basingstoke, 2005), pp. 202-4 and 214.

2 Catastrophe and Collaboration: The Crimean War

1. *Queen Victoria's Journals Online*, 16 Apr. 1855, Vol. 39, p. 210.
2. *Queen Victoria's Journals Online*, 17 Apr. 1855, Vol. 39, p. 218.
3. Theo Aronson, *Queen Victoria and the Bonapartes* (Cassell: London, 1972), p. 40.
4. Ibid., p. 48.
5. *Queen Victoria's Journals Online*, 18 Aug. 1855, Vol. 40, pp. 94-5.
6. *Queen Victoria's Journals Online*, 18 Aug. 1855, Vol. 40, p. 100.
7. Aronson, *Queen Victoria and the Bonapartes*, p. 51.
8. *Queen Victoria's Journals Online*, 20 Aug. 1855, Vol. 40, p. 105.
9. Albert quoted in, Parry, 'The Impact of Napoleon III on British Politics, 1851-1880', p. 152.
10. *Queen Victoria's Journals Online*, 20 Aug. 1855, Vol. 40, pp. 106-9; Aronson, *Queen Victoria and the Bonapartes*, pp. 59-66.
11. *Queen Victoria's Journals Online*, 20 Aug. 1855, Vol. 40, p. 110.
12. *Queen Victoria's Journals Online*, 22 Aug. 1855, Vol. 40, p. 120.
13. R. L. V. Ffrench Blake, *The Crimean War* (Sphere Books Limited: London, 1971), pp. 1-18; Alastair Massie, *The*

National Army Museum Book of the Crimean War: the untold stories (Sidgwick & Jackson: London, 2004), pp. 3-4; Saul David, *Victoria's Wars: the rise of empire* (Penguin Books: London, 2006), pp. 173-5.
14. M. Chamberlain, (2010, May 27). Gordon, George Hamilton-, fourth earl of Aberdeen (1784–1860), prime minister and scholar. *Oxford Dictionary of National Biography*. Ed. Retrieved 29 Mar. 2019, from http://www.oxforddnb.com.ezp.lib.cam.ac.uk/view/10.1093/ref:odnb/9780198614128.001.0001/odnb-9780198614128-e-11044.
15. Brison D. Gooch, *The New Bonapartist Generals in the Crimean War: distrust and decision-making in the Anglo-French alliance* (Martinus Nijhoff: The Hague, 1959), pp. 33 and 43-4.
16. Quoted in Massie, *The National Army Museum Book of the Crimean War*, p. 12.
17. Gooch, *The New Bonapartist Generals in the Crimean War*, p. 113.
18. Ibid., p. 115.
19. Ibid., p. 116.
20. Quoted in ibid., p. 116.
21. Gooch, *The New Bonapartist Generals in the Crimean War*, p. 120.
22. Massie, *The National Army Museum Book of the Crimean War*, pp. 32-4.
23. Baron de Bazancourt, *The Crimean Expedition, to the capture of Sebastopol. Chronicles of the war in the East, from its commencement to the signing of the Treaty of Paris*, Vol. I of II (Sampson Low, Son, & Co.: London), pp. 226-8 and 270.
24. Ibid., p. 270.
25. Ibid., p. 270.
26. Ibid., pp. 256 and 261.
27. Ibid., p. 272.
28. Raglan quoted in Massie, *The National Army Museum Book of the Crimean War*, p. 53.
29. Captain George quoted in, Massie, *The National Army Museum Book of the Crimean War*, p. 54.
30. W. H. Russell, *Complete History of the Russian War, from its commencement to its close: giving a graphic picture of the great drama of war* (John G. Wells: New York, 1856), pp. 60-1.

31. Ibid., p. 54.
32. Quoted in Gooch, *The New Bonapartist Generals in the Crimean War*, p. 136.
33. George Brown, *Memoranda and observations on the Crimean War, 1854-6, and notes on Mr. Kinglake's second volume* (James Watson: London, 1879), pp. 17-8.
34. (Anon.), *On the conduct of the war in the East. The Crimean Expedition. Memoir addressed to the government of H. M. the Emperor Napoléon III, by a General Officer* (W. Jeffs: London, 1855), p. 77.
35. Massie, *The National Army Museum Book of the Crimean War*, pp. 75-83.
36. Ibid., pp. 83-9.
37. Cecil Woodham-Smith, *The Reason Why* (Penguin Books: London, 1958), pp. 22-3.
38. Massie, *The National Army Museum Book of the Crimean War*, pp. 93-4.
39. Gooch, *The New Bonapartist Generals in the Crimean War*, p. 141.
40. Ibid., pp. 154-5.
41. Ibid., pp. 158-9.
42. *Queen Victoria's Journals Online*, 20 Aug. 1855, Vol. 40, pp. 105 and 111
43. Reid quoted in Joseph O. Baylen and Alan Conway (eds.), *Soldier-Surgeon: the Crimean War letters of Dr Douglas A. Reid, 1855-1856* (University of Tennessee Press: Knoxville, 1968), pp. 36 and 59.
44. Harry Powell, *Recollections of a young soldier during the Crimean War* (Upstone and Doe: Oxford, 1876), p. 25.
45. Frederick Robinson, *Diary of the Crimean War* (Richard Bentley: London, 1856), pp. 150-1.
46. Ibid., p. 160.
47. Ibid., p. 244.
48. Ibid., p. 241.
49. Ibid., p. 244.
50. Sue M. Goldie (ed.), *'I have done my duty': Florence Nightingale in the Crimean War, 1854-56* (Manchester University Press: Manchester, 1987), pp. 272-3.

51. Lynn McDonald, 'Florence Nightingale, statistics and the Crimean War', *Journal of the Royal Statistical Society*, Series A, 177, Part 3 (2014), pp. 569-86, 574-5.
52. Russell, *Complete History of the Russian War, from its commencement to its close*, p. 98.
53. Ibid., p. 74.
54. Baron de Bazancourt, *The Crimean Expedition, to the capture of Sebastopol. Chronicles of the war in the East, from its commencement to the signing of the Treaty of Paris*, Vol. II of II (Sampson Low, Son, & Co.: London), pp. 34-6.
55. Yakup Bektas, 'The Crimean War as a technological enterprise', *Notes and Records*, 71 (2017), pp. 233-62, 235-7, 238-42, and 244-8.
56. John Sinclair, *The war in 1855. A sermon, preached on Wednesday, March 21, 1855, in the parish church of St. Mary Abbotts, Kensington* (Rivingtons: London, 1855), pp 8-9 and 10.
57. H. G. Merriman, *God's power and a nation's presumption. A sermon, preached in the parish church of Badger Salop, on the first day, Wednesday, 21st of March, 1855* (John Henry Parker: London, 1855), p. 10.
58. Ibid., p. 11.
59. Alfred Barry, *The Lessons of the war, and the duties of the peace. A sermon preached at the parish church, Leeds, on the evening of Sunday, May 4th, 1856, being the day appointed for public thanksgiving on the restoration of peace* (Thomas Harrison: Leeds, 1856), p. 10.
60. George Croly, 'The Preacher No. III. England's Greatness. A Sermon, delivered on Sunday morning, May 4, 1856', *The Penny Pulpit*, No. 2,592, 5 June 1856 (London, England), pp. 388-92.

3 Projections of Global Power: Cultivation and Commerce in China and Suez

1. Ferdinand De Lesseps, *The History of the Suez Canal: a personal narrative* (William Blackwood and Sons: Edinburgh, 1876), pp. 3-6; (Anon.), 'Ferdinand de Lesseps', *Nature*, 13 Dec. 1894, No. 1311, Vol. 51 (London, England) pp. 155-6.
2. Ibid., pp. 19-20.
3. Ferdinand De Lesseps, *The Isthmus of Suez Question* (Longman, Brown, Green, and Longman's: London, 1855), pp. 7-9.

4. De Lesseps, *The History of the Suez Canal*, p. 24.
5. De Lesseps, *The Isthmus of Suez Question*, p. 14.
6. Ferdinand De Lesseps, *Inquiry into the opinions of the commercial classes of Great Britain on the Suez ship canal* (John Weale: London, 1857), pp. 1-16 and iv.
7. De Lesseps, *The History of the Suez Canal*, pp. 32-3.
8. Ibid., p. 49.
9. De Lesseps, *Inquiry into the opinions of the commercial classes of Great Britain on the Suez ship canal*, p. 126.
10. Quoted in, Ibid., p. 125.
11. De Lesseps, *The History of the Suez Canal*, pp. vi-ix.
12. Ibid., p. 31.
13. Ibid., p. 46.
14. (Anon.), 'While M. Lesseps was expatiating last week ...', *The Times*, 24 May 1860 (London, England), Issue 23628, p. 8.
15. De Lesseps, *The History of the Suez Canal*, pp. 54-5.
16. (Anon.), 'Egypt', *The Times*, 21 Jun. 1859, (London, England), Issue 23338, p. 11.
17. On the Suez Canal opening see James R. Fichter, 'Britain and France, connected empires', in James R. Fichter (ed.), *British and French Colonialism in Africa, Asia and the Middle East: connected empires across the eighteenth to the twentieth centuries* (Palgrave Macmillan: Basingstoke, 2019), pp. 1-15, 5-7.
18. (Anon.), 'Ferdinand de Lesseps', *Nature*, 13 Dec. 1894, No. 1311, Vol. 51 (London, England) pp. 155-6.
19. De Lesseps, *The History of the Suez Canal*, p. 23; for a history of the Canal see D. A. Farnie, *East and West of Suez: the Suez Canal in History, 1854-1956* (Oxford University Press: Oxford, 1969).
20. Geoffrey Hicks, 'Disraeli, Derby and the Suez Canal, 1875: some myths reassessed', *History*, Vol. 97, No. 2 (326) (April 2012), pp. 182-203, 183-7.
21. In 1882 unrest in Egypt prompted Britain to invade, seizing complete control of the Suez Canal which remained a British possession until the canal's nationalisation in 1956.
22. Michael Mann, *China, 1860*, (Michael Russell: Salisbury, 1989), p. 12; on Anglo-French involvement in China at this time see Robert Bickers, *The Scramble for China: foreign devils in the Qing Empire, 1832-1914* (Penguin: London, 2012), pp. 147-150.

23. Ibid., pp. 1-3; David, *Victoria's Wars*, pp. 359-62.
24. Hope Grant quoted in Mann, *China, 1860*, p. 4.
25. (Anon.), *A foreigner's evidence on the China question* (Smith, Elder & Co.: London, 1859) p. 4.
26. (Anon.), *Some remarks on our affairs in China* (James Ridgway: London, 1860), pp. 11 and 26-7.
27. Karl Marx, 'Persia-China', *New York Daily Tribune*, 5 Jun. 1857, in Dona Torr (ed.), *Marx on China, 1853-1860: articles from the New York Daily Tribune* (Lawrence & Wishart: 1968), pp. 45-51, 50-1.
28. Karl Marx, 'Free trade and monopoly', *New York Daily Tribune*, 25 Sep. 1858, in Torr (ed.), *Marx on China, 1853-1860*, pp. 56-9, 56-5 and 58; Karl Marx, 'Another civilization war', *New York Daily Tribune*, 10 Oct. 1859, in Torr (ed.), *Marx on China, 1853-1860*, pp. 78-82, 80.
29. John Stuart Mill, *On Liberty and The Subjection of Women* (Penguin Books: London, 2006), pp. 81-2.
30. Mann, *China, 1860*, pp. 29-33.
31. Quoted in ibid., pp. 35-6.
32. Charles Rathbone Low, *General Lord Wolseley (of Cairo), G.C.B., G.C.M.G., D.C. L., LL.D. A memoir* (Richard Bentley and Son: London, 1883), p. 128.
33. Wolseley quoted in Mann, *China, 1860*, p. 42.
34. Elgin quoted in Mann, *China, 1860*, p. 56.
35. Mann, *China, 1860*, pp. 72-91.
36. G. Allgood, *China War, 1860: letters and journal* (Longman's, Green, and Co.: London, 1901), pp. 48-9.
37. (Anon.), 'The Third China War', *New York Times*, 27 Jul. 1860 (New York, United States), p. 4.
38. (Anon.), 'The China War', *The Examiner*, 1 Dec. 1860 (London, England), No. 2757; p. 753.
39. (Anon.), 'The Third China War', *New York Times*, 17 Nov. 1860 (New York, United States), p. 4.
40. Low, *General Lord Wolseley*, pp. 41-2.
41. G. J. Wolseley, *Narrative of the war with China in 1860* (Longman, Green, Longman, and Roberts: London, 1862), p. 224.
42. Ibid., p. 227.
43. Gordon quoted in David, *Victoria's Wars*, p. 394.

44. Victor Hugo, 'The Chinese Expedition: Victor Hugo on the sack of the Summer Palace – letter from Hugo to Captain Butler', 25 Nov., 1861.
45. Wolseley, *Narrative of the war with China in 1860*, p. 233.
46. Ibid., pp. 234-5.
47. David, *Victoria's Wars*, p. 394.
48. Ibid., p. 395.
49. Wolseley, *Narrative of the war with China in 1860*, p. 227.
50. Low, *General Lord Wolseley*, p. 144.
51. Wolseley, *Narrative of the war with China in 1860*, pp. 272-4.
52. Ibid., p. 274.
53. Samuel Mossman, *General Gordon's private diary of his exploits in China; amplified* (Sampson Low, Marston, Searle, & Rivington: London, 1885), pp. 23-30.

4 Peace Secured: Free Trade and the Cobden-Chevalier Treaty

1. Geoffrey Hicks, 'The Struggle for Stability: the fourteenth earl and Europe, 1852-1868', in Geoffrey Hicks (ed.), *Conservatism and British Foreign Policy, 1820-1920: the Derbys and their world*, (2011), pp. 81-98, 81 and 87; David Brown, 'Palmerston and Anglo-French Relations, 1846-1865', *Diplomacy and Statecraft*, 17:4, (2006), pp. 675-92, 683.
2. Brown, 'Palmerston and Anglo-French Relations, 1846-1865', p. 683.
3. (Anon.), 'France and England', *Littell's Living Age* (1844-1896); 17 Apr. 1858; 725; American Periodicals, pg. 224.
4. Paul Kennedy, *The Rise and Fall of British Naval Mastery*, 3rd edition (FontanaPress: London, 1991), p. 204.
5. David Todd, 'A French Imperial Meridian, 1814-1870', *Past and Present*, No. 210, (Feb. 2011), pp. 155-86, 177.
6. On naval rivalry see C. I. Hamilton, *Anglo-French Naval Rivalry, 1840-1870*, (Clarendon Press: Oxford, 1993); Don Leggett, *Shaping the Royal Navy: technology, authority and naval architecture, c. 1830-1906* (Manchester University Press: Manchester, 2015).
7. Derby quoted in Hicks, 'The Struggle for Stability: the fourteenth earl and Europe, 1852-1868', p. 91.
8. Palmerston quoted in Parry, 'The Impact of Napoleon III on British Politics, 1851-1880', pp. 157-61.

9. M. Taylor, (2009, May 21). Cobden, Richard (1804-1865), manufacturer and politician. Oxford Dictionary of National Biography. Ed. Retrieved 29 Mar. 2019, from http://www.oxforddnb.com.ezp.lib.cam.ac.uk/view/10.1093/ref:odnb/9780198614128.001.0001/odnb-9780198614128-e-5741.
10. Cobden quoted in Nicholas C. Edsall, *Richard Cobden: Independent Radical*, (Harvard University Press: Massachusetts, 1986), p. 326.
11. Todd, 'A French Imperial Meridian, 1814-1870', pp. 175-8.
12. Edsall, *Richard Cobden*, p. 331.
13. 'Richard Cobden to Michel Chevalier, 14 Sep. 1859', in Anthony Howe and Simon Morgan (eds.), *The Letters of Richard Cobden*, Vol. 3 of 4 (Oxford University Press: Oxford, 2012), pp. 454-57, 456.
14. 'Richard Cobden to William Gladstone, 11 Oct. 1859', in Howe and Morgan (eds.), *The Letters of Richard Cobden*, Vol. 3 of 4, pp. 465-66, 465.
15. 'Richard Cobden to Michel Chevalier, 14 Sep. 1859', in Howe and Morgan (eds.), *The Letters of Richard Cobden*, Vol. 3 of 4, pp. 454-57, 456; for a critic of England as a free trader before 1860 see, John V. C. Nye, *War, Wine, and Taxes: the political economy of Anglo-French trade, 1689-1900* (Princeton University Press: Princeton, 2007), pp. 89-109.
16. 'Richard Cobden to John Bright, 12 Sep. 1859', in Howe and Morgan (eds.), *The Letters of Richard Cobden*, Vol. 3 of 4, pp. 453-4, 454.
17. 'Richard Cobden to John Bright, 17 Oct. 1859', in Howe and Morgan (eds.), *The Letters of Richard Cobden*, Vol. 3 of 4, pp. 467-69, 467.
18. 'Richard Cobden to William Gladstone, 12 Jan. 1860', in Anthony Howe and Simon Morgan (eds.), *The Letters of Richard Cobden*, Vol. 4 of 4 (Oxford University Press: Oxford, 2015), pp. 5-6, 5.
19. 'Richard Cobden to John Bright, 10 Feb. 1860', in Howe and Morgan (eds.), *The Letters of Richard Cobden*, Vol. 4 of 4, pp. 14-19, 14-5.
20. 'Richard Cobden to William Gladstone, 1 Jan. 1860', in Howe and Morgan (eds.) *The Letters of Richard Cobden*, Vol. 4 of 4, pp. 3-4, 3.

21. Edsall, *Richard Cobden*, p. 332.
22. Ibid., p. 337.
23. 'Richard Cobden to John Crawford, 25 Oct. 1859', in Howe and Morgan (eds.), *The Letters of Richard Cobden*, Vol. 3 of 4, pp. 469-71, 470.
24. David Todd, *Free Trade and its Enemies in France, 1814-1851* (Cambridge University Press: Cambridge, 2015), pp. 5-6 and 89-90.
25. Ibid., pp. 190-1.
26. A. A. Iliasu, 'The Cobden-Chevalier Commercial Treaty of 1860', *The Historical Journal*, XIV, 1 (1971), pp. 67-98, 72-4; on the Italian Question see William E. Echard, *Napoléon III and the Concert of Europe* (Louisiana State University Press: Baton Rouge, 1983), pp. 107-28.
27. Edsall, *Richard Cobden*, p. 334.
28. 'Richard Cobden to William Gladstone, 11 Nov. 1859', in Howe and Morgan (eds.), *The Letters of Richard Cobden*, Vol. 3 of 4, pp. 477-8.
29. Iliasu, 'The Cobden-Chevalier Commercial Treaty of 1860', pp. 80-2.
30. Ibid., pp. 88-92.
31. 'Economist', 'The Treaty with France', *The Times*, 6 Feb. 1860 (London, England) Issue 23535, p. 7.
32. (Anon.), 'The Treaty of Commerce was signed at Paris...', *The Times*, 24 Jan. 1860 (London, England) Issue 23524, p. 8.
33. Edsall, *Richard Cobden*, p. 340.
34. Antonio Tena-Junginto, Markus Lampe, and Felipe Tâmega Fernandes, 'How much trade liberalization was there in the world before and after Cobden-Chevalier', *Journal of Economic History*, Vol. 72, No. 3, (Sep. 2012), pp. 708-40, 732; on the economic impact of the treaty see Markus Lampe, 'Explaining nineteenth-century bilateralism: economic and political determinants of the Cobden-Chevalier network', *Economic History Review*, 64:2 (2011), pp. 644-668.
35. Edsall, *Richard Cobden*, p. 341; on the Treaty's signing see Arthur Louis Dunham, *The Anglo-French Treaty of Commerce of 1860 and the progress of the industrial revolution in France* (University of Michigan Press: Ann Arbor, 1930), pp. 79-102.

36. M. Taylor, (2009, May 21). Cobden, Richard (1804-1865), manufacturer and politician. Oxford Dictionary of National Biography. Ed. Retrieved 29 Mar. 2019, from http://www.oxforddnb.com.ezp.lib.cam.ac.uk/view/10.1093/ref:odnb/9780198614128.001.0001/odnb-9780198614128-e-5741.

5 The Measure of Nations: Liberalism and the Metric System

1. Crosbie Smith, *Coal, Steam and Ships: engineering, enterprise and empire on the nineteenth-century seas* (Cambridge University Press: Cambridge, 2018), pp. 288-94; Edward Gillin, 'Prophets of Progress: authority in the scientific projections and religious realizations of the "Great Eastern" steamship', *Technology and Culture*, Vol. 56, No. 4, (October, 2015), pp. 928-56.
2. Smith, *Coal, Steam and Ships*, pp. 292-3.
3. For a history of these companies and the problem of coal consumption see Smith, *Coal, Steam and Ships*.
4. On PSNC see Smith, *Coal, Steam and Ships*, pp. 204-23, 304-22.
5. Ken Alder, 'A Revolution in Measure: the political economy of the Metric System in France', in M. Norton Wise (ed.), *The Values of Precision* (Princeton University Press: Princeton, 1995), pp. 39-71.
6. Quoted in Simon Schaffer, 'Metrology, Metrication, and Victorian Values', in Bernard Lightman (ed.), *Victorian Science in Context* (University of Chicago Press: Chicago, 1997), pp. 438-74, 445.
7. Edward Franklin Cox, 'The Metric System: a quarter-century of acceptance (1851-1876)', *Osiris*, Vol. 13 (1958), pp. 358-79, 362-5.
8. Maurice Crosland, *Gay-Lussac: scientist and bourgeois*, (Cambridge University Press: Cambridge, 1978), pp. 190-3.
9. Pierre Duplais, *A treatise on the manufacture and distillation of alcoholic liquors* (Henry Carey Baird: Philadelphia, 1871), pp. 253-4.
10. 'Richard Cobden to William Gladstone, 21 Nov. 1859', in Howe and Morgan (eds.), *The Letters of Richard Cobden*, Vol. 3 of 4, pp. 485-6; 'Richard Cobden to William Gladstone, 28 Nov. 1859', in Howe and Morgan (eds.), *The Letters of Richard Cobden*, Vol. 3 of 4, pp. 488-91.
11. 'Richard Cobden to William Gladstone, 5 Dec. 1859', in Howe and Morgan (eds.), *The Letters of Richard Cobden*, Vol. 3 of 4, pp. 491-2; 'Richard Cobden to William Gladstone, 29 Dec.

1859', in Howe and Morgan (eds.), *The Letters of Richard Cobden*, Vol. 3 of 4, pp. 505-6; on wine see, Dunham, *The Anglo-French Treaty of Commerce of 1860 and the progress of the industrial revolution in France*, pp. 277-293.
12. Quoted in Simon Schaffer, 'Metrology, Metrication, and Victorian Values', p. 446.
13. Bernard Semmel, 'Parliament and the Metric System', *Isis*, Vol. 54, No. 1 (Mar. 1963), pp. 125-33, 127.
14. Cox, 'The Metric System: a quarter-century of acceptance (1851-1876)', pp. 368-9.
15. *Report from the Select Committee on weights and measures; together with the proceedings of the committee, minutes of evidence, appendix, and index*, House of Commons Paper 411 (1862), p. iv.
16. Ibid., p. x.
17. Ibid., pp. viii-ix and 130-1.
18. *Weights and Measures. A bill for decimalizing our existing system of weights and measures, and for establishing an accordance between them and those of foreign countries*, House of Commons Papers 120 (1863), p. 3.
19. *Debate in the House of Commons on the proposed introduction of the Metric System of Weights and Measures, 1ˢᵗ July, 1863, corrected by the respective members who took part in the discussion* (Bell and Daldy: London, 1863), pp. 9 and 11.
20. Ibid., p. 16.
21. Ibid., p. 17.
22. Ibid., pp. 25-6.
23. Semmel, 'Parliament and the Metric System', p. 129.
24. *Debate in the House of Commons on the proposed introduction of the Metric System of Weights and Measures, 1ˢᵗ July, 1863, corrected by the respective members who took part in the discussion*, (Bell and Daldy: London, 1863), p. 34.
25. Ibid., p. 29.
26. Ibid., p. 29.
27. Ibid., p. 31.
28. 'Richard Cobden to Richard Rickard, 30 Sep 1864', in Howe and Morgan (eds.), *The Letters of Richard Cobden*, Vol. 4 of 4, p. 546.

29. *Debates in both houses of Parliament on the Metric Weights & Measures Bill. Session 1864* (Bell and Daldy: London, 1864), pp. 4 and 7.
30. Schaffer, 'Metrology, Metrication, and Victorian Values', pp. 449-59.
31. Cox, 'The Metric System: a quarter-century of acceptance (1851-1876)', pp. 372-5.
32. 26.Fanny Gribenski and Edward Gillin, 'The politics of musical standardization in nineteenth-century France and Britain', *Past and Present*, Vol. 251, Issue 1 (May 2021), pp. 153-87; I am grateful to Fanny Gribenski for discussions on Anglo-French efforts to unify pitch.
33. (Anon.), 'An Imperial Pitchfork', *The Spectator*, 28 Aug. 1858, (London, England), pp. 910-11.
34. 'Uniform musical pitch. Minutes of a meeting of musicians, amateurs, and others interested in music, held at the house of the society of arts, when the report of the committee appointed by the council of the society was received and adopted', *The Journal of the Society of Arts* 8, no. 417 (1860), pp. 1-8, 8.
35. (Anon.), 'Tuning-forks and musical pitch', *Chamber's Journal of Popular Literature Science and Arts*, Vol. 34, No. 346, Jul.–Dec. 1860 (London, England), 18 Aug. 1860, pp. 98-101, 100-1.
36. 'Uniform musical pitch.', pp. 1-8, 5.
37. Ibid., pp. 1-8, 6.

6 Entente Diminished: The Fall of Palmerston and Napoléon

1. (Anon.), 'The Entente Cordiale', *Punch*, Vol. 38 (31 Mar. 1860), p. 127.
2. (Anon.), 'Fox-hunting in France', *Punch*, Vol. 42 (8 Nov. 1862), p. 188.
3. Roger Price, *The French Second Empire: an anatomy of political power* (Cambridge University Press: Cambridge, 2001), pp. 41-94; Fenton Bresler, *Napoléon III: a life* (Harper Collins Publishers: London, 1999), pp. 306-7; On Palmerston's failure to work with Napoléon see Parry, 'The Impact of Napoleon III on British Politics, 1851-1880', p. 162.
4. Todd, 'A French Imperial Meridian, 1814-1870', pp. 182-3.
5. 'T. M. J.', 'The Schleswig-Holstein difficulty: is a general European war probable?', *The Merchants' Magazine and Commercial Review* (1839-1870); 1 Feb. 1864; 50, 2, p. 119.

6. Keith A. P. Sandiford, 'The British Cabinet and the Schleswig-Holstein Crisis, 1863-1864', *History*, Vol. 58, No. 194 (1973), pp. 360-83, 361-2.
7. *Denmark and Germany. No. 2. Correspondence respecting the affair of the Duchies of Holstein, Laurenburg, and Schleswig* (Harrison and Sons: London, 1864), p. 131.
8. Ibid., p. 620.
9. 'T. M. J.', 'The Schleswig-Holstein difficulty: is a general European war probable?' *The Merchants' Magazine and Commercial Review* (1839-1870); 1 Feb. 1864; 50, 2, p. 119.
10. W. E. Mosse, 'Queen Victoria and Her Ministers in the Schleswig-Holstein Crisis 1863-1864', *English Historical Review*, Vol. 78, No. 304 (Apr., 1963), pp. 263-83, 264-6.
11. Victoria quoted in ibid., p. 271.
12. Ibid., pp. 275-8.
13. Ibid., pp. 280-1.
14. D. Steele (2009, May 21). Temple, Henry John, third Viscount Palmerston (1784–1865), prime minister. *Oxford Dictionary of National Biography*. Ed. Retrieved 29 Mar. 2019, from http://www.oxforddnb.com.ezp.lib.cam.ac.uk/view/10.1093/ref:odnb/9780198614128.001.0001/odnb-9780198614128-e-27112.
15. (Anon.), 'The Schleswig-Holstein War', *The Round Table: a Saturday Review of politics, finance, literature, society, and art* (1863-1869), 27 Feb. 1864; 1; p. 161.
16. Geoffrey Wawro, *The Franco-Prussian War: the German conquest of France in 1870-1871*, (Cambridge University Press: Cambridge, 2003), pp. 16-18; Dora Neill Raymond, *British Policy and Opinion during the Franco-Prussian War* (Columbia University: New York, 1921), pp. 21-3.
17. Parry, 'The Impact of Napoleon III on British Politics, 1851-1880', pp. 167-8.
18. On the advocates of the acts see, Judith Walkowitz, *Prostitution and Victorian Society: women, class, and the state* (Cambridge University Press: Cambridge, 1980), pp. 69-89.
19. On Butler see ibid., pp. 113-36.
20. Josephine Elizabeth Grey Butler, *Recollections of George Butler* (J. W. Arrowsmith: London, 1892), p. 221.

21. Quoted in Parry, 'The Impact of Napoleon III on British Politics, 1851-1880', p. 166.
22. Walkowitz, *Prostitution and Victorian Society*, pp. 90-112.
23. T. G. Otte, *The Foreign Office Mind: the making of British foreign policy, 1865-1914* (Cambridge University Press: Cambridge, 2011), pp. 23-4; Cannadine, *Victorious Century*, pp. 317-8.
24. Wawro, *The Franco-Prussian War*, pp. 19-20.
25. Ibid., p. 25.
26. Ibid., pp. 20-1.
27. Ibid., pp. 22-3.
28. Ibid., p. 27.
29. Ibid., pp. 27-9.
30. Ibid., pp. 31-8.
31. Napoléon Bonaparte quoted in Michael Howard, *Franco-Prussian War: German Invasion of France, 1870-1871* (Routledge: London, 1991), p. 253.
32. On the siege see Wawro, *The Franco-Prussian War*, pp. 230-56; Howard, *Franco-Prussian War*, pp. 252-93.
33. (Anon.), 'The Siege of Paris', *Pall Mall Gazette* (London, England), 14 Nov., 1870; Issue 1795.
34. Raymond, *British Policy and Opinion during the Franco-Prussian War*, pp. 130-3 and 319-20.
35. Wawro, *The Franco-Prussian War*, pp. 301 and 304.
36. Bismarck quoted in ibid., p. 305.
37. Ibid., 305.
38. Raymond, *British Policy and Opinion during the Franco-Prussian War*, pp. 403-4.
39. Wawro, *The Franco-Prussian War*, p. 25.
40. Ibid., p. 314; Raymond, *British Policy and Opinion during the Franco-Prussian War*, p. 386.
41. Parry, 'The Impact of Napoleon III on British Politics, 1851-1880', p. 170.

7 Imperial Rivals: The Anglo-French Divergence, 1871–98

1. Stephen Kern, *The Culture of Time and Space, 1880-1918* (Harvard University Press: Harvard, 2003), p. 12; Derek Howse, *Greenwich Time and the Longitude* (Philip Wilson: London, 1997), p. 120.
2. Howse, *Greenwich Time and the Longitude*, p. 124.
3. Ibid., p. 135.

4. Ibid., pp. 133-43; on French resistance at the conference see Allen W. Palmer, 'Negotiation and Resistance in Global Networks: 1884 International Meridian Conference', *Mass Communication and Society*, Vol. 5, Iss. 1, (2002), pp. 7-24.
5. Howse, *Greenwich Time and the Longitude*, p. 136.
6. 'J. P.', 'The result of the Washington Conference', *Graphic* (London, England), 1 Aug. 1885; Issue 818.
7. Howse, *Greenwich Time and the Longitude*, p. 136.
8. Ibid., p. 120.
9. Quoted in Kern, *The Culture of Time and Space, 1880-1918*, p. 13.
10. Joseph Conrad, *The Secret Agent: a simple tale* (Penguin: London, 2012), pp. 27-9.
11. Philip Taylor, https://www.rmg.co.uk/discover/explore/astronomers-and-anarchist-bomber.
12. Kern, *The Culture of Time and Space, 1880-1918*, pp. 13-4.
13. Parry, 'The Impact of Napoleon III on British Politics, 1851-1880', pp. 170-3.
14. Jörg Lehman, 'Civilization versus Barbarism: the Franco-Prussian War in French History Textbooks, 1875-1895', *Journal of Educational Media, Memory & Society*, Vol. 7, No. 1 (Spring, 2015), pp. 51-65, 53-6.
15. Ibid., p. 52.
16. Derby quoted in T. G. Otte, 'From "War-in-Sight" to Nearly War: Anglo-French relations in the age of high imperialism, 1875-1898', *Diplomacy & Statecraft*, Vol. 17, Issue 4 (2006), pp. 693-714.
17. Salisbury quoted in ibid. pp. 693-714.
18. Ibid., pp. 693-714.
19. R. C. Mowat, 'From Liberalism to Imperialism: the case of Egypt 1875-1887', *The Historical Journal*, XVI, 1 (1973), pp. 109-24, 112.
20. Ibid., p. 113.
21. Ibid., p. 114.
22. Ibid., p. 114.
23. Granville quoted in Otte, 'From "War-in-Sight" to Nearly War: Anglo-French relations in the age of high imperialism, 1875-1898', pp. 693-714.
24. On the invasion of Egypt see Anthony G. Hopkins, 'The Victorians and Africa: a reconsideration of the occupation of Egypt,

1882', *Journal of African History*, 27.2 (1986), pp. 363–391; John Newsinger, 'Liberal Imperialism and the Occupation of Egypt in 1882', *Race & Class*, 49.3 (2008), pp. 54–75; Martin Thomas and Richard Toye, 'Arguing about intervention: a comparison of British and French rhetoric surrounding the 1882 and 1956 invasions of Egypt', *Historical Journal*, 58.4 (2015), pp. 1081–1113.

25. *Correspondence respecting the Anglo-French financial control* (Houses of Parliament Paper: Egypt, No. 20, 1882), (Harrison and Sons: London, 1882), p. 2
26. Ibid., pp. 5-6.
27. Ibid., p. 7.
28. Ibid., p. 10.
29. Ibid., p. 22.
30. Ibid., p. 23.
31. (Anon.), 'France and Egypt', *Morning Post* (London, England), 11 Jan. 1883; Issue 34492; p. 5.
32. (Anon.), 'The Anglo-French Agreement', *Morning Post* (London, England) 28 June 1884; Issue 34950; p. 5.
33. Quoted in (Anon.), 'France and Egypt', *The Daily News* (London, England), 30 Sep. 1886; Issue 12628.
34. Mowat, 'From Liberalism to Imperialism: the case of Egypt 1875-1887', pp. 110-11; for historical debates over the cost of empire see Patrick K. O'Brien, 'The Costs and Benefits of British Imperialism, 1846-1914', *Past & Present*, Vol. 120 (Aug. 1988), pp. 163-200; Paul Kennedy, 'The Costs and Benefits of British Imperialism, 1846-1914', *Past & Present*, Vol. 125 (Nov. 1989), pp. 186-192.
35. Mowat, 'From Liberalism to Imperialism: the case of Egypt 1875-1887', pp. 109-11.
36. Ibid., p. 116.
37. Ibid., pp. 118-20.
38. Kennedy, *The Rise and Fall of British Naval Mastery*, p. 213.
39. Ibid., p. 210; on imperial rivalry see Prosser Gifford and William Roger Louis (eds.), *France and Britain in Africa: imperial rivalry and colonial rule* (Yale University Press: New Haven, 1972).
40. Spencer quoted in Otte, 'From "War-in-Sight" to Nearly War: Anglo-French relations in the age of high imperialism, 1875-1898', pp. 693-714.
41. Salisbury quoted in ibid., pp. 693-714.

42. Ibid., pp. 693-714; also see James R. Fichter, 'Imperial Interdependence on Indochina's Maritime Periphery: France and coal in Ceylon, Singapore, and Hong Kong, 1859-1895', in James R. Fichter (ed.), *British and French Colonialism in Africa, Asia and the Middle East: connected empires across the eighteenth to the twentieth centuries* (Palgrave Macmillan: Basingstoke, 2019), pp. 151-79; Frederick Verney, 'Note on the Anglo-French Convention in Siam', *The Nineteenth Century: a monthly review* (Mar. 1877-Dec. 1900); Feb. 1896; 39, 228; pp. 332-4, 332.
43. Granville quoted in Phares M. Mutibwa, 'Britain's "Abandonment" of Madagascar: the Anglo-French Convention of August 1890', *Transafrican Journal of History*, Vol. 3, No. 1/2 (1973), pp. 96-111, 96.
44. Ibid., p. 98.
45. (Anon.), 'French at Fashoda', *Lloyd's Illustrated Newspaper* (London, England) 18 Sep. 1898; Issue 2913.
46. Quoted in T. W. Riker, 'A Survey of British Policy in the Fashoda Crisis', *Political Science Quarterly*, Vol. 44, No. 1 (Mar. 1929), pp. 54-78, 55.
47. Ibid., pp. 56-7.
48. Grey quoted in ibid., p. 58.
49. On Marchand see, Hillas Smith, *The Unknown Frenchman: the story of Marchand and Fashoda* (Book Guild Publishing: Lewes, 2001).
50. Otte, 'From "War-in-Sight" to Nearly War: Anglo-French relations in the age of high imperialism, 1875-1898', pp. 693-714; also see James Hubbard Goode, 'The Fashoda Crisis: a survey of Anglo-French Imperial Policy on the Upper Nile Question, 1882-1899' (PhD thesis: North Texas State University, 1971).
51. Sir Hubert von Herkomer and Frederick Goodall, 'Kitchener, Horatio Herbert, Earl Kitchener of Khartoum (1850–1916).' *Oxford Dictionary of National Biography*. 23 Sep. 2004; Accessed 2 Apr. 2020. https://www.oxforddnb.com/view/10.1093/ref:odnb/9780198614128.001.0001/odnb-9780198614128-e-1001401.
52. Quoted in Riker, 'A Survey of British Policy in the Fashoda Crisis', p. 66.
53. (Anon.), 'Marchand leaves Fashoda', *Western Mail* (Cardiff, Wales) 29 Oct. 1898; Issue 983.

54. Riker, 'A Survey of British Policy in the Fashoda Crisis', pp. 70-3; also see, David Levering Lewis, *Race to Fashoda* (Henry & Company: New York, 2001); Darrell Bates, *The Fashoda Incident of 1898: encounter on the Nile* (Oxford University Press: Oxford, 1984); Roger Glenn Brown, *Fashoda Reconsidered: the impact of domestic politics on French policy in Africa, 1893-1898* (John Hopkins University Press: Baltimore, 1970).
55. Winston Spencer-Churchill, 'The Fashoda Incident', *The North American Review*, Vol. 167, No. 505, (Dec. 1898), pp. 736-43, 737.
56. Ibid., p. 741.
57. Ibid., p. 742.
58. On Britain and France in Nigeria see Barbara M. Cooper, '"Our Anglo-Saxon Colleagues": French administration of Niger and the Constraining embrace of Northern Nigeria', in James R. Fichter (ed.), *British and French Colonialism in Africa, Asia and the Middle East: connected empires across the eighteenth to the twentieth centuries* (Palgrave Macmillan: Basingstoke, 2019), pp. 35-64; (Anon.), 'Anglo-French Niger-Nile Convention', *New York Times* (New York, United States), 13 May 1899; p. 7; (Anon.), 'The Anglo-French Agreement', *York Herald* (York, England), 28 Mar. 1899; Issue 14195, p. 5.
59. Wells, H. G., *Classics Collection 1: The Time Machine, The Island of Doctor Moreau, The War of the Worlds, The First Men in the Moon, The Invisible Man* (Gollancz: London, 2010), p. 295.
60. Michael T. Kiernan, *The Engineers of Cornwall at the Mines of Pontgibaud in France* (Redruth Cornish Global Migration Programme: Redruth, undated), pp. 1-4.
61. Ibid., pp. 28-32.
62. Kenneth McConkey, 'Forbes, Stanhope Alexander (1857–1947), genre painter.' *Oxford Dictionary of National Biography.* 23 Sep. 2004; Accessed 2 Apr. 2020. https://www.oxforddnb.com/view/10.1093/ref:odnb/9780198614128.001.0001/odnb-9780198614128-e-33194.
63. Forbes quoted in Lionel Birch, *Stanhope A. Forbes A.R.A., and Elizabeth Stanhope Forbes, A.R.W.S.* (Cassell: London, 1906), pp 25-6; also see, Caroline Fox, *Stanhope Forbes and the Newlyn School* (David & Charles: Newton Abbot, 1993);

Charles Lewis Hind, *Stanhope A. Forbes, Royal Academician* (Virtue & Company: London, 1911).
64. On the Barbizon School see Steven Adams, *The Barbizon School & the Origins of Impressionism* (Phaidon Press: New York, 1994); on artistic, poetic, and literary exchanges see, Ian Small and Ceri Crossley (eds.), *Studies in Anglo-French cultural relations* (Palgrave Macmillan: Basingstoke, 1988).
65. Rachel Rich, *Bourgeois Consumption: food, space and identity in London and Paris, 1850-1914* (Manchester University Press: Manchester, 2011), pp. 3 and 9.
66. René Studio, 'Ritz, César Jean (1850–1918).' *Oxford Dictionary of National Biography*. 23 Sep. 2004; Accessed 2 Apr. 2020. https://www.oxforddnb.com/view/10.1093/ref:odnb/9780198614128.001.0001/odnb-9780198614128-e-1005507; F. Ashburner, 'Escoffier, Georges Auguste (1846–1935), master chef and writer on cookery'. *Oxford Dictionary of National Biography*. 23 Sep. 2004; Accessed 2 Apr. 2020. https://www.oxforddnb.com/view/10.1093/ref:odnb/9780198614128.001.0001/odnb-9780198614128-e-50441.
67. Robert Graham Harding, 'The Establishment of Champagne in Britain, 1860-1914' (DPhil., thesis: University of Oxford, 2018), pp. 35 and 50-5; I would like to thank Robert Harding for his invaluable discussions on this subject at St Cross College.
68. Ibid., pp. 12-3.
69. Ibid., pp. 79-80.
70. Ibid., pp. 12, 17-18, and 29.
71. Ibid., pp. 36-46.
72. Ibid., p. 161.
73. Ibid., p. 163-4.
74. Ibid., p. 163.
75. Ibid., p. 34.
76. Kennedy, *The Rise and Fall of British Naval Mastery*, pp. 223-4.
77. Ibid., p. 228.

8 Entente Renewed: The Drift to Global War
1. Vicky Albritton and Fredrik Albritton Jonsson, *Green Victorians: the simple life in John Ruskin's Lake District* (University of Chicago Press: Chicago, 2016), pp. 21-2.

2. John Ruskin, *Our fathers have told us. Part 1: The Bible of Amiens* (George Allen: Sunnyside, Orpington, 1881), p. 2; thanks to William Whyte for directing me to Ruskin's discussion of Amiens.
3. Ibid., pp. 6-7.
4. Ibid., p. 2.
5. Ibid., p. 15.
6. On Amiens Cathedral see Hans Jantzen, *High Gothic: a comparative analysis of the Great Gothic Cathedrals of Chartres, Rheims, and Amiens* (Constable and Co.: Letchworth, 1962).
7. Cynthia Gamble, 'France and Belgium', in Francis O'Gorman (ed.), *The Cambridge Companion to John Ruskin* (Cambridge University Press: Cambridge, 2015), pp. 66-80, 71-2.
8. Ruskin quoted in ibid., p. 67.
9. Ibid., pp. 67-71.
10. Ibid., pp. 74-5.
11. Richard Macksey, 'Introduction', in Marcel Proust, *On Reading Ruskin: prefaces to La Bible d'Amiens and Sésame et Les Lys with selections from the notes to the translated texts*, (trans.) Jean Autret, William Burford, and Phillip J. Wolfe (Yale University Press: New Haven, 1987), pp. xiii-liii, xv.
12. Marcel Proust, 'Preface to John Ruskin's *Bible of Amiens*', in Marcel Proust, *On Reading Ruskin: prefaces to La Bible d'Amiens and Sésame et Les Lys with selections from the notes to the translated texts* (trans.) Jean Autret, William Burford, and Phillip J. Wolfe (Yale University Press: New Haven, 1987), pp. 5-71, 9.
13. Ibid., pp. 19-21.
14. Quoted in Stuart Eagles, 'Political Legacies', in Francis O'Gorman (ed.), *The Cambridge Companion to John Ruskin* (Cambridge University Press: Cambridge, 2015), pp. 249-62, 260-1.
15. Quoted in Kennedy, *The Rise and Fall of British Naval Mastery*, p. 244.
16. Marsden and Smith, *Engineering Empires*, pp. 221-2.
17. Quoted in Kennedy, *The Rise and Fall of British Naval Mastery*, p. 244.
18. Ibid., p. 247.

19. Keith M. Wilson, *The Policy of the Entente: essays on the determinants of British Foreign Policy, 1904-1914* (Cambridge University Press: Cambridge, 1985), p. 8.
20. Gregory D. Miller, *The Shadow of the Past: reputation and military alliances before the First World War* (Cornell University: Ithaca, 2012), pp. 67-8; Wilson, *The Policy of the Entente*, p. 5.
21. John Albert White, *Transition to Global Rivalry: alliance diplomacy and the Quadruple Entente, 1895-1907* (Cambridge University Press: Cambridge, 1995), p. 17.
22. M. B. Hayne, *The French Foreign Office and the Origins of the First World War, 1898-1914* (Oxford University Press: Oxford, 1993), p. 96.
23. Ibid., pp. 97-8.
24. Ibid., p. 102.
25. Ibid., pp. 103-6.
26. Loubert quoted in Robert K. Massie, *Dreadnought: Britain, Germany, and the Coming of the Great War*, (Jonathan Cape: London, 1992), p. 344.
27. On the Edwardian Foreign Office see chapter five of Otte, *The Foreign Office Mind*, pp. 240-313.
28. White, *Transition to Global Rivalry*, p. 27.
29. (Anon.), 'King Edward in Rome and Paris', *The Independent* (London, England), 17 May 1903; 55, 2840, p. 1059.
30. Massie, *Dreadnought*, pp. 344-5; on Edward VII's state visits see, Matthew Glencross, *The State Visits of Edward VII: reinventing royal diplomacy for the twentieth century* (Palgrave Macmillan: Basingstoke, 2015).
31. (Anon.), 'Anglo-French Entente Worries Germany: agreement over Morocco rouses the Pan-German Party', *New York Times* (New York, United States), 17 Apr. 1904; p. 4.
32. *Anglo-French Convention. A bill for approving and carrying into effect a convention between His Majesty and the President of the French Republic* (House of Commons Papers: No. 205, 1904), pp. 1-5; on Morocco see (Anon.), 'The Anglo-French Convention and its sequel, by Sir Harry Johnston', *The Review of Reviews*, June 1904; 29, 174; p. 583.
33. James K. Hiller, 'The 1904 Anglo-French Newfoundland Fisheries Convention: another look', *Acadiensis*, Vol. 25:1 (Autumn, 1995), pp. 82-98, 83-4.

34. Ibid., pp. 86-9 and 98; Miller, *The Shadow of the Past*, p. 84.
35. (Anon.), 'Anglo-French Relations', *Outlook* (London, England), 5 July, 1913; 104: 10; p. 493.
36. (Anon.), 'L'Entente Cordiale', *The Hospital* (London, England), 8 Oct., 1904, p. 20.
37. Miller, *The Shadow of the Past*, pp. 75-80.
38. Miller, *The Shadow of the Past*, p. 94; White, *Transition to Global Rivalry*, p. 162.
39. Bülow quoted in White, *Transition to Global Rivalry*, p. 162.
40. Roosevelt quoted in ibid., p. 164.
41. Edward VII quoted in ibid., p. 168.
42. Balfour quoted in ibid., p. 170.
43. Ibid., pp. 186-9; on the Algeciras Conference see Miller, *The Shadow of the Past*, pp. 95-115.
44. White, *Transition to Global Rivalry*, p. 193.
45. Keith Robbins, 'Grey, Edward, Viscount Grey of Fallodon (1862–1933), politician, countryman, and author.' *Oxford Dictionary of National Biography*. 23 Sep. 2004; Accessed 2 Apr. 2020. https://www.oxforddnb.com/view/10.1093/ref:odnb/9780198614128.001.0001/odnb-9780198614128-e-33570.
46. White, *Transition to Global Rivalry*, p. 203.
47. Miller, *The Shadow of the Past*, pp. 127-31.
48. T. G. Otte, 'Entente diplomacy v détente, 1911-1914', in Dominik Geppert, William Mulligan, and Andreas Rose (eds.), *The Wars Before the Great War: conflict and international politics before the outbreak of the First world war* (Cambridge University Press: Cambridge, 2015), pp. 264-82, 269-71; Fredrich Kießling, 'Anglo-French relations and the wars before the war', in Dominik Geppert, William Mulligan, and Andreas Rose (eds.), *The Wars Before the Great War: conflict and international politics before the outbreak of the First world war* (Cambridge University Press: Cambridge, 2015), pp. 283-97, 285-6.
49. Kießling, 'Anglo-French relations and the wars before the war', pp. 295-7.
50. Otte, 'Entente diplomacy v détente, 1911-1914', pp. 275-6.
51. Grey quoted in ibid., p. 279; also see, Kießling, 'Anglo-French relations and the wars before the war', pp., 289-90.

52. Elizabeth Greenhalgh, *Victory Through Coalition: Britain and France during the First World War* (Cambridge University Press: Cambridge 2005), p. 285.
53. Grey quoted in Wilson, *The Policy of the Entente*, p. 35.
54. Ibid., pp. 121-3.
55. Ibid., p. 126.
56. Ibid., pp. 130-4.
57. William J. Philpott, 'The making of the military entente, 1904-14', *English Historical Review*, Vol. CXXVIII, No. 534 (Oct. 2013), pp. 1155-85.
58. Ibid., p. 1156.
59. Ibid., p. 1161.
60. Ibid., pp. 1162-3.
61. General Durand quoted in ibid., p. 1164.
62. Ibid., p. 1170.
63. Ibid., pp. 1174-5.
64. Ibid., p. 1176.

Epilogue: An Anglo-French World Order?
1. Wilson, *The Policy of the Entente*, pp. 137-43.
2. Greenhalgh, *Victory Through Coalition*, p. 1.
3. William Philpott, 'Britain and France go to war: Anglo-French relations on the Western Front, 1914-1918', *War in History*, 2:1 (1995), pp. 43-64, 44.
4. Ibid., pp. 47-8; on the Somme and Verdun see Greenhalgh, *Victory Through Coalition*, pp. 43-74.
5. John French quoted in Philpott, 'Britain and France go to war', p. 56.
6. Kitchener quoted in ibid., p. 49.
7. Ibid., p. 57.
8. Ibid., p. 54.
9. Esher quoted in ibid., p. 54.
10. Greenhalgh, *Victory Through Coalition*, p. 282.
11. Martin Horn, 'External finance in Anglo-French relations in the First World War, 1914-1917', *The International History Review*, Vol. 17, No. 1 (Feb. 1995), pp. 51-77, 52-3.
12. Ibid., pp. 54-5.
13. Selborne quoted in ibid., p. 54.
14. Ibid., pp. 59-63.
15. Keynes quoted in ibid., p. 67.

16. Ibid., pp. 68-9.
17. Ibid., p. 69.
18. Ibid., pp. 76-7.
19. Kenneth O. Morgan, 'Lloyd George and Clemenceau: Prima Donnas in Partnership', in Antoine Capet (ed.), *Britain, France and the Entente Cordiale since 1904*, (Palgrave: London, 2006), pp. 28-40, 39.
20. Hardinge quoted in Robert Boyce, 'Behind the façade of the Entente Cordiale after the Great War', in Antoine Capet (ed.), *Britain, France and the Entente Cordiale since 1904* (Palgrave: London, 2006), pp. 41-63, 53-4.
21. Explored in Robert Tombs and Emilie Chabel (eds.), *Britain and France in Two World Wars: truth, myth and memory* (Bloomsbury: London, 2013).
22. Harry J. Mace, 'The Eurafrique Initiative: Ernest Bevin and Anglo-French relations in the Foreign Office, 1945-1950', *Diplomacy & Statecraft*, Vol. 28, Issue 4 (2017), pp. 601-18; Eric T. Jennings, 'Britain and free France in Africa, 1940-1943', in James R. Fichter (ed.), *British and French Colonialism in Africa, Asia and the Middle East: connected empires across the eighteenth to the twentieth centuries* (Palgrave Macmillan: Basingstoke, 2019), pp. 277-96; John Kent, *The Internationalization of Colonialism: Britain, France, and Black Africa, 1939-1956* (Clarendon Press: Oxford, 1992).
23. Tony Chafer and Gordon Cummin, 'Beyond Fashoda: Anglo-French security cooperation in Africa since Saint-Malo', *International Affairs (Royal Institute of International Affairs, 1944-)*, Vol. 86, No. 5, (Sep., 2010), pp. 1129-47; Alan Sharp and Glyn Stone (eds.), *Anglo-French relations in the twentieth century: rivalry and cooperation* (Routledge: Abingdon, 1999); P. Chassaigne and M. Dockrill (eds.), *Anglo-French relations, 1898-1998: from Fashoda to Jospin* (Palgrave Macmillan: Basingstoke, 2002).
24. Argued in Antoine Capet (ed.), *Britain, France and the Entente Cordiale since 1904* (Palgrave: London, 2006).

INDEX

Aberdeen (Scotland) 82
Aberdeen, Lord 33, 59, 73–4
Abdülmecid, Sultan 58
Afghanistan 162–3, 201
Africa 13, 80, 107–8, 172, 177, 179–80, 183, 208
Airy, George Biddell 127
Albert, Prince 33, 38, 44, 53–6, 103, 126, 142
Alert (boat) 217
Alexander II 78, 165
Alexandra, Princess 140–41
Alexandria, Queen 202
Alexandria (Egypt) 17, 167, 169–70, 198
Algeciras Conference 209–10
Algeria 60, 145, 159–60
Allah, Muhammad Ahmad bin Abd 178
Allgood, George 95–6
American Civil War 169
Amiens Cathedral 194–8
Anderson, Elizabeth Garrett 147

Anglo-French Mediterranean agreement 213
anti-Semitism 19
Antoinette, Marie 32
Antwerp (Belgium) 186, 212–13, 219
Argentina 126
Arrow (ship) 89
Arts and Crafts movement 49
Ascension Isle 17
Asia 107–8, 110
Asquith, Herbert 200–1, 210, 212, 215, 218
Australia 13, 20–1, 78–9, 120
Austria 32, 57, 87, 113, 142–3, 150, 166, 210–1, 218
Austro-Hungarian Empire 138, 140, 144, 159, 164, 167, 176–7, 210–11, 217–8

Babbage, Charles 31
Balaklava 65, 67–8, 72–3
Balfour, Arthur 209
Balkan League 211

Balkans 210–11, 215
Bank of England 221
Bank of France 221
Barbizon (France) 186
Barbizon School 186–7
Baring, Evelyn 167, 169, 174
Barry, Alfred 76–7
Barry, Charles, 17, 76
Bastiat, Frédéric 113
Battle of the Alma 62–5, 70
Battle of Austerlitz 35
Battle of Britain 14
Battle of Inkermann 67
Battle of Königgrätz 144
Battle of Omdurman 180–82
Battle of Sedan 152
Battle of Tell-El-Kebir 170
Battle of Waterloo 13, 28–9, 54, 59–60, 85, 191, 207
Bazancourt, César Lecat de 62–3, 73
Belfast (Ireland) 82
Belgium 126, 128, 150, 159, 176, 183–4, 190, 195, 212–5, 218–9, 222
Bennett, Winifred 219
Berlin (Germany) 207, 212–3
Between the Tides (Langley) 185
Biot, Jean-Baptiste 29
Birmingham (England) 18, 82
Bismarck, Otto von 140, 144, 150, 152–4, 164–6
Boer Wars 199–204, 215
Bombay (India) 82
Bonaparte, Joséphine 34
Bonaparte, Napoléon 13, 16, 22–3, 28–31, 34–6, 53–4, 59, 80, 115, 122, 150, 152
Bonaparte, Pierre-Napoléon 151
Borghese, Pauline 23

Bosnia 166
Bosnia-Herzegovina 210
Bosquet, Pierre François 67
Boulanger, George Ernest 176
Bourdin, Martial 161
Bourges Cathedral 196
Bowring, John 89
Branagh, Kenneth 119
Brazil 39, 126, 158
Breton Children in an Orchard—Quimperlé (Forbes) 185
Bright, John 126
Bristol (England) 82, 118, 157
Britain, 17, 35–6, 39–40, 45, 55, 57–9, 63, 65, 68, 73–4, 86, 89, 92–6, 106, 113–14, 120, 138–9, 150, 153–4, 166, 193, 195–6, 220
Africa, marking spheres of influence in 183
'Age of Equipoise' 14–15
alcohol 124–5, 188
architecture in 19–20
British Army 14
Burma, annexing of 176
champagne 188–90
Continental Europe, strained relationship with 12
Cornwall, mining district of 29–30, 184–5
credit, collapse of 223
decline of 191–2, 199, 224–5
diapason normal 134–5
Egyptian question 168–75, 178, 191–2, 203, 206
entente cordiale, with France 33, 88, 110–1, 191, 204, 207–8, 211–2, 216, 224–5, 227

European influence, embracing of 27
'finest hour' of 14
as first among nations 37–8
France, bankrolling of during World War I 222–3
France, collaboration with 78, 103, 184–5, 197, 198, 207
France, cultural connections 90–1
France, drifting apart 145, 162, 173, 191, 211
France, as global competitor 176–7
France, general relationship with 12, 20–21, 23–27, 50, 56, 107, 109–10, 116–17, 212, 222
France, renewed friendship with 206–7
France, rivalry between 103–4, 162
French armies, relations between 213–6
free trade 110, 112–13, 115, 124, 126, 136
French food 187
French invasion, fear of 110–12, 226
French time, as symbolic of French disorder 160
'Gallo-mania' 130
German Empire, at war with 218
global dominance 13, 18, 225–6
global position, uncertainty of 12–13
globalisation of 121
imperial expansion of 175, 191

industrialization of 15, 28–9, 42, 44, 47–9
influence of, diminished 155
information network of 198–9, 217
international influence, inflated sense of 12
international peace, threat to 202
invasion panics 37, 155, 183, 226
isolation of 14, 144, 155
laissez-faire system 26, 127, 136, 160–1, 167, 173, 200, 207
liberalism and free trade 109
liberal reforms 31
metric system 122–4, 126–8, 130–3, 135–6, 159
Morocco 208–10, 212
musical standard 133–5
as mutually dependent, with France 221
national debt 77–8
as 'nation of shopkeepers' 115
naval power of 16, 81, 104–5, 199
naval race 175–6, 200
nouveau riche 189–90
overseas territories 16
Pax Britannica, age of 15–16
place in world, as uncertain 225
poverty in 18
prostitution in 145–7, 149
Pyramidology 132
railway network, expansion of 14–15
reform, clamour for 18
as religious nation 42

Index

restraint of 189
Roman global dominance, as heir to 19–20
rotten boroughs 31–2
Royal Navy 78, 201
Russia, alliance with 208
Schleswig-Holstein crisis 141–3
as second tier of nations 13–14
standardised measurements 122–3
as standing alone 13–14
steam power 28–30, 38, 42, 75
Sudan 180–82
Suez Canal 79–82, 84–5, 87–8, 167, 172–4, 177
Summer Palace, sacking of 11–12, 97–100
'superiority' of 41
as superpower 13–15
technology 77
telegraphy, expansion of 14–15, 50–52
'War-in-Sight' crisis 165
welfare state 14
World War I 217, 221
as world's timekeeper 156–7, 161
working-class unrest 14–15, 32–3
xenophobia in, 176
See also England
British Commonwealth 12
British Empire 12, 16–7, 31, 52, 82, 175, 198, 202
imperial expansion, as incompatible with domestic reform 174
time, as gem of 161
British Expeditionary Force (BEF) 212–16, 219–20

Brittany (France) 185–7
Brown, George 65
Bruce, James, 8th Earl of Elgin 90
Brunel, Isambard Kingdom 17, 118–21
Brussels (Belgium) 124
Buenos Aires (Argentina) 16–7
Bulgaria 166, 211
Bülow, Bernard von 199–200, 208–9
Burghersh, Lord 63
Burma 175–6
Burn, W. L. 14
Butler, Josephine 148–9

Cairo (Egypt) 13, 167, 170, 178
Caisse de la Dette Publique 167
Calcutta (India) 92, 95–6, 120
Cambon, Pierre Paul 204, 206
Campbell-Bannerman, Henry 200, 212
Canada 13, 78, 108–9, 158, 199
Canrobert, François 64, 67, 69
Canton (China) 89, 106–7
Cape Town (South Africa) 13, 17, 178, 198
Cardigan, Lord 66–7, 72–3
Carlton Hotel 187–8
Carlyle, Thomas 24
Carnot, Sadi 30
Casablanca (Morocco) 209
Casablanca Agreement 210
Ceylon 17
Chad 178
Chadwick, Edwin 126
Chaillot Works 30
Chamberlain, Joseph 203
Chartres Cathedral 194, 196
Chartists 32–3

Cherbourg (France) 103–5
Chester, Harry 135
Chevalier, Michel 45, 107–10,
　112, 117, 125, 177
Chicago (Illinois) 107
Childers, Hugh 149
Chile 126
China 15–17, 20, 26, 39, 80, 88,
　90–95, 102, 106, 110–12, 199
　invasion of 96–97, 101, 103
　Summer Palace, sacking of
　　11–12, 97–101, 225
　xenophobia in 89, 101
Christian IX 140, 202
cholera 75–6, 94
Christie, Agatha 29
Church of England 42
Churchill, Winston 119, 181–3,
　200, 213, 217–9
Cixi, Empress Dowager 101
Clemenceau, Georges 210
Club Anatomies 161
Cobden-Chevalier Free Trade
　Treaty 116–17, 122, 124, 126,
　137, 174, 188
Cobden, Richard 106–7, 109–5,
　117, 124–6, 131, 134, 136,
　174, 177
Collins, Wilkie 149
Commission of Liquidation
　168–9
Conan Doyle, Arthur 29
Conrad, Joseph 160–1
Congress of Berlin 162–3, 165–6,
　168
Congress of Vienna 57, 140
Conspiracy to Murder Bill 104
Constable, John 186
Contagious Diseases Acts 145–7,
　149

Cooke and Wheatstone system
　50
Cork (Ireland) 82
Corn Laws 112–3
Cornwall (England) 185–7
Court, Charles à 215
Cousin-Montauban, Charles 90,
　94, 97
Cowley, Lord 114–5
Crampton, Thomas 50
Crimea 26, 61, 65, 68–9, 79, 88,
　91
Crimean War 56, 84, 91, 96–7,
　103, 105–6, 109, 112, 146,
　155, 162
　British army, as national
　　embarrassment 71–2
　British and French
　　collaboration, importance of
　　78
　British officers, incompetence
　　of 66–8
　casualties of 74
　'Charge of the Light Brigade'
　　66
　cholera 75–6, 94
　as first industrial conflict 74
　French soldiers, as respected 72
　Light Brigade 69, 72–3
　medical treatment during 71–2
　national debt 77–8
　93rd Highlanders 65–6
　photography, use of 73
Croley, George 77
Cromwell, Oliver 66
Cuba 108–9
Cultural Revolution 99
Cunard 120–1
Cyprus 17, 162, 163, 166
Crystal Palace 38, 44–5, 50

Darwin, Charles 18
Daubigny, Charles-François 186
Décazes, Louis-Charles duc 165
de Gaulle, Charles 224
Delcassé, Théophile 179, 181, 201–4, 206, 208–9
Delonde, François 179
Denmark 139, 140–3, 158, 202
Derby, Earl of 36
Derby, Lord 165, 167
Dickens, Charles 24–5
Disraeli, Benjamin 21, 36, 87–8, 105, 154–5, 162, 165
Dover (England) 198
D'Oyly, Richard 187
Dreadnought (vessel) 200
Dreikaiserbund (Three Emperors' League) 164
Dublin (Ireland) 82
Duclerc, Charles Théodore Eugène 170–72, 174
Duke of Cádiz 33
Duke of Cambridge 90–1
Duke of Newcastle 59, 63
Duke of Wellington 23, 59–60, 64
Dupin, Baron Pierre Charles François 29
Dussard, Hippolyte 45

Earl of Malmsbury 36–7
Eastern Steam Navigation Company 119
East India Trading Company 82
Edinburgh (Scotland) 82
Edward VII 23, 204, 206, 208, 215–6
  Germany, dislike of 202–3
  as trend setter 202
Edwards, Humphrey 30
Egypt 20, 39, 56, 79, 80–2, 87, 132, 166, 190–2, 202, 204, 215
  bankruptcy of 167
  British control of 170–75, 178, 203, 206
  Commission of Liquidation 168–9
  coup in 169
  fellahin class 168
  Franco-British dual control of 168–71
  occupation of 173–4
  and Sudan 180
Elba 115
Elgin, Lord, 95, 97
Elgin Marbles 90
England 25, 28, 53, 77, 82–3, 106, 111, 113, 142, 148, 155, 175, 184, 188, 190, 194–6
  as parochial 226
  See also Britain
Esher, Lord 220
Escoffier, Georges Auguste 187–8
Eugénie, Empress 53–5, 86
Eurafrique 224
Europe 12–13, 20–1, 23, 27–8, 32, 34, 49–51, 53, 57, 77, 82, 86, 88–9, 91, 93–4, 106, 116, 126, 133, 135–6, 139, 155, 165–6, 190–1, 199, 224–5, 227
European Economic Community (EEC) 224
European Union (EU) 12–13
Ewart, William 126–8, 130–2, 136
Exposition du système du monde (Laplace) 31

Falklands 17
Fashoda (Sudan) 177–81, 190, 199, 201–2
Fashoda Crisis 191, 207
Faure, Félix 181
Ferdinand, Franz 217
Ferry, Jules 172
Fiji 17
First China War 89
First French Empire 13
First Opium War 20
Fisher, Jacky 198, 200, 212
Fleming, Sandford 158
Foch, Ferdinand 214
Forbes, Elizabeth 186
Forbes, Juliette de Guise 185
Forbes, Stanhope 185–86
Forbes, William 185
France 28, 30–31, 34–7, 39, 52, 54–5, 58–60, 63–5, 68, 73–5, 77, 89–96, 106, 108, 126, 128, 139, 144, 151–2, 165, 167, 186, 194, 196, 199, 201, 205–6, 211–3, 220, 222–3, 226
  alcohol 124–5, 188
  Alsace and Lorraine, loss of 154–5, 162, 164
  architecture in 21–2
  Bourbon monarchy, restoration of 32
  Britain, as allies 197–8
  Britain, collaboration with 78, 103, 184–5
  Britain, drifting apart 145, 162, 191
  Britain, as global competitor 177
  Britain, relationship with 12, 20–21, 23–7, 50, 56, 107, 109–10, 116–7
  Britain, rivalry between 103–4, 162
  Britain, breakdown of/torn apart 173
  British food 187
  Burma, treaty with 176
  cathedral architecture 195
  champagne 188–90
  decline of 156, 191–2, 224–5
  defeat of 154–5, 163
  diapason normal 133–5
  education system, reforms of 163–4
  Egyptian question 168–75, 191–2
  as enemy 176
  entente cordiale, with Britain 33, 88, 110–11, 191, 204, 216, 224–5, 227
  Europe, turn to 224
  Fashoda syndrome 183
  free trade 115, 124, 127, 177
  German Empire, at war with 218–9
  Germany, rivalry with 163
  global influence of 23
  Great Exhibition 44–5
  immorality of, accusations of 148–50
  'informal empire' of 23
  invasion of, by Germany 157
  invasion, British fear of by 107, 110
  as interventionist state 26, 127, 136, 172
  Madagascar, seize of 177

Index

metre, as symbol of French reason 122
metric system 124, 127, 130
as military threat 103–4
and Morocco 208–10
musical standard 133–4
nationalism of 176
as naval power 103–4
Ottoman Empire, secret treaty with 57
prostitution in 145–6
protectionism of 112–5
Russia, alliance with 175–6, 207
Schleswig-Holstein crisis 142–3
and Sudan 177–82
Suez Canal 79–85, 87
Summer Palace, sacking of 11–2, 97–100
time, regulating of 158–62
universities 164
as unreliable partner 172
World War I 221
xenophobia in 176
Franco-Prussian War 163–5, 169, 176, 180, 196
Franz Joseph 138, 144
Frederick VII 140
Frederick of Prussia, Prince 103, 140–1
free trade 110, 112–13, 115, 117, 124, 126, 131, 134, 138–9, 174, 188
French Empire 13, 99, 104, 142
French, John 214–5, 219–20
French Polynesia 163, 172
French Revolution 24, 28, 32, 122, 130, 154–5
French Revolution, the: a History (Carlyle) 24

Gambia 17, 206
Garnier, Joseph 45
Gay-Lussac, Joseph Louis 124–5
George III 53–4, 122
George V 207
German Confederation 140, 144, 151
German Empire 27, 139–40, 144, 154, 199, 217–8
German States 32
Germany 14–15, 87, 126, 152, 154–5, 159, 164–5, 176–7, 181, 189, 192, 200–202, 204, 206, 211–5, 217, 221–3
  Belgian neutrality, violation of 218–9
  France, rivalry with 163
  militarism, fear of 191, 216
  and Morocco 208–10
  naval expansion of 199
  Schleswig-Holstein crisis 142–3
  time, regulation of 157
  unification of 150
Gibraltar 198, 209
Gladstone, William Ewart 36–7, 105–6, 109–12, 114, 116, 124–5, 130–1, 153, 155, 163, 169–70, 172–3, 175, 178, 189
  free trade, commitment to 188
  'moral empire', hope of 174
  wine tariffs, slashing of 188
Glarétie, Jules 202
Glasgow (Scotland) 18, 22, 82
Gloire (ship) 105
Gong, Prince 11
Gordon, Charles 98, 101–2, 178, 180, 182
Grand Hotel 187
Grant, Hope 90–91, 94, 97

Granville 170–3, 177
Gray, Effie 47
Great Eastern (steamship) 17, 118–21
Great Exhibition 15, 21, 24, 38–40, 47, 50, 52, 122–3
    foreign competition, encouraging of 44–5
    hubris, as act of 44
    labourers, degrading of 48
    and religion 42
Great Pyramid 132
Great Reform Act 31–2, 112–3
Great Western Railway 157
Greece 19, 49, 56, 211
Greek Orthodox Church 57–8
Greenwich (England) 123, 156–7
Greenwich time
    Greenwich Mean Time 159–60
    Greenwich Meridian 156, 158, 162
    imperial prestige, 160–1
Grey, Edward 179, 209–12, 215, 218
Guiana 17
guillotine 33–4
Guizot, François 33

Haig, Douglas 220
Haldane, Richard 212, 215, 218
Hanotaux, Gabriel 179
Hardinge, Lord 223
Harding, Robert 190
Haussman, Georges-Eugéne 22, 151
Heligoland 176, 202, 212
Henley, Joseph 130
Herschel, John 31, 123
Herschel, William 123
Herzegovina 166

Holstein 140, 142–3
Hong Kong (China) 12, 17, 20, 89–90, 94–6, 120–1
Hope, James 90
Howard, Harriet 150
Hubbard, John 130
Hugo, Victor 98–100
Hull (England) 82
Hullah, John 135
Hungary 32

Illinois Railway Company 107
India 10, 13, 18, 40–41, 56, 78–80, 86, 89–93, 120, 169, 174, 177
Indian Mutiny 90, 95, 97
indigenous peoples: capitalism, 121
Indochina 163, 172, 177
International Association for Obtaining a Uniform Decimal System of Measures, Weights, and Coins 124
International Meridian Conference 156
International Statistical Congress 124, 126
invasion panics 23–4, 37, 104
Ireland 18–9, 82
Isabella, Queen 33
Isle of Wight (England) 32
Italy 39, 87, 113–4, 126, 152, 159, 167, 176–7, 222

Japan 199, 207–8
Jerusalem 57
Joffre, Joseph 219–20
J. P. Morgan & Co 223
Joubert, R. 168

Kennedy, Paul 15–7
Kenya 175
Keynes, John Maynard 222
Kingscote, Nigel 60
Kitchener, Herbert 180–2, 220

Labour Party 14, 50
Lacornée, Jacques 21
Ladies' National Association for the Repeal of the Contagious Diseases Act (LNA)
   crusade against Frenchness 148
   as publicity masterpiece 149
Lagos 17
L'Aigle (yacht) 86
Langley, Walter 185
Laplace, Pierre-Simon 31
La Touche, Rose 47
Lavisse, Ernest 164
Leith (Scotland) 82
Lemoinne, John-Marguerite-Émile 39–40
Leopold of Saxe-Coburg, 33
Lesseps, Ferdinand de 79–80, 86
   charm offensive of 81–3
   death of 87
   public subscription, launch of 84–5
Leveson-Gower, Granville (second Earl Granville) 169
liberalism 37, 128, 134–5, 148, 160, 163, 207, 226
   free trade 109–10
   minimal government, cornerstone of 127
Liberal Party, 37, 106–7, 218
Liddell, John 146
Liprandi, Pavel 65, 67
Liverpool (England) 18, 82, 107

Lloyd George, David 200, 218, 222
London (England) 11, 14, 17–18, 22–3, 25–6, 38, 40, 42, 44, 47, 51–2, 55, 61, 73, 82, 92, 109, 118, 156–7, 159–60, 167, 176, 206, 223
   champagne, popularity in 188–9
   eating habits, revolution in 187–8
   as financial hub 221
   French doctors, visits by 207
Loubert, Émilie 203–4
Louis Napoléon 34, 36, 58–60, 62, 64, 73–4, 78, 90, 111
   coup d'état of 35
   See also Napoléon III
Louis Philippe 113
Louis XVI 32, 55, 122
Louis-Napoléon 57
Louis Philippe, King 32–3
Lucan, Lord 66–7
Luisa Fernanda 33
Luxembourg 150, 218
Lyon (France) 114
Lyons, Viscount 170–71, 176

Macmillan, Harold 224
Madagascar 163, 172, 177
Mahdi 178
Mahmud II 56
Malacca 17
Malaya 175
Mali 178
Mallet, Louis 174
Manchester (England) 14, 18, 82
Mao Zedong 99
Marchand, Jean-Baptiste 179–81
Marie Antoinette 54

283

Marie Louise 34
Marx, Karl 50, 92–4, 102
Maximilian 138–9
Melbourne, Lord 35
Merriman, H. G. 75–6
metric system 122–4, 128–32
Metric System Bill 128–9, 130–32
Mexico 108–9, 138, 145
Mikhailovich, Aleksandr 164–5
Millais, John Everett 47
Millet, Jean-François 186
Mill, John Stuart 93–4
Moldavia 57–8, 74
Molte, Helmuth von 144, 157
Mombasa 17
Morocco 20, 201, 204, 206, 208–10
Moroccan Crisis 212–3
Montenegro 166, 211
Montevideo (Uruguay) 16–7
Morris, William 49
Morse Code 50
Murders in the Rue Morgue, The (Poe) 29

Napoléon II, 34
Napoléon III 12, 20–22, 24, 36–7, 51, 53–5, 61, 65, 94, 98, 103, 105–6, 109, 111, 115, 117, 136–7, 144–5, 151, 163, 165, 192, 216, 226–7
  abdication of 155
  assassination attempt 104
  death of 155
  fall of 152
  diapason normal decree 133–4
  exile of 155
  free trade 110, 113–14
  Mexican monarchy 138–9, 142
  Schleswig-Holstein crisis 143
  as unreliable partner 27, 138
  waning of 150
  See also Louis Napoléon
Napoléon, Prince 61, 65
Napoleonic Wars 28–9, 31, 57, 65
Nares, George 86
Naval Defence Act 175
Nelson, Horatio 105
Netherlands 87, 126, 159
Newcastle (England) 82
Newcomen, Thomas 29
Newfoundland 204–5
Newlyn (England) art colony 185
Newlyn Art School 185–87
Newport (vessel) 86
Newton, Isaac 30–31
New York City 107, 118–9, 223
New Zealand 13
Nice (France) 115
Nicholas I 56–9, 78
Niger 178
Nigeria 175, 183, 206
Nightingale, Florence 71, 77, 146, 148
  sanitary reforms of 72
Nightingale Fund 76
Nolan, Louis 65
North Africa 208
North America 19, 108–9, 119–20
Notre-Dame Cathedral 196

Oceanic (steamship) 118
On Liberty (Mill) 93
On the Origin of Species (Darwin) 18
Opium 89, 92–3
Orange Free State 175

Index

Orsini, Felice 104
Ottoman Empire 56, 74, 162–3, 165–7, 207–8, 211
　bankruptcy of 87
　France, secret treaty with 57
Oxford (England) 157

Pacifico, David 19
Pacific Steam Navigation Company (PSNC) 120–1
Palace of Versailles 154
Palestine 57
Pallu, Alphonse 184
Palmerston, Lord 18–20, 27, 33, 36–7, 59, 73–4, 89–90, 94, 104–7, 114, 116–7, 137, 139–40, 153, 155, 165, 192, 216, 226–7
　death of 144
　as pragmatist 35
　Schleswig-Holstein crisis 142–3
Panama Canal 86–7
Panama Canal Company 86
Paris (France) 11, 25–6, 30, 32, 47, 51–2, 54, 61, 73, 109, 112–4, 148–9, 152–3, 159–60, 167, 173, 176, 186, 196, 203, 207, 213, 218, 221, 223
　beauty of 55, 204
　eating habits, revolution in 187
　radical socialism, as centre of 154
　rebuilding of 55
　as time centre 161–2
　transformation of 22–3
Paris Commune 154
Paris Observatory 158
Paris Peace Conference 223
Parry, Jonathan 37
Pasha, Isma'il 167–8

Pasha, Tewfik 168, 170
Paxton, Joseph 38
Peace of Paris 74, 76, 103, 109
Peacock, George 31
Peel, Robert 33
Peking (China) 11, 15, 89–90, 92, 95–6, 100–101, 110
Peninsula and Oriental Steam Navigation Company (P&O) 82, 120–21
Peninsular War 85
Persia 40–41, 58, 201
Peru 126
Petty-Fitzmaurice, Henry, 5th Marquess of Lansdowne 204, 206, 209–10
Plymouth (England) 111, 157
Poe, Edgar Allan 29
Poincaré, Raymond 162, 206–7
Poland 139
Pontgibaud Silver-Lead Mining and Smelting Company 184–5
Portsmouth (England) 111
Portugal 59–60, 108–9, 115, 126, 128, 188
poverty 18, 25, 108–9
Powell, Harry 69–70
prostitution
　French immorality, association between 149
　regulation of 145–6
　speculum, use of 145, 147–8
Proust, Marcel 196–7
Prussia 57, 103, 113, 139–45, 150–53, 155, 164, 202
Pugin, Augustus 17
Punch (periodical) 51, 137–8
Pyramidology 132

Qing Dynasty 92, 96–7, 101

Raglan, Lord 59–60, 62–7, 69
Rambaud, Alfred 164
Ranavalona III 177
Reflections on the motive power of fire (Carnot) 30
Reform Act 147
Reid, Douglas 69
Reign of Terror 24, 33
Reims Cathedral 196
Reuter, Paul Julius 51–2
Revanchism 176
Revolutionary War 28
Revue historique (journal) 164
Rhodes, Cecil 178
Rhodesia 175
Ribot, Alexandre 221–2
Rickard, Richard 131
Ritz, César 187
Ritz Hotel 187
Robinson, Frederick 70–1
Roman Catholicism 57–8
Roman Empire 20
Romania 166, 211
Rome (Italy) 16, 19, 145
Roosevelt, Theodore 208–9
Rothschilds 163
Rouen Cathedral 196
Rousseau, Théodore 186
Rouvier, Maurice 209
Royal Academy 185
Royal Commission 146–7
Royal Navy 13, 61, 78, 86, 104–5, 183–4, 192, 200, 208, 218, 221–2
  supremacy of 16, 213
  Two-Power Standard, launch of 175
Royal Observatory 156, 158, 160–1
Royal Society 131
Royal Standards Commission 133
Royal Steam Packet Company (RMSP) 120–21
Ruskin, John 47, 193–5, 198
  Amiens cathedral 197
  architecture and nature, link to 48
  French architecture, celebration of 197
  Gothic, appreciation of 48–9, 196
  influence of 50
  religious principles, and architecture 48–9
  romantic socialism of 197
Russell, John Scott, 119
Russell, Lord John 33–6, 141–3
Russell, Lord Odo 165
Russell, William 64, 72–3
Russia 11, 15, 20, 56–9, 74, 76–9, 88, 91–2, 103, 106, 115, 155, 162, 164–5, 189–90, 199, 201, 209–11, 215, 217–8, 222
  Britain, alliance with 208
  debts of 222
  France, alliance with 175–6, 207
  Schleswig-Holstein crisis 142–3
  Suez Canal 207–8
  See also Soviet Union
Russo-Turkish War 165–6

Saint-Arnaud, Jacques Leroy de 60–4
Saine-Chapelle Cathedral 196
Salisbury, Lord 166, 168, 176, 180, 182–3

Two-Power Standard, launch of 175, 200–201
San Domingo 158
Savoy (France) 115
Savoy Hotel 187
Say, Jean-Baptiste 28–9
Saxe-Lauenburg 143
Schleswig, 140, 142–3
Schleswig-Holstein crisis 140–44
science 17–8, 76
  'scientist,' coining of 40
Scott, George Gilbert 19–20
Sebastopol 58–9, 61–2, 64–6, 69–70, 72, 74, 76, 79
Second Empire 151
Secret Agent, The (Conrad) 160–61
Seignobos, Charles 164
Selborne, Lord 221–2
Senegal 178
Serbia 166, 217–8, 222
Seychelles 17
Shanghai (China) 16–17, 89–90, 94, 101, 121
Siam 177
Sierra Leone 17
Sinclair, John 75
Singapore 17, 121, 198–9
Slavery 31, 85
Smyth, Charles Piazzi 132
Society of Arts 124, 134–5
Somaliland 178
South Africa 155, 162–3, 199
  Boer population in 199
  concentration camps 199
South America 16, 121, 209
Soviet Union 13–14
  See also Russia
Spain 39, 59–60, 87, 108–9, 188, 210
Spencer, Lord 175–6
spheres of influence 177, 182–3, 208
Stansfield, James 149
State Bank of Morocco 210
Stephenson, Robert 84
St Helena 22, 28, 53, 152
St Hilaire, Bathélemy 83
St Lucia and Tobago 17
Stones of Venice, The (Ruskin) 48
St Paul's Cathedral 38
Street in Brittany, A (Forbes) 185
Submarine Telegraph Company 51
Sudan 177–9
  British capture of 180
  French withdrawal from 181–2
Suez Canal 20–21, 79–85, 87–88, 163, 167–9, 172–4, 177
  invasion of 170
  opening ceremony 86
Suez Canal Company 86–8, 121
Suez Crisis 224
Sweden 32
Switzerland 32, 34, 128, 152
Syria 56–7

Tai-ping Rebellion 101
Taku forts incident, 90, 94–6
Tale of Two Cities, A (Dickens) 24–5
Tangier (Morocco), 208, 210
Taylor, John 184–5
telegraphs 51–2, 73–4, 198–9
  progress, as symbol of 50
Tempest, The (Shakespeare) 119
Thibaw Min (king of Burma) 176
Third China War 102

Third Republic 154, 163–4, 171, 181, 183, 191, 201
Thunder Child (torpedo-ram) 183–4
Tirpitz, Alfred von 199–200
Toulon (France) 104–5, 111
Transvaal 175
Treaty of Bucharest 57
Treaty of London 140, 142
Treaty of Nanking 89
Treaty of Tientsin 89–90
Treaty of Utrecht 205
Trevithick, Richard 29
Trident Nuclear Deterrent 12
Tunis (Tunisia) 166
Turkey 39, 58, 77, 106
   decline of 56–7
   as 'Sick Man of Europe' 56, 74

Uganda 175
United States 12–15, 39, 45, 52, 87, 107–9, 126, 157, 182, 190–2, 199, 208–9, 217, 221–5
University of Cambridge mathematical education, as centre of 31
'Urabi, Ahmed 169–70
Uranus 123
Uruguay 126

Valparaiso (Spain) 16–7
Venice (Italy) 196
Victoria, Queen 12–3, 19, 23, 32, 38, 50, 53–6, 59, 69, 73, 78, 86, 88, 98, 103, 106, 138, 140–42, 155, 165, 202–3
Vienna (Austria) 207
Violett-le-Duc, Eugène 194

Waddington, William Henry 166
Wallachia 57–8
Warrior (vessel) 105
War of the Worlds, The (Wells), 183
Washington Conference 157–8, 160
Washington, DC 107
Watt, James 29
Weights and Measures Act 123
Wells, H. G. 183–4
West Africa 16, 163
West Indies 13, 21, 78, 121
Whewell, William 40–41
Wilhelm I 140, 152, 154
Wilhelm II 103, 199, 201–4, 208
Wilson, Harold 224
Wilson, Henry J. 149, 214
Windham, Charles 64, 68
Wolseley, Garnet 95, 97, 99–101, 170, 215
Wolstenholme, Elizabeth 148
women's suffrage campaign 149
Woolf, Arthur 29–30
World War I 13, 74, 157, 197, 217
   Anglo-French finance, as bedrock of 222
   as 'high noon' of entente 223
   trench warfare 219, 222
   Western Front 198, 221
World War II 13, 223–4
Wren, Christopher 38

Yizhu (Xianfeng Emperor) 11, 89–90, 101

Zanzibar 17, 175–7, 202
Zulus 155